The Jewels of the Qur'an

THE JEWELS OF THE QUR'AN

Al-Ghazali's Theory

A translation, with an introduction and annotation
of al-Ghazali's Kitāb Jawāhir al-Qur'an

MUHAMMAD ABUL QUASEM

IBT
Islamic Book Trust
Kuala Lumpur

First published 1977
Dr M.A. Quasem, Selangor

This new edition 2013
Islamic Book Trust
607 Mutiara Majestic
Jalan Othman
46000 Petaling Jaya
Selangor, Malaysia
www.ibtbooks.com

Islamic Book Trust is affiliated with The Other Press.

Perpustakaan Negara Malaysia Cataloguing-in-Publication Data

Quasem, Muhammad Abul
The jewels of the Quran : al Ghazali's theory / by Muhammad Abul Quasem.
Includes index
Bibliography: p. 211
ISBN 978-967-5062-97-1
1. Ghazzali, 1058-1111. 2. Koran--Criticism, interpretation, etc. I. Title.
297.1226

Printed by
Academe Art & Printing Services Sdn. Bhd.
No. 7, Jalan Rajawali 1A
Bandar Baru Puchong
Batu 8, Jalan Puchong
47100 Selangor

In the name of God, Most Gracious, Most Merciful

Surely this Qur'an guides you to the way which is most firm and right, and gives the believers who do good deeds the glad tidings that they shall have a great reward and warns that for those who do not believe in the Hereafter We have prepared a grievous chastisement. (Qur'an, 17:9-10)

Contents

Introduction

وَنُنَزِّلُ مِنَ الْقُرْآنِ مَا هُوَ شِفَاءٌ وَرَحْمَةٌ لِلْمُؤْمِنِينَ.

> We revealed of the Qur'an that which is a spiritual healing and a mercy for the believers. (Qur'an, 17:82)

The Qur'an is the Holy Scripture of Islam revealed to Prophet Muḥammad (ṣ) through the angel of revelation, Gabriel, in approximately twenty-three years of his lifetime (610 AD—632) in Makkah and Madīnah. Seven hundred million human beings who call themselves Muslims have accepted it as the Creator's final message or revelation to mankind and jinn (*infra,* p. 30, n. 74), two intelligent species charged with religious and moral responsibilities. Muslims not only read and study the Qur'an for drawing guidance in all aspects of their life, but also recite it for other purposes, such as the obtaining of reward from God and gaining the blessings which come from uttering the divine speech. Recitation for these purposes is made at different times and on various occasions, e.g. in the morning, at night, on completion of every ritual prayer, at the start of sermons, in ceremonies and in pious gatherings. Thus the Qur'an is practically inseparable from the life of a Muslim. Many non-Muslims have also been interested in the Qur'an and most of them have regarded it with reverence as the Holy Scripture of a great faith; the reasons for their interest in the Scripture of another religion, however, are obviously not identical with those of Muslims.

The Qur'an is purely divine but its understanding is completely human—a statement often made by Muslim scholars of recognized authority. The understanding of the Qur'an concerns not only the meaning and significance of its verses, but also several broad problems related to it as a whole. Scholars sometimes differ in understanding some aspects of the Qur'an. Non-Muslims differ from Muslims primarily in apprehending certain fundamental issues concerning the Scripture, e.g. its authority, its source, and the nature of its appeal to human beings—whether this appeal is universal or limited to some particular sections of humanity—and they differ mainly because their religious beliefs and ideological convictions are different. Among the Muslim scholars themselves differences have also occurred in respect of the meaning and import of several categories of verses and also in respect of apprehending certain basic Qur'anic problems, such as the eternity or created nature of the Qur'an, and the methods of understanding it. Thus the Sunnites, the Shīʿites, the Muʿtazilites, the Ashʿarites, the Literalists, the Sufis, the Philosophers, and the Modernists are not always found to be in agreement on Qur'anic interpretation and in their views on some Qur'anic problems of importance. The reasons why they differ among themselves in understanding the Scripture are rooted in their disagreement on other matters.

One of the leading Muslim thinkers who adheres mainly to the Sunnites, the Ashʿarites and the Sufis and who is strongly opposed to the Shīʿites, the Muʿtazilites, the Literalists and part of the theories of his contemporary philosophers, is Abū Ḥāmid al-Ghazālī (d. 505 AH/1111 AD). He has sometimes been acclaimed in both East and West as the greatest religious authority of Islam after the prophet Muḥammad, and he is by no means unworthy of this dignity. Muslims have given him the title of the Proof of Islam (*ḥujjah al-Islām*) and the Ornament of Religion (*zayn al-dīn*). His accomplishments have spread over many diverse branches of learning including Islamic jurisprudence, theology, logic, metaphysics, ethics, Sufism, and Qur'anic studies. At an advanced age, when he had already composed numerous works on many of these Islamic intellectual disciplines and when he had already completed traversing the Sufi path and thus had already ascended to the highest peak of intellectual and spiritual achievement, he expressed his own understanding of the Qur'an through the composition of a work, *Jawāhir al-Qur'ān,* which, in the following chapters, has been translated into English under the title *The Jewels of the Qur'an.*

This book is the source for much of what we know concerning al-Ghazālī's own views on our religious Scripture. It is of course not a commentary on the Qur'an in the general usage of the term, although it does comment upon certain important Qur'anic sūrahs and verses in various connections. It presents us with al-Ghazālī's own understanding of some basic problems concerning the Qur'an—problems which are of equal interest to both Muslim and non-Muslim students of the Scripture. Throughout the book there is an emphasis—a strong emphasis—upon employing what the author considers to be the correct method of apprehending the Holy Book, i.e. upon penetrating into the depth of the inner, hidden meanings of the Qur'anic verses, without merely being content with their outward meanings, like a diver's diving down to the depths of a fathomless ocean in order to bring out the hidden pearls and treasures. A very clear-cut and complete, but brief, theory concerning the aims (*maqāṣid*) of the Qur'an is given in this book—a theory which is recognized as important and is often quoted by al-Suyūṭī (d. 911 AH) and other later scholars of the Qur'an. Inseparably connected with this theory is another, in which al-Ghazālī demonstrates that all diverse branches of Islamic learning have stemmed from the Qur'an; this is a demonstration of the view usually held by Muslims that the Holy Scripture constitutes the sole source of all forms of Islamic knowledge. In this book there is also an effort to demonstrate the truth of the statements of the prophet Muḥammad on the excellence of some Qur'anic sūrahs and verses over others—e.g. his statements: The Sūrah of Yā Sīn is the heart of the Qur'an, the Throne Verse is the chief of all Qur'anic verses, the Sūrah of Sincerity equals the merit of one-third of the entire Qur'an, the Opening Sūrah is the key to all the doors of Paradise, and so on. The second part of the book presents us with all 'jewel' verses and all 'pearl' verses—

verses which are concerned with the two most important of the six principal aims of the Scripture. The separation of these verses from all the other verses which concern the remaining aims of the Qur'an is unprecedented in the history of Qur'anic literature and must be regarded as a significant contribution to Qur'anic studies. These are the main problems discussed in this book. In connection with them other minor but important problems have also been dealt with, one of them being the relationship between the world of perception and the world of the unseen; this relationship is reminiscent of Plato's well known theory of forms—a reason why students of al-Ghazālī sometimes tend to think of Plato's influence upon him.

The writing in the first part of the book is mostly allegorical; this is needed in order to facilitate the exposition of the lofty and magnificent nature of the Qur'an. The truth underlying the major allegories employed is explained, and sometimes separate sections are devoted to this task; yet allegories are to be found here and there unexplained, demanding the reader's own effort to grasp their underlying meaning and significance. The treatment of the book is serious, deep, penetrating and, above all, so logical that one chapter follows another automatically and smoothly. This logical arrangement of material is in complete agreement with al-Ghazālī's usual method of composition.

Since this English version of the book is the translation of the Arabic original it seems necessary to mention the methods employed in making this translation. It is not a strictly literal rendering of the original; rather it is the presentation of the meaning of the original in easy, modern English; in presenting this meaning, however, efforts are made to be very close to the original. Sometimes materials are added in the text for clarification of the meaning, and these are put between square brackets. Where an expression of the original is likely to affect the flow of reading, such an expression is put between round brackets. All footnotes are added by the translator, sometimes to clarify difficult concepts, phrases and words, and sometimes to provide the reader with more relevant information. In the numbering of the Qur'anic verses appearing in this book the official Egyptian edition of the Qur'an is consistently followed. The terms Qur'an and sūrah are occasionally abbreviated as Q. and S. respectively.

In respect of the translation of more than fifteen hundred Qur'anic verses which appear in this book, the reader will notice a sharp deviation from the archaic English of earlier Biblical translations. This style influenced many English translations of the Qur'an which are, as a result, clumsy, obscure or incomprehensible, especially to the general reader, despite the Qur'an's repeated claim to be a clear, easy book of guidance. This disadvantage of the older Biblical style of translation was also pointed out by A.J. Arberry more than two decades ago; he himself retained what he considered to be "a minimal obedience to tradition" (*The Holy Koran: An Introduction With Selections,* London, 1953, p. 31). In the last twenty-four years Islam expanded greatly, especially in Africa, Europe, Canada and the United States of America, but many new converts have been heard to express their weariness at the Biblical style of Qur'an-translation and their desire for translations in regular, modern, free-flowing English, which would not only be scholarly but also interesting and enjoyable. Such a translation of more than fifteen hundred Qur'anic verses has been attempted in this book. The reader will also notice that the present translation has tried to retain the emphasis which Qur'anic verses contain very often through various linguistic subtleties. This emphasis aims at eliciting positive response on the part of the hearer, and forms one of the special characteristics of the Scripture of Islam. Most of the Qur'an-translators have neglected this emphasis. In respects other than this and the style, the present translation sometimes agrees with the existing ones to which it is indebted. It is hoped that this small book of al-Ghazālī will be of great help to the English speaking reader in his understanding of the Qur'an.

The first part of this English version of the book was prepared in Edinburgh in June, 1973 on completion of my doctoral studies in the ethics of al-Ghazālī under the supervision of Professor W. Montgomery Watt. I should like to record my thanks to Mrs Phyllis Graham for carefully going through the manuscript of that part and to Dr Roger Card of the National University of Malaysia for reading the manuscript of the entire book and making some valuable suggestions. My thanks are also due to Mr Syed Zulflida, Mr Peter Mooney, Mr Lee Gray and Mr Moxie Craus of the National University of Malaysia for editing the manuscript and for reading the proofs.

M. Abul Quasem
Kuala Lumpur, Dhū al-Ḥijjah 1397
November 1977

Contents of the book in detail

In the name of God, Most Gracious, Ever Merciful

All types of perfect praise belong to God alone, the Lord of all the worlds. May His blessings be on His prophet Muḥammad, on all [members of] his family, and on all his companions!

This section concerns the content of the book we have named *the jewels of the Qur'an.*

Know (may God guide you to the right path!) that we have arranged this book in three parts: One on introductory matters, one on aims, and one on the matters connected with the aims.

The first part which is on introductory matters comprises nineteen chapters:

1. The Qur'an is [like] an ocean which covers many types of jewels and valuables.
2. The limiting of the aims of the Qur'an and its valuables to six divisions of which three are important principles and three follow them and complete them.
3. The explanation of these six divisions one by one. They branch off so that they become ten.
4. The process by which all sciences branch off from these ten divisions. The sciences of the Qur'an are divided into the science of the outer shell and the science of the inner jewels. An explanation of the grades of sciences.
5. How the sciences of the ancients and the moderns branch off from the Qur'an.[1]
6. The meaning of the statement that the Qur'an comprises red brimstone, the greatest antidote, the strongest musk, and all other valuables and pearls. This can only be known by

1. This oblique sign is used throughout this book in order to indicate the termination of a page of the Arabic original.

one who knows the relationship between the visible world and the invisible world.

7. The reasons why the entities of the invisible world are illustrated in the Qur'an by means of similitudes derived from the visible world.
8. The comprehension of the connection existing between the visible world and the invisible world.
9. Analysis of the allegories underlying red brimstone, the greatest antidote, the strongest musk, aloe-wood, corundums, pearls, and so on.
10. The benefit of employing these allegories.
11. How some verses of the Qur'an excel others when the whole of it is the speech of God (may He be exalted!).
12. The secrets of the Sūrah of Opening[1] (الْفَاتِحَة) (*al-Fātiḥah*) and how it comprises eight of the ten types of the valuables of the Qur'an. The description of part of the meaning of "Most Gracious (الرَّحْمَن), Ever Merciful" (الرَّحِيم) in relation to the nature of animals.
13. That the eight doors of Paradise are opened through the Sūrah of Opening (الْفَاتِحَة) and that it is the key to all of them.
14. Why the Verse of the Throne (آيَة الْكُرْسِيّ) (*Āyah al-Kursī*)[2] is regarded as the chief of Qur'anic verses, and why it is nobler than the verses, "God bears witness"[3] (شَهِدَ اللهُ), "Proclaim: He is God, the Single"[4] (قُلْ هُوَ اللَّهُ أَحَدٌ), the beginning of the Sūrah of Iron[5] (أَوَّلُ الْحَدِيد), the end of the Sūrah of the Gathering[6] (أَوَّلُ الْحَشْر), and all other verses.
15. An investigation into the reason why the [value of the] Sūrah of Sincerity (سُورَةُ الإِخْلاص) (*Sūrah al-Ikhlāṣ*)[7] is equal to [the value of] a third part of the Qur'an.
16. Why the Sūrah of Yā Sīn[8] (سُورَةُ يس) is regarded as the heart of the Qur'an.

---

1. Sūrah 1.
2. Qur'an, 2:255
3. Qur'an, 3:18.
4. Qur'an, 112:1.
5. Qur'an, 57:1-6.
6. Qur'an, 59:22-24.
7. Sūrah 112.
8. Sūrah 36.

17. Why the Prophet (ṣ) specified the Sūrah of Opening (الْفَاتِحَة) as the best sūrah of the Qur'an and the Verse of the Throne (آيَة الْكُرْسِيّ) as the chief of the Qur'anic verses, and why this was better than its opposite.
18. The condition of the gnostics (*al-'ārifūn*). In this world they are as if in 'a Paradise the breadth of which is greater than the heavens and the earth';[9] 'the clusters of the fruits of their' present 'Paradise are near to gather'[10] and 'are unfailing and unforbidden'.[11]
19. The secret reason for stringing the jewels of the Qur'an on one string and its pearls on another.

These are the nineteen chapters [which constitute the first part of the book].

The second part deals with the aims, and comprises the pith of the Qur'anic verses which are of two kinds. The first consists of the jewels which are the verses revealed especially concerning the essence of God (to Him belong glory and power). His attributes and works. This is the cognitive part (*al-qism al-'ilmī*). The second consists of the pearls which are verses on the description of the straight path (الصِّرَاط الْمُسْتَقِيم) and verses which urge man to follow it. This is the practical part (*al-qism al-'amalī*).

A chapter explaining the reason why the Qur'anic verses have been confined to this sum total.[12]

---

9. Qur'an, 3:133.
10. Qur'an, 69:23.
11. Qur'an, 56:32-33.
12. At this place thirty-four lines of the original Arabic text have not been translated because they describe the contents, not of *The Jewels of the Qur'an,* but of another work of al-Ghazālī, *The Book of the Forty on the Principles of Religion* (*Kitāb al-Arba'īn fī Uṣūl al-Dīn*).

Part One
Introductory Matters

This part deals with several important problems about the Qur'an. It comprises nineteen chapters some of which concern problems about the Qur'an as a whole, while others treat problems related to some of its specific parts. These chapters are arranged by al-Ghazālī so logically and systematically that one chapter leads the reader to another automatically and smoothly.

1

The Qur'an—an ocean with jewels and valuables

أَفَلَا يَتَدَبَّرُونَ الْقُرْآنَ أَمْ عَلَىٰ قُلُوبٍ أَقْفَالُهَا.

> Do they not ponder over the Qur'an in order to understand its deep meaning, or is it that their minds are locked up from within? (Qur'an, 47:24)

In the name of God, Most Gracious, Ever Merciful

After mentioning the name of God, I glorify Him with His praise which should constitute the beginning of every book. May His blessings be upon His messengers!—a prayer which should form the completion of every discourse.

I then wish to rouse you from your sleep, O you who recite the Qur'an to a great length, who take its study as an occupation, and who imbibe some of its outward meanings and sentences.[13] How long will you ramble on the shore of the ocean, closing your eyes to the wonders of the meanings of the Qur'an? Was it not your duty to sail to the midst of the fathomless ocean of these meanings in order to see their wonders, to travel to their islands in order to gather their best produce, and to dive into their depths so that you might become rich by obtaining their jewels? Do you not feel ashamed of being deprived of their pearls and jewels by your persistence in looking at their shores and outward appearances?

Has it not come to your knowledge that the Qur'an is [like] an ocean and that it is from the Qur'an that the sciences of the

---

13. In this chapter al-Ghazālī asks man neither to devote himself wholly to the recitation of the Qur'an, nor to be content with understanding its outward meaning, but to make a serious endeavour to know the deep meanings hidden under Qur'anic verses. The Qur'an is like an ocean. As in the bottom of an ocean, pearls remain hidden, so also are hidden

ancients and the moderns branch off,[14] just as rivers and brooks branch off from the shores of an ocean? Why do you not emulate those people who waded through their waves and thus gained red brimstone,[15] dived into their depths and thus drew out red corundum, shining pearls and green chrysolite, travelled along their coasts and thus gathered grey ambergris and fresh blooming aloe-wood, and became attached to their islands and thus derived from their animals the greatest antidote and the strongest musk? Take notice that, fulfilling the duty of [Islamic] brotherhood and hoping the blessing of your prayer to God, I now wish to guide you to the manner of the journey of these people, of their diving and of their swimming.

---

the wonderful meanings behind the Qur'anic verses. It is the duty of a Muslim to understand these meanings. If he fails to fulfil this duty he should be ashamed of his conduct.

14. The phrase 'sciences of the ancients and sciences of the moderns' (*'ulūm al-awwalīn wa 'ulūm al-ākharīn*) here means all Islamic subjects of study that came into existence from early Islam up to al-Ghazālī's time. How these subjects stemmed off from the Qur'an is demonstrated in the fourth and fifth chapters of this book. The term 'science' is used in this book in a loose sense; it means knowledge, subject of study or intellectual discipline; it does not mean that science which is opposite of arts. The words *awwalīn* and *ākharīn* are taken from Tradition (*ḥadīth*) where they occur; see Ibn Mājah. *Sunan,* Fitan, 20.

15. The allegories underlying red brimstone, red corundum, and so on are analysed in chap. 9.

2

The aims of the Qur'an and its valuables

The secret of the Qur'an, its purest pith, and its ultimate aim consist in calling people to God, the Most Powerful, the Lord of this world and the Hereafter,[16] the Creator of the heavens above and the layers of earth below, and of whatever is between them and whatever is under the moist subsoil[17]. For this reason the sūrahs of the Qur'an and its verses are limited to six types of which three are precedents and important principles and [the remaining] three follow them, enrich them and complete them.

As to the three important divisions, they concern the definition of God to Whom men are called, the definition of the straight path[18] perseverance in which is required in advancing towards Him, and the definition of the condition at the time of attaining to Him.

As to the three divisions which enrich them and complete them, one describes the conditions of those who answer to the call to God, and His delicate dealings with them, the secret and the purpose of this being to excite [in others] a desire [for the attainment of these conditions] and to encourage them [to it]. It also describes the conditions of those who shrink from answering to the call and the manner of the suppression and punishment of them by God, the secret and the purpose of this being to provoke consideration and fear. The second division narrates the conditions of those who deny God, and reveals

16. Qur'an, 53:25.
17. Qur'an, 20:6
18. Qur'an, 1:6.

their disgrace and their ignorance in disputing and arguing against the truth. The secret and the purpose of all this being, on the side of falsity, to make manifest and to create aversion, and, on the side of truth, clear apprehension, confirmation and constraint. The third division defines the stages of the path to God and the manner of taking provision and preparation for it.

3

An explanation of the six aims of the Qur'an

The first division of Qur'anic verses concerns the definition of the One to Whom men are called. It is an explanation of knowledge (*maʿrifah*) of God (may He be exalted!), and it is the red brimstone. This knowledge comprises knowledge of the essence of the True One, knowledge of His attributes, and knowledge of His works, and these three are to be called corundum, since these are the most special of the benefits derived from the red brimstone.

Just as corundums have grades—among them are red, bluish-grey and yellow; some of them are more precious than others—so these three forms of knowledge are not of the same grade. On the contrary, the most precious of them is knowledge of God's essence, and hence this should be called the red corundum. Next to this is knowledge of God's attributes, and this is the bluish-grey corundum. Contiguous to this is knowledge of God's works, and this is the yellow corundum.

As the most precious of these corundums is the greatest and the most rare to find, and because of its rarity [even] kings can only get possession of a little of it whereas they may sometimes gain much of what is inferior to it, so also knowledge of divine essence is the narrowest in scope, most difficult to acquire, most puzzling to thought, and furthest from receiving discussion. This is the reason why the Qur'an contains only notes and indications of this knowledge, and references to it amount to [a] the mention of absolute sanctification such as the words of God (may He be exalted!), "Like Him there is nothing"[19]

19. Qur'an, 42:11.

(لَيْسَ كَمِثْلِهِ شَيْءٌ), and the Sūrah of Sincerity[20], (سُورَةُ الإِخْلَاصِ) and [b] the mention of absolute greatness such as His words, "Glory be to Him! High be He exalted above that which they [i.e. polytheists] describe of Him! The Originator of the heavens and the earth!"[21] (سُبْحَانَهُ وَتَعَالَىٰ عَمَّا يَصِفُونَ ۞ بَدِيعُ السَّمَاوَاتِ وَالْأَرْضِ)

As to the divine attributes their scope is wider, and the girdle of speech concerning them is broader. This is the reason why the verses describing divine knowledge, power, life, speech, wisdom, hearing, seeing, and so on, are numerous.

As for divine works they are [comparable to] a sea the shores of which are very broad and the bounds of which cannot be ascertained by inquiry. Rather there is nothing in existence except God and His works. All that exists besides Him is His works; the Qur'an, however, includes the obvious of them existing in the visible world such as the mention of the heavens, the stars, the earth, mountains, trees, animals, seas, plants, sending down of sweet water [from the clouds] and all other means of maintaining plants and [other forms of] life. These are the divine works obvious to the senses. The noblest of His works, the most wonderful of them, and those which point most clearly to the glory of their Maker are those which are not obvious to the senses, but belong to the invisible world (*'ālam al-malakūt*). They are the angels, the incorporeal beings, the spirit, and the soul, i.e. that part of man which knows God (may He be exalted!); these last two are also among the sum total of the unseen and invisible world and are outside the world of possession and sense perception. Among the divine works not obvious to the senses are the terrestrial angels entrusted with [the care of] mankind, and they are those angels who prostrated themselves before Adam. Among them are also the devils who have been given power over mankind, and they are those who refused to prostrate themselves before Adam. [Further,] among them are the celestial angels the highest of whom in rank are the archangels (*al-karūbiyyūn*) who are secluded in Paradise

20. Sūrah 112.
21. Qur'an, 6:100-101.

(*ḥaẓīrah al-quds*) giving no attention to human beings; rather they give no attention to anything other than God (may He be exalted!) because of their absorption in the beauty of His Lordly Excellency and its glory; they confine their gaze to Him, glorifying Him day and night without tiring.[22] Do not consider it improbable that among the servants of God there may be someone whom His glory diverts from giving attention to Adam and his children. Man cannot magnify himself to this extent. Truly, the Messenger of God (may He bless him and greet him!) said, "Surely God has a white earth where the journey of the sun is of thirty days similar to the days of this world; it is filled thirty times more [than this world] with creatures who do not know that God is disobeyed in the earth, nor do they know that God (may He be exalted!) has created Adam and Iblīs.[23] Ibn 'Abbās[24] narrated this Tradition. The kingdom of God is indeed wide!

Know that the majority of people are not aware of most of the works of God, especially the noblest of these works. Rather their understanding is confined to the worlds of sense and imagination, which form the last of the results of the invisible world and are like the rind most distant from the purest pith. One who has not gone beyond this stage has, as it were, seen nothing of the pomegranate except its rind, or of man's wonders except his outward shape.

These, then, constitute the sum total of the first division of Qur'anic sūrahs and verses, and in them are present different types of corundums. We shall soon recite to you the verses revealed concerning them especially,[25] since they are the essence of the Qur'an, its heart, its pith, and its secret.

The second division concerns the definition of the path of advancing towards God (may He be exalted!). This is by

---

22. Qur'an, 21:20.
23. Unidentified.
24. 'Abdallāh ibn 'Abbās was a cousin and a great companion of the prophet Muḥammad; he died in 68 AH/687-688 AD See al-Dhahabī, *Tadhkirah al-Ḥuffāẓ*, Hyderabad, India, 1333, I, 37; Ibn 'Abd al-Barr, *al-Istī'āb*, Egypt, 1960, III, 933-939.
25. Pt. II, chap. 1.

devoting oneself to the service of God as He (may He be exalted!) said, "Devote yourself to Him very devoutly"[26] (وَتَبَتَّلْ إِلَيْهِ تَبْتِيلًا). Devotion to Him is achieved by advancing towards Him and turning away from things other than Him; and this is expressed in His words, "There is no God but He; so take Him for a guardian."[27] (لَا إِلَٰهَ إِلَّا هُوَ فَاتَّخِذْهُ وَكِيلًا) Advancement towards Him can only be achieved by perseverance in remembrance of Him, while turning away from things other than Him is effected by opposing passion, by cleansing oneself from the troubles of this world, and by purification of the soul from them. The result of this purification is prosperity in the Hereafter[28] as God (may He be exalted!) said, "He indeed has achieved prosperity who has purified himself and remembers the name of his Lord and so performs the ritual prayer"[29] (قَدْ أَفْلَحَ مَنْ تَزَكَّىٰ ۝ وَذَكَرَ اسْمَ رَبِّهِ فَصَلَّىٰ). Thus the path is supported by two matters, namely, perseverance and opposition—perseverance in remembrance of God (may He be exalted!) and opposition to that which diverts from Him. This is the journey (*al-safar*) to God.[30]

In this journey to God there is movement neither from the side of the traveller nor from the side of Him to Whom he travels, since both are together. Have you not heard the words of God (may He be exalted!)—and He is the most truthful of all those who speak—"We are nearer to him [i.e. man] than his jugular vein (وَنَحْنُ أَقْرَبُ إِلَيْهِ مِنْ حَبْلِ الْوَرِيدِ)"[31]

The truth is that the seeker and the Sought are comparable to a picture present in a mirror: The picture is not revealed in

26. Qur'an, 73:8.
27. Qur'an, 73:9.
28. For a discussion of al-Ghazālī's conceptions of other worldly happiness, prosperity, success and salvation, see Muhammad Abul Quasem, "Al-Ghazālī's Conception of Happiness," *Arabica,* XXII, 153-161.
29. Qur'an, 87:14-15.
30. This is a technical term of Sufism. The meanings of this and other technical terms such as path (*ṭarīq*), traveller (*musāfir, sālik*) are briefly described in al-Ghazālī's book *al-Imlā' 'alā Ishkālāt al-Iḥyā'*, in *Iḥyā' 'Ulūm al-Dīn,* Beirut, V, 15-16.
31. Qur'an, 50:15.

it because of rust on its surface; when, however, you polish the mirror the picture is revealed in it, neither by the movement of the picture towards it nor by its movement towards the picture, but by the removal of the veil. God (may He be exalted!) is revealed by His essence and is not concealed, for concealment of light is impossible, and by light everything which is concealed becomes obvious, and God is the light of the heavens and the earth.[32] The concealment of light from the pupil of the eye is only caused by one of two matters—either by turbidness in the pupil of the eye, or by weakness in it since it is unable to tolerate the great dazzling light just as the eyes of bats are unable to tolerate the light of the sun. Nothing, then, is incumbent upon you except to cleanse turbidness from the eye of the soul and to strengthen its pupil. In that case God will be in the soul as the picture is in the mirror, so that when He suddenly reveals Himself in the mirror of the soul you hasten to say that He is inside the soul and that the human nature (*nāsūt*) has put on the divine nature (*lāhūt*),[33] until God strengthens you with the firm word[34] so that you realize that the picture is not [really] inside the mirror, but [only] reflected in it. If the picture were to rest inside the mirror it would be inconceivable that it could be reflected in many mirrors at one time; rather [the case would be that] at that time when it rested inside one mirror, it moved from another. Such, however, is not the fact in the least, for God reveals Himself to many of the gnostics at the same time. It is true that He reveals Himself to some mirrors [of the soul] most perfectly, most obviously, most directly and most clearly, and to others most secretly and indirectly, and this [difference] is commensurate with the clarity of the mirror, its polish, the correctness of its shape and the right width of its surface. This is why the Prophet (ṣ) said "God certainly reveals Himself to people generally, but to Abū Bakr

32. Qur'an, 24:35.
33. This is al-Ghazālī's criticism of the Christian belief that the divine nature and the human nature are blended in Jesus Christ.
34. Qur'an, 14:27.

especially."[35]

Knowledge of advancement [towards God] and attainment of Him (*wuṣūl*) is also [like] a deep sea from the seas of the Qur'an. We shall soon gather for you the verses which will guide you to the path of advancement [towards God] so that you may reflect over them in their entirety.[36] It may be that what should be opened will be opened to you. This division [of Qur'anic sūrahs and verses] constitutes the shining pearls.

The third division defines man's condition at the time of attaining to God. It includes the mention of repose and delight which he will encounter. The word which is comprehensive of all the types of repose is Paradise, and the highest of these is the pleasure of looking upon God (may He be exalted!). It [also] includes the mention of humiliation and punishment to be suffered by those who are veiled from Him through neglecting to traverse [the path to Him]. The word which is comprehensive of all the types of pain is Hell, and the most intense of them is the pain caused by the veil (*ḥijāb*) [from God] and removal to a distance (*ib'ād*) [from Him]; (may God protect us from it!). For this reason He mentioned it first in His words (may He be exalted!), "No indeed. On that Day they will most certainly be veiled from their Lord. Then they shall roast in Hell."[37]

This division further includes the mention of the preceding conditions of both groups, [i.e. the people of Paradise and the people of Hell]. These conditions are expressed as resurrection, raising of the dead, reckoning, the balance, and the bridge. These have obvious outward meanings, which occupy the place of food, for common men; these have [also] obscure secrets, which occupy the place of life, for the special people. A third part of the verses of the Qur'an and its sūrahs concerns the details of these. We do not intend to gather them [in this book], because they are more than can be gathered and

35. Unidentified. For the biography of Abū Bakr al-Ṣiddīq see Ibn Ḥajar al-'Asqalānī, *Tahdhīb al-Tahdhīb,* Hyderabad, India, 1325 AH, V, 315-316.
36. See *infra,* Pt. II, chap. 2.
37. Qur'an, 83:15.

counted. In their case there is scope for thought and search. This third division constitutes the green chrysolite.

The fourth division [of Qur'anic sūrahs and verses] concerns the conditions of those who have traversed [the path to God] and those who have denied Him and deviated from His path. The conditions of the former are [expressed in the] stories of Adam, Noah (Nūḥ), Abraham (Ibrāhīm), Moses (Mūsā), Aaron (Hārūn), Zachariah, John the Baptist (Yaḥyā), Jesus ('Īsā), Mary (Maryam), David (Dāwūd), Solomon (Sulaymān), Jonah (Yūnus), Lot(Lūṭ), Enoch (Idrīs), Khaḍir, Shu'ayb, Elias, Muḥammad (ṣ), Gabriel, Michael, [other] angels, and so on. The conditions of those who have denied God and have deviated from His path are like the stories of Nimrod, Pharaoh, 'Ād, people of Lot, people of Tubba', men of the Grove (Aykah), infidels of Makkah, worshippers of idols, the devils, and so on. The benefit of this division lies in the arousal of fear, the giving of warning and the promotion of consideration. This division also includes secrets, indications and hints, which require prolonged reflection. Grey ambergris and fresh blooming aloe-wood are to be found in the description of the conditions of these two groups of people. The verses revealed concerning them are so many that there is no need to seek them and gather them.

The fifth division [of Qur'anic sūrahs and verses] concerns the arguments of the infidels against the truth, clear explanation of their humiliation by obvious proofs, and the striking disclosure of their falsehood and self-deceit. Their falsehood is of three kinds: One consists in speaking of God (may He be exalted!) in terms which do not befit Him, such as that the angels are His daughters,[38] that He has a child, that He has partners, and that He is 'a third of the three'.[39] The second is to consider God's Messenger (ṣ) as a sorcerer, soothsayer and a liar, to refuse to believe in

---

38. This was the belief of the pagan Arabs of the time of the prophet Muḥammad; see Qur'an 17:40, 43:19, 52:27.
39. This refers to the Christian doctrine of the Trinity. See Qur'an 5:73, 4:171.

his prophethood, and to say that he is a man like other people so that he does not deserve to be followed. The third is the denial of the Last Day, the denial of the resurrection, raising the dead, Paradise, Hell, and the denial of the consequences of obedience and disobedience to God. In His (may He be exalted!) arguments substantiated with proofs against the infidels are present subtleties and realities in which a great antidote is to be found. The verses concerning this [fifth] division also are obviously numerous.

The sixth division [of Qur'anic sūrahs and verses] defines the fulfilment of obligations at the stages of the path [to God] and the manner of taking provision and of seeking preparedness by making ready the weapons which will repel the bandits and brigands at the stages. The explanation of this is that the world is one of the stages of those who travel to God[40] (may He be exalted!), and the body is a vehicle. The man who neglects the management of the stage and the vehicle cannot complete his journey. So long as he does not set in order the affairs of his livelihood, the task of complete devotion to God (may He be exalted!) which is identical with traversing the path to Him, cannot be attained. This devotion [in turn] cannot be complete until his body is sound and his offspring continued. These two become complete by the means of preservation of their existence and by the means of repelling those things which corrupt them and destroy them. As to the means of preservation of their existence, they are eating and drinking which are for the continuance of the body and for sexual intercourse which is for the continuance of offspring. Food is created as a means of life, and females as a means of continuation of species. But edibles and women are not special for some eaters [and some men] on the authority of their innate quality. Should this matter be left without defining the rules of making them special [for some only], people would have neglected it and fought among themselves, and this would have diverted them from traversing the path [to God]; indeed this would have led them to destruction. The Qur'an,

40. See *supra*, p. 10, n. 30.

therefore, has explained the rules of speciality in regard to wealth in the verses dealing with sales, usury, giving and receiving of loans, division of inheritances, the causes of required expenditures, the division of booty, charities, marriages, emancipation of slaves, *kitābah*,[41] the possession of slaves and the taking of prisoners in battle. The Qur'an has [also] defined the manner of speciality in regard to wealth, at the time of accusation, by confession, oaths and witnesses. As for speciality with regard to females, it is described in the verses concerning marriage, divorce, withdrawal from divorce, the legal period of retirement assigned to a widow or divorced woman before she may marry again, *khul'*[42], dowry, *īlā'*,[43] *ẓihār*,[44] *li'ān*,[45] and also in the verses concerning those women with whom marriage is unlawful because of blood relationship, suckling, and relationship through marriage.

---

41. *Kitābah* literally means writing. In Islamic religious law it is a form of buying oneself free. It is a contractual liberation where the slave pays his owner a certain amount of money or its equivalent in two or three instalments. The owner is the *mukātib* and the slave is the *mukātab*. The latter alone can annul the contract if he wishes. See Qur'an 24:33.
42. According to traditional Ḥanafī law, a wife may obtain a divorce by providing the husband with some money, usually the dower money which she received from him on her marriage, for her release. This form of divorce is known as *khul'*. It is an extra-judicial method of divorce, not requiring any decree of the court. But since it is a divorce by mutual agreement, the free consent of the husband is essential for its validity. The Qur'anic verse (2:229) upon which the institution of *khul'* is grounded is: If you fear that the husband and wife will not be able to observe the limits prescribed by God there will be no sin to either of them in respect of that which the wife may surrender for her release.
43. A form of divorce in which a man vows not to have any sexual intercourse with his wife for a period of not less than four months. See al-Jurjānī, *al-Ta'rīfāt*, ed. G. Flügel. Leipzig, 1845, p. 42; Qur'an 2:226: al-Bukhārī, *Ṣaḥīḥ*, Ṭalāq, 21; Ibn Mājah, *Sunan*, Ṭalāq, 24.
44. *Ẓihār* is a form of divorce by the formula 'you (i.e. wife) are to me as my mother's back' (*anti 'alayya ka ẓahri ummī*). This is reminiscent of pre-Islamic practice. Cf. Qur'an 58:2; al-Bukhārī, *Ṣaḥīḥ*, Ṭalāq, 23; Ibn Mājah, *Sunan*, Ṭalāq, 25.
45. *Li'ān* is a form of divorce which takes place under the following circumstances: If a man accuses his wife of adultery and does not prove it by

The means of repelling those elements which corrupt both the soundness of the body and the continuance of offspring are the punishments which restrain man from those elements. These punishments are like war with the infidels and unjust people and incitement to it, penalties, indemnities, reproofs, atonements, blood-ransoms and retaliation. Retaliation and blood-ransom are prescribed as a deterrent from [a man's] effort to destroy the life and limb [of another]. The penalties for theft and highway robbery are prescribed as a means of repelling that which destroys wealth, which is the means of livelihood. The penalties for adultery, homosexuality and false accusation are prescribed as deterrents from that which disorders the matters of offspring and lineages and corrupts the means of the continuance of the human species and successive generations. War with the infidels is enjoined as repelling that which will be caused by the deniers of truth, namely, disorder of the means of livelihood and worship, by both of which the [task of] attaining to God is accomplished. War with unjust people is ordered to repel the confusion which will appear when the disobedient people slip from the control of the religious government which is entrusted to the one [i.e. the king][46] who guards those who traverse [the path of God] and support the righteous, as a deputy of the Messenger of the Lord of all the worlds. The verses revealed concerning these matters are not hidden from you. They embody fundamental principles, advantages, wisdom, and benefits, which all are

---

four witnesses, he must swear before God that he is telling the truth and then add, "If I am a liar may God curse me". The wife then says, "I swear before God that my husband lies", and then adds "may God's wrath be upon me if this man be telling the truth". After this the divorce takes place *ipso facto.* Cf. Qur'an 24:6; al-Bukhārī, *Ṣaḥīḥ*, Ṭalāq, 4, 25, 27-36; Ibn Mājah, *Sunan,* Ṭalāq, 27.

46. The king's function in the ideal Islamic community is, according to al-Ghazālī, to create such an atmosphere as is conducive to the cultivation of religion and morality by the people. Thus politics lies at the background of ethics and religion. The king guards and supports the righteous, saints and Sufis. He works as the deputy of the Prophet (ṣ). In Islam kingship is something divine.

comprehended by the one who reflects upon the beauties of the revealed law which describes the bounds of judgements concerning the matters of this life. This sixth division [of the Qur'anic verses also] include that which is termed lawful, unlawful, and the bounds of God. It is in the verses falling under this division that the strongest musk is to be found.

These [six divisions] then form the confluence of those teachings which are contained in the sūrahs of the Qur'an and their verses. Should you thread these six divisions together with their intended branches on one string, you will find that there are ten types. [They concern] the divine essence, divine attributes, divine works, the life to come, the straight path (الصِّرَاطَ الْمُسْتَقِيم) i.e. the purification and beautification [of the soul], the conditions of the saints, the conditions of God's enemies, [His] arguments with the infidels, and [finally] the bounds of legal judgements.

4

Divisions of sciences of the Qur'an

You now, I suppose, long to know the manner of branching off of all these sciences[47] from these ten divisions [of Qur'anic verses] and [also] the grades of these sciences in respect of nearness and remoteness from their intended purpose. Then, know that the realities we hinted at have secrets and jewels; [but also] they have sea-shells, and the sea-shell is that which appears first. Some of the people who reach the sea-shells, know [only] these, while others break the shells and carefully examine the pearls [inside them]. Likewise, the shell of the jewels of the Qur'an, its garment, is the Arabic language. From this shell branch off five sciences which are the sciences of the rind, the shell and the garment [of the Qur'an], Thus from the words of the Qur'an, stemmed off the science of Arabic language; from the desinential syntax of the words, stemmed off the science of syntax of Arabic grammar; from the various desinential syntaxes of the Qur'an, stemmed off the science of readings; from the manner of pronouncing Qur'anic letters, stemmed off the science of outlets of letters. This is because the first of the parts of meanings with which speech is united is the sound; then by being shaped the sound becomes letters; then the assemblage of letters makes a word; the specification of some of the assembled letters makes the Arabic language; then the process of shaping of letters attributes to it the quality of desinential syntax; then the specification of one of the different desinential syntaxes makes a reading ascribed

47. For the meaning of the word science see *supra,* p. 4, n. 14.

to the seven standard readings; then when there is a proper Arabic word to which desinential syntax is applied, it has become the indicator of a meaning; then it demands outward exegesis, and this is the fifth science. These are the sciences of the shell and the rind of the Qur'an.

These sciences, however, are not of the same grade. On the contrary, a sea-shell has a face towards its inward part, and this face encounters the pearl face to face and nearly resembles it because of the proximity of its neighbourhood and continuance of its contact with the pearl; the sea-shell has also a face towards its outward part, and this face nearly resembles all other stones because of the remoteness of its neighbourhood and its lack of contact with the pearl. Likewise is the shell of the Qur'an. Its outward face is the sound, and the man entrusted with the knowledge of correcting its outlets in transmission and pronunciation is a man who possesses knowledge of letters. Thus he is the possessor of the knowledge of the outward rind which is removed from the inward part of the shell, let alone the pearl itself. Ignorance of a group of people has indeed reached to the extent that they have imagined the Qur'an to be mere letters and sounds, and on this belief they have based the theory that the Qur'an is created, since letters and sounds are created. What is most fitting for these people is that they should be stoned to death, or, [if it were possible] their intellect should be stoned. To reprimand them or to be severe with them is not enough for them as a calamity; nothing of the worlds of the Qur'an and the stages of its heavens appeared to them except its remotest rind.[48] This will acquaint you with the rank of knowledge of the Qur'an reader, for he only knows the correction of outlets of letters.

Contiguous to it in rank is the science of the language of the Qur'an. This is a science which includes, for example, the translation of the Qur'an and that which is near to it, i.e. the

48. This criticism of al-Ghazālī is directed against the Mu'tazilites who hold the theory that the Qur'an is created (*ḥādith*). All other Muslims believe that the Qur'an is the eternal and uncreated (*qadīm*) speech of God.

science of the strange words of the Qur'an. Near to the science of the Qur'anic language is the science of the desinential syntax of language, and this is the syntax of grammar. In one respect this science falls after the science of language, for the desinential syntax is after that to which it is applied. When compared to that science in respect of value also, it is below that, for it is like that which follows the language. Then near to the science of desinential syntax is the science of readings. This is a science by which the different ways of desinential syntax and various types of modes of pronunciation are known. It is more special to the Qur'an than philology and syntax of grammar, but it is among the superfluous things which are not needed, whereas philology and syntax of grammar are such that man is in need of them. Thus the philologist and the grammarian are at a higher rank than one who knows only the science of readings. All these people, however, turn round the shell and the rind of the Qur'an, although their grades are different.

Near to the science of readings is the science of outward exegesis of the Qur'an. This is the last grade of the shell of the Qur'an, which is near to contact with the pearl. This is the reason why its resemblance with the pearl has become strong, so that some people imagine that it is the pearl [itself] and that beyond it there is nothing more valuable than it. It is with it that most people are content. How great are their deception and deprivation, for they have imagined that there is no rank beyond the rank of theirs![49] However, in relation to those who possess the knowledge of [other] sciences of the shell, they are at a rank high and noble, since the science of exegesis is mighty when compared to other sciences of the shell, because it is not meant for them while they are meant for it.

When people at these five grades fulfil the stipulations of

49. Al-Ghazālī here minimizes the importance of those exegetes who confine themselves to the outward meaning of the Qur'anic verses. He exalts those exegetes who try to disclose the deep and hidden meanings of the verses of the Qur'an—meanings which he compares to the pearls that remain hidden in the bottom of a fathomless ocean. Also see *supra*, chap. 1.

their sciences, preserving them and transmitting them in a complete manner, God will appreciate their efforts and cleanse their faces, as His Messenger (ṣ) prayed, "May God grant an easy life to the man who heard my saying, then took it in, and then transmitted it as he heard it! It may be that a bearer of knowledge bears it to one who is not learned, and it may be that a bearer of knowledge bears it to one who is more learned than he."[50] They [i.e. the people of the five grades just mentioned] heard and transmitted and will, consequently, obtain the reward of bearing [what they heard] and transmitting it to one who is more learned than them or to one who is not learned. The exegete who is confined, in the science of exegesis, to narrating that which is related (*al-manqūl*) to him is a bearer and transmitter, just as one who has memorized the Qur'an and Traditions is a bearer and transmitter.

Likewise, the science of Tradition branches off into these parts, except reading and the correction of the outlets of letters. The grade of one who memorizes Traditions and transmits them is like that of one who teaches the Qur'an and memorizes it. The grade of one who knows [only] the outward meanings of Traditions is like that of an exegete. The grade of one who concerns himself with the science of names of transmitters of Traditions is like the grade of a grammarian or philologist. This is because the chain of transmission of Traditions and narration of them constitute the instrument of their transmission to us, and upright conditions of the transmitters form a stipulation for the soundness of the instrument of transmission; thus knowledge of the transmitters and knowledge of their conditions amount to the knowledge of the instrument and the stipulation of the instrument.

These, then, are the sciences of the shell of the Qur'an.

The second type is the sciences of the pith [of the Qur'an]. It has two grades. The lower grade is of the sciences of the three [Qur'anic] divisions which we have termed as those that follow

---

50. Ibn Mājah, *Sunan,* Muqaddimah, 18, Manāsik, 76; Aḥmad ibn Ḥanbal, *Musnad,* IV, 80, 82.

and complete [the more important three divisions[51]. These lower sciences are as follows].

The first concerns the knowledge of the stories [narrated] in the Qur'an and of what is related to the prophets, to the deniers [of God] and to His enemies. Story-tellers, preachers, and some of the Traditionists (*al-muḥaddithūn*) are responsible for this kind of knowledge. The need for this knowledge is not universal.

The second concerns God's argument with the infidels and His dispute with them. From this division stems the science of theology (*'ilm al-kalām*) intended to repel errors and heresies [with regard to Islamic religious beliefs] and to remove doubts [related to them]. Theologians are responsible for this science. We have explained this science at two levels. The lower level we have explained in *The Epistle from Jerusalem,*[52] and the higher level in *The Mean in Belief.*[53] This science is meant to guard the layman's religious belief against the confusion created by the heretics. This science does not concentrate on the intuitive knowledge (*kashf*) of realities. With this kind of science are related [a] the book we composed on the incoherence of the philosophers,[54] [b] that which we set forth in

51. See *infra,* chap. 2.
52. *Epistle from Jerusalem* (*al-Risālah al-Qudsiyyah*) al-Ghazālī wrote in Jerusalem. His stay at this holy place was part of his ten year life of solitude devoted to vigorous Sufi practices. In Jerusalem he used to enter the precinct of the Dome of the Rock every day and shut himself in. The *Epistle* he later incorporated in the second book of the first part of his *Iḥyā'*. The articles of faith set forth in the *Epistle* constitute the lower level because they are combined with their simple proofs only.
53. *The Mean in Belief* (*al-Iqtiṣād fi al-I'tiqād*) was written in the pre-Sufi period of al-Ghazālī's life, in Baghdad. In this work the articles of faith are set forth, having been combined with their deeper realities, complex of proofs involving deeper investigation, subtle questions and difficulties. It is published in Cairo.
54. This refers to al-Ghazālī's *Tahāfut al-Falāsifah* composed in 1095 AD when he was not a Sufi. In this book he was concerned with the negative aspect of the articles of faith, i.e. with those beliefs which, in reality, were wholly or partly unIslamic but which were considered by his contemporary Muslim philosophers to be fully Islamic.

the denial of Bāṭinism[55] in the book surnamed *The Mustaẓhirī,*[56] and in the book entitled *The Proof of the Truth and Fragments of Bāṭinism,*[57] and [c] the book *The Explanation of Disagreement on the Principles of Religion.*[58] This science has an instrument[59] by which one knows the methods of debate, indeed, the methods of dispute by true argument. These we dealt with in the book *The Touchstone of Reflection*[60] and in the book *The Standard of Knowledge,*[61] in such a way as not to be found in the [works of] Jurists and theologians, and he who is not acquainted with these two books cannot be confident in regard to the real nature of argument and doubt.

The third concerns the knowledge of the bounds [of legal judgements] laid down for specialization with regard to wealth and woman in order to seek help for the continuance of life and offspring. The jurists are entrusted with this knowledge. [That part of jurisprudence which is known as] 'the quarter of

---

55. Bāṭinism is identical with Ismā'īlism, a branch of Shī'ism. The Shī'ites are condemned as heretics by the main body of Muslims. Al-Ghazālī wrote several books directed in whole or in part against the Bāṭinites and completely exposed the falsity of their heretical beliefs.
56. At the request of the caliph al-Mustaẓhir who came to the throne in February, 1094, al-Ghazālī wrote this book in 1095 before his conversion to Sufism, in refutation of the Bāṭinites or the Ta'līmites. It was dedicated to the caliph.
57. *The Proof of the Truth and Fragments of Bāṭinism* (*Ḥujjah al-Ḥaqq wa Qawāṣim al-Bāṭiniyyah*) al-Ghazālī wrote in reply to the criticisms by the Ta'līmites made against him in Baghdad. It is lost.
58. *Mufaṣṣal al-Khilāf fī Uṣūl al-Dīn* is lost. Al-Ghazālī wrote this book in reply to criticisms by the Ta'līmites made against him in Hamadan.
59. By this instrument is meant Aristotelian logic as transmitted to the Muslim world by al-Ghazālī's contemporary philosophers, especially al-Fārābī and Avicenna. Al-Ghazālī approved of logic and made much more extensive use of it than did the Muslim theologians before him. In *al-Qisṭās al-Mustaqīm,* he justified logical principles by reference to the Qur'an.
60. *Miḥaqq al-Naẓar* was written before al-Ghazālī's conversion to Sufism. It is an exposition of logic used in theology. It is published in Cairo.
61. *Mi'yār al-'Ilm* was also written before al-Ghazālī became a Sufi. It too is an exposition of logic; it explains the technical terms used in *Tahāfut.* It was published in Cairo in 1329 AH.

jurisprudence on a man's dealing with others' (*rub' al-mu'āmalāt*) explains the specialization with regard to wealth. 'The quarter on marriage' (*rub' al-nikāḥ*) explains the specialization regarding the means of production of human species, i.e. women. 'The quarter on crimes' (*rub' al-jināyāt*) explains the restraint of those who bring disorder to these two. The need for this kind of knowledge is universal, because it is connected first with the goodness of this world and then with the goodness of the life to come. This is why one endowed with this knowledge is distinguished by the possession of great fame and reverence and by being held in preference to others, such as preachers, story-tellers, and theologians. For this same reason much research has been done on this science—so much so that it has exceeded the necessary measure; as a result of this, numerous books have appeared on this subject, especially on its disputed problems, although disagreement is near and error is not far from truth; everyone who makes independent legal judgements (*mujtahid*) comes near to be called right or to be said to have earned one reward should he make a mistake and his opponent [is said to have] two [because he is right]. But since great influence and renown are achieved by this science the motive for excess in deducing branches from it multiplied. We [ourselves] wasted a good part of our life writing books on its disputed problems, and we spent much of our life composing works on creeds and arranging them in our books *The Simple,*[62] *The Mediator,*[63] and *The Concise,*[64] despite exaggeration and excess in deducing branches and consequences. The amount of discussion we set forth in the

62. *Al-Basīṭ* is unpublished; see Ibn Khallikān, *Wafayāt al-A'yān wa Anbā' Abnā' al-Zamān,* Cairo, 1299, II, 246. It is a summary of Imām al-Ḥaramayn's *Nihāyah al-Maṭlab.*

63. *Al-Wasīṭ* is also unpublished; it is a summary of *al-Basīṭ*. See Ibn Khallikān, *Wafayāt,* II, 246.

64. *Al-Wajīz* was published in Cairo in 1317 AH. It is divided into two parts each of which consists of two hundred and ninety-six pages excluding the pages of contents which are ten and nine respectively. It is a summary of Shāfi'ī law.

book *The Essence of the Abridged*[65] is sufficient. This is the fourth book [of ours on this science] and is the smallest of all these works. The early generations (*al-awwalūn*) used to give legal judgements on problems but they did not preserve more than the content of this book. They gave right judgements through God's grace or suspended judgement saying: We do not know. They did not engage their whole life in this; on the contrary, they were preoccupied with the important [sciences] and turned this matter to others. This, then, is the manner in which jurisprudence stemmed off from the Qur'an.

From among jurisprudence, the Qur'an, and Tradition there originates a science named the principles of jurisprudence (*uṣūl al-fiqh*). It concerns the control of the rules of seeking information, by Qur'anic verses and prophetic traditions, about the judgements of the revealed law.

It should not be hidden from you that the ranks of story-tellers and preachers are below the ranks of jurists and theologians so long as the former group is content with mere stories and the like of them. The ranks of jurists and the theologians are close [to one another]; the need for jurists, however, is more universal, while that for the theologians is much stronger, and both are needed for the well-being of this world. Jurists are needed for the preservation of judgements with regard to the specialization of food and women. Theologians are needed for repelling, by argument and dispute, the harm done by heretics in order that their evil may not be spread and their harm may not become common. The relationship of jurists and theologians to the path [to God] and to what is aimed at is [as follows]: The relationship of jurists[66] is similar to the relationship of those who build and maintain houses of refuge and provide facilities along the way to Makkah to the

65. *Khulāṣah al-Mukhtaṣar* is lost. This book is al-Ghazālī's rearrangement of *al-Mukhtaṣar al-Ṣaghīr* (printed in Bulaq in 1321-1326 AH) of Abū Ibrāhīm Ismā'īl ibn Yaḥyā al-Muzanī (264 AH/878 AH). See al-Ghazālī, *Iḥyā'*, I, 40.

66. For more information on this relationship see Quasem, *The Ethics of al-Ghazālī: a Composite Ethics in Islam*, 1975, pp. 22-24, 26.

pilgrimage. The relationship of the theologians is similar to the relationship of squandered things on the path of pilgrimage and of its guard to the pilgrims. Should the jurists and the theologians add to their occupations the traversing of the path to God (may He be exalted!), by abstaining from the [blame-worthy aspect of the] world and by advancing towards God (may He be exalted!), then their excellence over others would be like the excellence of the sun over the moon. If, however, they confine themselves [only] to their occupations, their rank will be very low.

The higher grade of the sciences of the pith [of the Qur'an] consists in those important sciences which are the precedents and roots [of the three sciences already mentioned]. The noblest of these higher sciences is knowledge of God and the Last Day, for this knowledge is of that which is intended. Below this is knowledge of the straight path and of the manner of traversing it. This is the knowledge of [a] purification of the soul and removal of the obstacles of the destructive qualities, and of [b] making the soul beautiful with the saving qualities. We discussed these forms of knowledge in the [forty] 'books'[67] of *The Revival of Religious Sciences.* Thus in its 'Quarter on the Destructive Qualities' are discussed the vices from which the purification of the soul is required, namely, greed, anger, pride, ostentation, conceit, envy, love of influence, love of wealth, and so on. In 'the Quarter on the Saving Qualities' appear the praiseworthy qualities with which the soul should be made beautiful, such as asceticism, trust in God, satisfaction with divine decrees, love of God, truthfulness, sincerity, and so forth. In short, *The Revival* comprises forty 'books' each of which will guide you to one of the obstacles of the carnal soul together with the method of its removal, and to one

67. *The Revival* (*Iḥyā'*) is divided into four parts, each of which is called a 'quarter' (*rub'*). Each quarter is subdivided into ten parts, each of which is called a book (*kitāb*). For reasons why the *Revival* is divided into four parts see *Iḥyā'*. I, 3-4: Nabih Amin Faris, "The Iḥyā' 'Ulūm al-Dīn of al-Ghazzāli," *Proceedings of the American Philosophical Society,*" LXXI (1939), 15-19.

of the veils of the carnal soul along with the method of lifting it. This is a science [the rank of] which is above the sciences of jurisprudence, theology, and what is before these, for this is the science of the manner of traversing the path to God [itself], while the others are [merely] the sciences of the instrument of traversing, of repairing its stages and of resisting those which corrupt it when they appear.

The highest and noblest knowledge is the knowledge of God (may He be exalted!), because all other forms of knowledge are sought for the sake of it and it is not sought for anything else. The manner of progression in regard to it is to advance from divine works to divine attributes, and then from divine attributes to divine essence; thus there are three stages. The highest of these stages is knowledge of divine essence, and it is not possible for most people to understand this. That is why they have been commanded, "Reflect on God's creation, and do not reflect on His essence."[68] This progression is indicated by the gradual advance of God's Messenger (ṣ) in his observation, when he said, "I seek the protection of Your forgiveness from Your punishment."[69] This is his observation of divine work. Then he said, "I seek the protection of Your pleasure from Your displeasure." This is his observation of divine attributes. Finally he said, "I seek the protection of You against You." This is his observation of divine essence. Thus he was advancing step by step towards nearness [to God]. Then, at the time of reaching the extreme stage he admitted his inability by saying, "I do not understand Your praise; You are as You have praised Yourself."[70]

This [i.e. knowledge of God] is the noblest of all forms of knowledge, and it is followed in excellence by knowledge of the life to come, which is knowledge of final return to God, as we have already mentioned in our discussion of the three divisions

68. Unidentified.
69. Al-Nasā'ī, *Sunan,* Isti'ādhah, 62.
70. Muslim, *Ṣaḥīḥ,* Ṣalāh, 222; al-Tirmidhī, *Sunan,* Da'wāt, 75, 112; al-Nasā'ī, *Sunan,* Ṭahārah, 119; Abū Dāwūd, *Sunan,* Ṣalāh, 148; Ibn Mājah, *Sunan,* Iqāmah, 117.

[of the Qur'an].[71] This knowledge is connected with the science of gnosis (*'ilm al-ma'rifah*), and its real meaning is knowledge of man's relation to God (may He be exalted!) at the time of being drawn near to Him through knowledge or being veiled from Him by ignorance. Some of the principles of these four types of knowledge—i.e. knowledge of divine essence, attributes and works, and knowledge of the future life—and their confluence, which are that measure of knowledge with which we have been provided despite our short life, many works and calamities, and few helpers and companions, we set forth in some of [our] works[72] but did not disclose. [The reason for not disclosing it is that] most people's understanding would be wearied by it, and the weak, who are the most traditional in knowledge (*mutarassimīn bi al-'ilm*), would be harmed by it. Indeed, its disclosure is only beneficial to him, who has brought his knowledge of outward acts (*'ilm al-ẓāhir*) to perfection, and has followed the path to God removing evil qualities from the carnal soul and [undergoing] the methods of mortification, with the result that his carnal soul has become trained and is in good condition on the straight path so that he has no longer any pleasure in the [blameworthy aspect of the] world and only searches for the True One. In addition to these, he is provided with illuminating prudence, critical natural disposition, sharp intelligence and clear understanding. It is unlawful for those into whose hands that book falls, to disclose it except to one who combines [in oneself all] these qualities.

This, then, is the confluence of the sciences stemming from the Qur'an and their grades.

---

71. *Supra*, pp. 12-13.
72. This seems to refer to al-Ghazālī's book *al-Maḍnūn bih 'alā Ghayr Ahlih* published in Cairo in 1309 AH. This book mentions *The Revival* and is itself mentioned in *The Book of the Forty.*

5

Sciences of ancients and moderns from the Qur'an

Perhaps you will say: [Tell me the reason why you have limited sciences[73] to these only, when] there are many sciences besides them, i.e. the Science of Medicine, of the stars (Astronomy), of the shapes of the universe (Geography), and of the shapes of the animal's body and the anatomy of its limbs (Anatomy), and the science of magic, of talisman, and others.

[As a reply to this enquiry] know that we only indicated the religious sciences the existence of the origin of which in the universe is necessary in order that traversing the path to God and journeying towards Him may become easy. As to those sciences which you have indicated, they are sciences [no doubt], but the well-being of this life and of the next does not depend on knowledge of them, and this is why we did not mention them. Besides the sciences you have enumerated, there are [still] others the meanings of which are known, and the universe is not destitute of those who know them, and there is no need to mention them.

Rather I should say that through clear insight free from doubt, it has become apparent to us that in possibility and potentiality there are sciences which have not yet come into existence, although it is in man's power to grasp them. There are [other] sciences which [once] came into existence, but have now been effaced so that at this time such a man who knows them can never be found on the surface of the earth. There are [still] other sciences the understanding and acquisition of

73. For the meaning of the word 'sciences' see *supra*, p. 4, n. 14.

which are by no means in the power of human beings but which are possessed by some of the angels drawn near [to God], because possibility is limited in the case of human beings, while in the case of the angels it is limited to the relatively highest perfection,[74] as in the case of animals it is limited to the utmost imperfection. Only God (glory be to Him!) is He in Whose case knowledge has no limit, and our knowledge departs from the knowledge of the True One in two ways. One is the negation of its highest degree, and the other is that in His case sciences are not such as are in potentiality and possibility awaiting coming into existence; on the contrary, they are [already] existent and present—in His case every possibility of perfection is present and existent.

The principles of those sciences which we have enumerated and of those which we have not specified, are not outside the Qur'an, for all of these sciences are drawn out of one of the seas of knowledge of God (may He be exalted!), i.e. the sea of [knowledge of His] works. We have already mentioned[75] that the Qur'an is [like] a sea which has no shore, and that 'if the ocean became ink for [transcribing] the words of my Lord, surely the ocean would be exhausted before the words of my Lord came to an end'.[76] Among the works of God (may He be exalted!) which [for their vastness can be called] the sea of His works are, for instance, recovery and disease, as He (may He be exalted!), narrating the words of Abraham, said, "When I fall ill it is He Who restores me to health"[77] (وَإِذَا مَرِضْتُ فَهُوَ يَشْفِينِ). This single work can only be known by him who knows the science of medicine completely, for this science means nothing but the knowledge of all aspects of diseases together with their symptoms, and the knowledge of their cure and its means. Among the works of God are [also] the determination of [man's] knowledge of the sun and the moon and of their stages according to a fixed reckoning, as God (may

74. Among the creatures of God, only the angels, man and jinn are endowed with intelligence. Man's position is below that of the angels, whose qualities he should try to acquire. See al-Ghazālī, *Iḥyā'*, I, 236.
75. *Supra*, chaps. 1, 3.
76. Qur'an, 18:109.
77. Qur'an, 26:80.

He be exalted!) said: [At His will] the sun and the moon move according to a fixed reckoning[78] (الشَّمْسُ وَالْقَمَرُ بِحُسْبَانٍ). He [also] said: He ordained stages for the moon so that you might learn the method of calculating years and determining time[79] (قَدَّرَهُ مَنَازِلَ لِتَعْلَمُوا عَدَدَ السِّنِينَ وَالْحِسَابَ). He [further] said: [When....the moon is eclipsed, and the sun and the moon exhibit the same phenomenon.] on that Day man will say: Is there a place of refuge?[80]. He [further] said: He merges the night into the day, and merges the day into the night[81] (يُولِجُ اللَّيْلَ فِي النَّهَارِ وَيُولِجُ النَّهَارَ فِي اللَّيْلِ). He also said: The sun is moving towards an appointed goal; this is the decree of the Almighty, the All-knowing[82] (وَالشَّمْسُ تَجْرِي لِمُسْتَقَرٍّ لَهَا ذَلِكَ تَقْدِيرُ الْعَزِيزِ الْعَلِيمِ). The real meaning of the movements of the sun and the moon according to a fixed reckoning and of the eclipse of both, of the merging of the night into the day and the manner of the wrapping of one of them about the other, can only be known by him who knows the manner of the composition of the heavens and the earth, and this itself is a science [i.e. astronomy].

Likewise, the complete meaning of God's words, "O man, what has deceived you concerning your Gracious Lord, Who created you, then perfected you, then proportioned you aright? He fashioned you in whatever form He pleased"[83] (يَا أَيُّهَا الْإِنْسَانُ مَا غَرَّكَ بِرَبِّكَ الْكَرِيمِ ۞ الَّذِي خَلَقَكَ فَسَوَّاكَ فَعَدَلَكَ ۞ فِي أَيِّ صُورَةٍ مَا شَاءَ رَكَّبَكَ), can only be known by him who knows the anatomy of man's limbs and internal organs, their number, their kinds, their underlying wisdom, and their uses. God indicated these in many places of the Qur'an, and [knowledge of] these belongs to the sciences of the ancients and the moderns;[84] [in fact] in the Qur'an lies the confluence of the sciences of the ancients and the moderns.[85] In the same way the complete meaning of God's words, "I perfected his

78. Qur'an, 55:5.
79. Qur'an, 10:5.
80. Qur'an, 75:7-10.
81. Qur'an, 35:13.
82. Qur'an, 36:38.
83. Qur'an, 82:6-8.
84. For the phrase 'sciences of the ancients and the moderns' see *supra*, p. 4, n. 14.
85. See *supra*, chap. 4.

[i.e. Adam's] shape and breathed My spirit into him" (فَإِذَا سَوَّيْتُهُ وَنَفَخْتُ فِيهِ مِنْ رُوحِي), cannot be known so long as perfection of shape, breath and spirit are not known. There are such obscure sciences behind these as the occupation of which most people are heedless; sometimes they [even] fail to understand these sciences if they hear these from one who knows them. Should I go on narrating the details of divine works to which the verses of the Qur'an point, it would take a long time. Only an indication of their confluence is possible [here], and we have done this where[86] we have mentioned that knowledge of divine works is among the sum total of knowledge of God (may He be exalted!). That sum total includes these details. Likewise, every division we have briefly described will, if further divided, be branched off into many details. Reflect, then, on the Qur'an and seek its wonderful meanings, so that by chance you may encounter in it the confluence of the sciences of the ancients and the moderns and the sum total of their beginnings. Reflection on the Qur'an is intended only for reaching from the brief description of these sciences to their detailed knowledge which is [like] an ocean that has no shore.

---

86. *Supra,* chap. 3, pp. 8-9.

6

Explaining allegories about the Qur'an

Perhaps you will say: You have indicated in some of the divisions of sciences [already described][87] that there is found in some of them the greatest antidote, in others the strongest musk, and in [still] others red brimstone and other valuables; these are traditional allegories giving hints and indications [towards hidden meanings underlying them. Unveil these meanings with a view to facilitating my understanding].

Know that affectation and traditionalism are hateful to men of serious endeavour. In every sentence which has occurred, there are hints and indications of a hidden meaning understood by him who understands the relationship between the world of possession and perception and the world of the unseen and dominion, since everything in the former world is only a form of something spiritual in the unseen world, as if that thing which is in the world of possession and perception were the same as that which is in the world of the unseen and dominion, in respect to its spirit and meaning though not in respect to its shape and form. The physical form from the world of perception is included in the spiritual meaning of that world. This is why this world constitutes one of the stages of the path to God—a stage indispensable for man—since just as it is impossible to reach the core except by way of the rind, so it is impossible to advance towards the world of spirits except through the form of the world of bodies. This relationship can only be known by an example: Consider that which is revealed

87. *Supra,* chap. 3.

to a sleeping man in a true dream which is a forty-sixth part of prophethood,[88] and how it is revealed to him through imaginative forms. The man who teaches wisdom to those who are unworthy of it sees in his sleep that he is hanging pearls round the necks of pigs. A certain man dreamt that there was a ring in his hand with which he was sealing women's genitals and men's mouths. Ibn Sīrīn[89] said to him [in its interpretation]: You are a man who calls out to prayer (*adhān*) in the lunar month Ramaḍān before dawn. The man said: Yes. Another man dreamt that he was pouring oil into olive oil. Ibn Sīrīn said to him: If you have a slave women she is [in fact] your mother; she was captured in a war and sold, and you bought her without knowing [your relationship with her]. This was the fact. Observe, then, that sealing mouths and genitals with a ring agrees with calling out to prayer before dawn, in respect of the spirit of the ring which is prohibition, although the former differs from the latter in respect of form. Compare the other two dreams with this which we have just mentioned.

Know that the Qur'an and Traditions include many [instances] of this kind. Consider the words of the Prophet (*ṣ*), "The mind of a believer in God lies between two of the Fingers of the Most Gracious."[90] The spirit of the finger is ability for rapid movement; the believer's mind is assuredly a meeting-place of the angel and of Satan—the latter misleads him and the former guides him to the right path; through these two, God (may He be exalted!) changes man's minds as you change things with your two fingers. Observe, then, how the relationship of these two appointed beings with God (may He be exalted!) corresponds

---

88. Al-Bukhārī, *Ṣaḥīḥ*, Ta'bīr, 2, 4, 10, 26; Muslim, *Ṣaḥīḥ*, Ru'yā, 7, 8, 9.
89. Muḥammad Ibn Sīrīn (d. 110 AH/728 AD), a Follower (*tābi'ī*), was the first renowned Muslim interpreter of dreams. He was also a great Traditionist, a jurist and an ascetic of Baṣrah. As a Traditionist he acted more seriously than as an interpreter of dreams, although it is as this latter that he finally came to be well known. For more information on him see T. Fahd, "Ibn Sīrīn," *EI* 2 III, 947-948.
90. Muslim, *Ṣaḥīḥ*, Qadar, 17; Ibn Mājah, *Sunan*, Du'ā', 2; Aḥmad ibn Ḥanbal, *Musnad*, VI, 251, IV, 182.

to that of your two fingers with the meaning of His two fingers, although they differ in form. From this, extract [the spiritual meaning of] the words of the Prophet (ṣ), "Surely God (may He be exalted!) created Adam in His form,"[91] and all verses and all other Traditions which are imagined by the ignorant to mean resemblance [between man and God]. One example is sufficient for an intelligent man; many examples only increase the perplexity of fools.

When you have learnt the meaning of the divine finger it is possible for you to advance towards [the understanding of] the divine pen, hand, right hand, face, and form. When you have taken all of these in their spiritual, and not corporeal, meaning, you will know that the spirit of pen and its reality which needs to be investigated when you have mentioned the definition of pen, lies in that with which [something] is written. So if there is anything in existence by means of which the forms of knowledge are engraved on the plates of human souls, it is most suitable that such a thing should be [called] the pen, for surely God (may He be exalted!) has taught by the pen, taught man that which he did not know'[92]. This pen is spiritual, since the spirit of pen and its reality are found in it, and it is only the form of pen and its shape that are wanting in it. A pen being made of wood or reed does not belong to the reality of pen, and this is why it is not found in the real definition of pen. Everything has a definition, a reality, which is its spirit; when you have found the spirit, you have become spiritual, and the doors of the unseen world are opened to you and you have become worthy of associating with the Highest Counsel (*al-mala' al-a'lā*) of the angels[93] who are indeed good companions.

It is not improbable that indications of this kind are present in the Qur'an, although you are unable to tolerate this kind of thing which strikes at your audition until its explanation is ascribed to the companions of the Prophet (ṣ). Should blind following (*taqlīd*) predominate in you, consider the commentators'

91. Al-Bukhārī, *Ṣaḥīḥ*, Isti'dhān, 1; Muslim, *Ṣaḥīḥ*, Birr, 115. Jannah, 28.
92. Qur'an, 96:4-5.
93. Qur'an, 37:8, 38:69.

explanation of the words of God (may He be exalted!), "God sends down water from the clouds so that valleys begin to flow according to their capacity, and the flood carries swelling foam on its surface; in the same way foam comes up from that which they [i.e. men] heat up in the fire, for the purpose of making ornaments or articles of domestic use..." (to the end of the verse)[94] (أَنْزَلَ مِنَ السَّمَاءِ مَاءً فَسَالَتْ أَوْدِيَةٌ بِقَدَرِهَا فَاحْتَمَلَ السَّيْلُ زَبَدًا رَابِيًا وَمِمَّا يُوقِدُونَ عَلَيْهِ فِي النَّارِ ابْتِغَاءَ حِلْيَةٍ أَوْ مَتَاعٍ زَبَدٌ مِثْلُهُ). Observe how God has likened knowledge with water, souls with valleys and springs, and error with foam. Then He has made you aware of the end of the verse, saying, "Thus God sets forth similitudes." This depth of discussion on this subject will suffice you. You are unable to understand more than this.

In short, know that everything which you are likely to understand is presented to you by the Qur'an in such a way that if in sleep you were studying the Protected Tablet (*al-lawḥ al-maḥfūẓ*) with your soul, it would be related to you through a suitable symbol which needs interpretation. Know that interpretation of the Qur'an (*ta'wīl*) occupies the place of interpretation of dreams (*taʿbīr*). This is why we have said that a commentator of the Qur'an (*al-mufassir*) is concerned with its rind,[95] since the man [i.e. the commentator] who translates the outward meaning of the ring, genitals and mouths is not like him who understands that the [real] meaning is calling out to prayer before dawn.

---

94. Qur'an, 13:17.
95. See *supra*, p. 20.

7

The invisible world through the visible world

Perhaps you will ask: Why have you set out these realities in these symbols and not clearly revealed them, as a result of which people may suspect you of [being in] the ignorance of 'resemblance' (*al-tashbīh*) and the error of 'imagination'?

[As a reply to this question] know that you will understand this when you know that the unseen is revealed from the Protected Tablet to a sleeping man only through symbols and not by clear revelation, as I have already narrated to you in an example.[96] This is something which is known to him who can comprehend the hidden connection between the visible world and the invisible. Then when you have known this, you will realize that in this world you are certainly asleep although you are awake. 'Men are asleep, and they wake up from their sleep when they die'.[97] At the time of awakening by death, the real meanings and spirits of what they heard in this life through symbols are revealed to them, and they know that those symbols are rinds and shells of these spirits; they also know with certainty the truthfulness of Qur'anic verses and of the words of God's Messenger (may He bless him and greet him!), in the same way as the man who calls out for the ritual prayer (*mu'adhdhin*) became convinced of the truthfulness of Ibn Sīrīn's words and of the correctness of his interpretation of the dream.[98] All these are revealed at the time of approach of

96. See *supra*, pp. 34.
97. Unidentified. The meaning of this prophetic tradition al-Ghazālī explains in this and the following paragraphs.
98. See *supra*, pp. 34.

death, and sometimes some of these are revealed in death pangs. At these times those who have denied God and the heedless lament, "Oh, would that we had obeyed God and obeyed the Messenger!"[99] (يَا لَيْتَنَا أَطَعْنَا اللَّهَ وَأَطَعْنَا الرَّسُولَا) On this theme God further said, "Do they look for anything else but its interpretation? On the Day of Judgement when its interpretation comes, those who had neglected it before will say, 'the Messengers of our Lord did indeed bring the truth. Have we then any intercessors who would intercede for us? Or, could we be sent back [to the world] that we might act differently from that which we used to do....?" (to the end of the verse).[100] (هَلْ يَنْظُرُونَ إِلاَّ تَأْوِيلَهُ يَوْمَ يَأْتِي تَأْوِيلُهُ يَقُولُ الَّذِينَ نَسُوهُ مِنْ قَبْلُ قَدْ جَاءَتْ رُسُلُ رَبِّنَا بِالْحَقِّ فَهَلْ لَنَا مِنْ شُفَعَاءَ فَيَشْفَعُوا لَنَا أَوْ نُرَدُّ فَنَعْمَلَ غَيْرَ الَّذِي كُنَّا نَعْمَلُ... الآية) "Woe is me! Would that I had never taken such a one as a friend!"[101] (يَا وَيْلَتَى لَيْتَنِي لَمْ أَتَّخِذْ فُلَانًا خَلِيلًا). "Would that I were mere dust!"[102] (يَا لَيْتَنِي كُنْتُ تُرَابًا) "O my grief over my remissness in respect of my duty to God!"[103] (يَا حَسْرَتَا عَلَىٰ مَا فَرَّطْتُ فِي جَنْبِ اللَّهِ) "Oh, the bitterness of our remorse at neglecting this Hour [of the Doom]!"[104] (يَا حَسْرَتَنَا عَلَىٰ مَا فَرَّطْنَا فِيهَا) "Lord, we have seen and we have heard, so now send us back [to the world] that we may do good deeds. Verily we have now sure faith in what we were told."[105] (رَبَّنَا أَبْصَرْنَا وَسَمِعْنَا فَارْجِعْنَا نَعْمَلْ صَالِحًا إِنَّا مُوقِنُونَ).

This is indicated by most of the Qur'anic verses connected with the explanation of the life to come—verses which we have called[106] green chrysolite. Then understand from this that so long as you are in this-worldly life you are asleep, and your waking up is only after death at which time you become fit to see the clear truth face to face. Before that time it is impossible for you to know the realities except when they are moulded in the form of imaginative symbols. Because of the concentration of your look upon the sensuous, you think

99. Qur'an, 33:66.
100. Qur'an, 7:53.
101. Qur'an, 25:28.
102. Qur'an, 78:40.
103. Qur'an, 39:56.
104. Qur'an, 6:31.
105. Qur'an, 32:12.
106. *Supra,* pp. 8-9.

that the sensuous has only imaginative meaning, and you become unmindful of its spirit, as you become unmindful of your own spirit and only understand your body.

8

Connection between invisible and visible worlds

Perhaps you will say: Disclose then the relationship existing between the two worlds, and the reason why a dream is through symbols and not by clear revelation, and why God's Messenger (may He bless him and greet him!) used to see [the angel] Gabriel (*Jibrīl*) often in a form other than his and only saw him twice in his own form.[107]

[As a reply to your enquiries] know that if you have imagined that this knowledge will be vouchsafed to you at once without your prior preparation for its acceptance through self-training in morals, mortification, renunciation of [the blame-worthy aspect of] the world completely, fleeing away from preoccupation with men, engrossment in the love of the Creator and seeking of the True One, then you have waxed proud and have ascended exceedingly high. Such knowledge will be withheld from a person like you, and it will be said :

> You both have come to know the secret of my good fortune,
> But you will find me slow in revealing the secret of my good fortune.

Abandon, therefore, your ambition for attaining this knowledge by correspondence, and seek it only through the door of mortification and righteousness. Then guidance will follow it and strengthen it, as God (may He be exalted!) said, "Most surely We will guide in Our ways those who strive hard after

107.Al-Bukhārī, *Ṣaḥīḥ*, Bad' al-Khalq, 7; Muslim, *Ṣaḥīḥ*, Īmān, 282, 287; Aḥmad ibn Ḥanbal, *Musnad*, VI, 236, 241.

Us"[108] (وَالَّذِينَ جَاهَدُوا فِينَا لَنَهْدِيَنَّهُمْ سُبُلَنَا). The Prophet (ṣ) said, "God bequeaths to him, who acts according to that which he knows, the knowledge of that which he did not know."[109]

Know with certainty that the secrets of the visible world are veiled from the souls which are defiled by love of the world and most of whose energies are fully absorbed in the pursuit of the present world. We only mentioned this much [of these secrets] in order to produce yearning for, and encouragement to, them, and in order to make known one of the secrets of the Qur'an to him who is unmindful of it and to whom the shells of the Qur'an are not opened at all to reveal its jewels. Then if your desire is true, you will endeavour to seek out these secrets and ask the help of men of insight, in these matters, and will receive help from them. I do not think that you will be successful [in this endeavour] should you apply yourself to it solely by your judgement and reason. How will you be able to understand these [secrets of the invisible world] when you do not understand the language in action? On the contrary, you suppose that in the universe there is only the language of statement. This is why you did not understand the meaning of the words of God (may He be exalted!), "There is not a thing but glorifies Him with His praise"[110] (وَإِنْ مِنْ شَيْءٍ إِلَّا يُسَبِّحُ بِحَمْدِهِ). Nor do you understand the meaning of the words of God (may He be exalted!), "They [i.e. the heavens and the earth] said, 'We have submitted [to You] willingly"[111] (قَالَتَا أَتَيْنَا طَائِعِينَ), unless you suppose that the earth has a language and life. Nor do you understand the statement of the speakers, "The wall asked the peg, 'Why do you pierce me?' It replied, 'Ask him who hammers me and does not leave me. Behind me is the stone which hammers me.'"[112] You do not

108. Qur'an, 29:69.
109. Unidentified.
110. Qur'an, 17:44.
111. Qur'an, 41:11.
112. This conversation has been quoted by al-Zamakhsharī with slight variation. His explanation of the Qur'anic verse under consideration is identical with that of al-Ghazālī. See al-Zamakhsharī, *al-Kashshāf,* Egypt, 1385/1966, III, 446.

understand that this statement is true and more correct than the language of words; so how will you understand the secrets which are behind it?

9

Meaning of allegories to describe the Qur'an

Perhaps you wish to be fully aware of the hints and indications that are deposited under the jewels which, as we have already mentioned,[113] the Qur'an includes.

So [I say:] Know that to people in the visible world red brimstone means the alchemy by which they are able to turn substances from their base qualities to precious qualities, so that by it stone becomes changed into corundum and copper into pure gold, and thus through these they obtain access to the pleasures of the world which are [in reality] turbid and disturbed at present and will pass away in the near future. Do you not, then, consider the question: Is that which turns the essence of the soul from the vices of a beast and the error of ignorance to the purity of the angels and their spirituality so that the soul may advance from the lowest depth to the highest and obtain by it nearness to the Lord of all the worlds and gaze upon His face always and perpetually—most deserving of the name red brimstone or not? This is why we have named it red brimstone. So think deeply, consult with yourself and be fair, so that you will realize that this name is the worthiest of this meaning and most correctly applicable to it. Then the most precious things obtained through alchemy are corundums the best type of which is the ruby. For this reason we have named[114] it knowledge of divine essence.

As to the greatest antidote, men understand it to mean that by which one is cured from destructive poisons entering the

113.*Supra,* chaps, 1, 3.
114.*Supra,* p. 7.

stomach, although the destruction resulting from it is only destruction in the case of the perishable world. Consider, therefore, that if the poisons of heresy, passions and errors entering the soul cause such a destruction that it always and perpetually stands between the elevation of the soul and the holy universe and the fount of delight and ease, and that [if] the Qur'anic verses which contain arguments cure men from these poisons and remove their harm—then are these verses most deserving of the name the greatest antidote or not?[115]

With regard to the strongest musk [let me point out that] in the visible world it means a thing which man carries and from which rises up a fragrant smell that makes it so much known and apparent that even if he wants to hide it, it does not become hidden but spreads. Consider, then, that if in the cognitive possession [of man] there is a thing from which fame spreads in the universe and by which its possessor becomes so famous that if he wants to disappear [from people] and prefers obscurity it makes him much more famous and exposes him—then is not the name of the strongest musk the worthiest and most correctly applicable to it? As you know, the science of jurisprudence, the knowledge of the judgements of the revealed law (sharī'ah), brings fame [to its possessors], increases attention [of others to them] and magnifies [their] influence [upon others][116], and the delight of fame and widespread influence which the soul obtains is much greater than the delight of fragrance of musk which the sense of smell obtains.

As to the aloe-wood, to people it means a solid substance by which man is not profited [so long as it is in its natural state] but, when it is charged with fire until it is burnt, smoke rises from it and reaches the sense of smell; then its benefits and uses become great, and the place where it is burnt and the place to which it is thrown become odorous. So if in the hypocrites and God's enemies there are shadows 'like blocks of wood propped up',[117] no benefit is derived from them. But when there falls upon them God's punishment and warning in

115. *Supra*, pp. 13-14.
116. *Supra*, pp. 23-24.
117. Qur'an, 63:4.

the form of thunderbolts, sinking of land, and earthquakes, so that they are burnt and the smoke rising from them reaches the sense of smell of [other people's] souls, there is a great benefit in exciting [others'] quest of the highest Paradise and of the near presence of the True One (glory be to Him and may He be exalted!), and in turning away from error, heedlessness and following of passion. If such be the case, then is not the name of aloe-wood the worthiest and most correctly applicable to it?. Be, therefore, satisfied with this degree of explanation of these indications and find out the remainder for yourself and solve the indication in it if you are able and are among such people.

> I could have made him hear had I called a living man.
> But there is no life in him whom I call.

10
The benefit of employing allegories in the Qur'an

Perhaps you will say: It has become clear to me that these indications are correct and true; is there any other benefit in them which you know?

[As a reply to your question] know that every benefit lies beyond these indications, for these are a sample presented here in order that you may know by them the definition of the road to spiritual meanings of the invisible world through the traditional words, so that the doors of the unveiling of the meaning of the Qur'an may be opened [to you] and the methods of diving in their seas may be known. We have seen many groups of people to whom outward aspects of the Qur'an became disordered and objections to these aspects came to their minds, and they imagined that which contradicts these. Consequently their basic belief in religion became corrupted, and this corruption produced in them a secret denial of the resurrection, raising of the dead, Paradise, Hell and return to God (may He be exalted!) after death. They nurtured these objections in their secret minds; the bridle of their fear of God and the tie of piety became loosened. They went to great lengths in seeking the vanities of the world, eating what is unlawful and following carnal desires; they limited their energies to the seeking of influence, wealth and all forms of enjoyment of the present world. They looked upon the pious with the eye of disdain, deeming them ignorant; if they saw piety in a man which they were unable to deny because of the abundance of his knowledge, the perfection of his reason and his piercing intelligence, they attacked him by saying that his motive was to deceive, to attract others and to turn their faces to himself; thus the sight of piety in the pious only increased their arrogance and error, although the sight of piety of religious people is among the greatest of the things which strengthen the belief of the believers.

All this happened because their intellect was confined to the study of shapes of things and their imaginative forms; their consideration was not extended to the spirit and realities of things, and they did not understand the parallelism between the visible world and the invisible. Since they did not understand that, and since the outward aspects of questions seemed to them contradictory, they themselves strayed from the right path and led others astray. Neither did they understand anything from the spiritual world through immediate experience (*dhawq*) such as the understanding of the special people (*khawāṣṣ*), nor did they believe in the unseen as is the belief of the layman. Thus their intelligence destroyed them. Ignorance is nearer to salvation than defective prudence and imperfect intelligence. We do not regard that as improbable; we have in fact stumbled in the extremities of these errors for a long time, because of the misfortune of evil companions and our association with them, until God took us away from the extremities of these faults and saved us from their abysses. To Him, therefore, belong all types of perfect praise, grace and bounty for directing us to the right way, granting this favour to us, doing this benefit to us, and preserving us from the abysses of ruin. This is not of those things which can be obtained through effort and wish. "Whatever of mercy God grants to men may be withheld by none, and whatever He withholds may not be released by anyone. He is the All-mighty, the All-wise."[118] (مَا يَفْتَحِ اللَّهُ لِلنَّاسِ مِنْ رَحْمَةٍ فَلَا مُمْسِكَ لَهَا وَمَا يُمْسِكْ فَلَا مُرْسِلَ لَهُ مِنْ بَعْدِهِ وَهُوَ الْعَزِيزُ الْحَكِيمُ).

118.Qur'an, 35:2.

11

Variance in the excellence of Qur'anic verses

Perhaps you will ask me: In these remarks you intend to state that some parts of the Qur'an are more excellent than others, whereas all are the speech of God (may He be exalted!). So how can some parts be distinguished from others and how can some parts be more excellent than others?

[As a reply to this question] know that if the light of insight (*nūr al-baṣīrah*)[119] does not guide you to the difference between the Verse of the Throne[120] (آيَةَ الْكُرْسِيِّ) and a verse concerning giving and receiving loans (آيَةَ الْمُدَايَنَاتِ), and between the Sūrah of Sincerity[121] (سُورَةُ الإخلاص) and the Sūrah of Destruction[122], and your mind which is empty and wholly absorbed in blindly following the opinions of others (*taqlīd*), lives in the comfort of mere belief in such differences, then follow the Messenger of God (may His blessing and greeting be upon him!), who is the man to whom the Qur'an was revealed. Prophetic traditions have pointed to the nobility of some verses and to the manifold multiplication of reward for recitation in the case of some revealed sūrahs. Thus the Prophet (ṣ) said, "The Sūrah of the Opening of the Book[123] is the best sūrah of the Qur'an."[124] He (ṣ) also said, "The Verse of the Throne is the chief of the Qur'anic verses."[125] He (may

119. The light of insight here means reason (*'aql*). Sometimes, however, it means the intuitive faculty of the mind—a faculty higher than reason.
120. Qur'an, 2:255.
121. Sūrah 112.
122. Sūrah 111.
123. Sūrah 1.
124. Unidentified.
125. Al-Tirmidhī, *Sunan,* Thawāb al-Qur'ān, 2.

God bless him and greet him!) further said, "The Sūrah of Yāsīn[126] is the heart of the Qur'an[127], and the sūrah beginning with 'Say: He is God, the Single'[128] is equal to a third part of the Qur'an in respect of value."[129] There are innumerable Traditions regarding the excellence of the striking verses of the Qur'an and regarding the specification of some verses and sūrahs as excellent and also regarding the great reward of their recitation. Seek them, if you like, from books on Tradition.

We shall now tell you the meaning of these four Traditions on the excellence of these sūrahs, although the arrangement of the divisions of the Qur'an and its branches and their grades which we have set forth will guide you to this meaning if you review them and reflect upon them. We have limited the divisions of the Qur'an and its branches to ten.[130]

126.Sūrah 36.
127.Aḥmad ibn Ḥanbal, *Musnad,* V, 26.
128.Sūrah 112.
129.Muslim, *Ṣaḥīḥ,* Musātīrīn, 260: al-Tirmidhī, *Sunan,* Ḥajj. 95.
130.*Supra,* chaps. 2, 3.

12
Secrets of Sūrah al-Fātiḥah

When you have considered, you will find that the Sura of Opening,[131] despite its shortness comprises eight well traced roads. Thus the words of God (may He be exalted!), "In the name of God, Most Gracious, Ever Merciful" (بِسْمِ اللَّهِ الرَّحْمَٰنِ الرَّحِيمِ), give information concerning His essence. His words, "Most Gracious, Ever Merciful," give information concerning one of His special attributes. The characteristic of this attribute is that it requires all other attributes, such as knowledge, power, and so on. This attribute is also connected with those men upon whom mercy is bestowed, in such a way that this connection familiarizes them with Him, Fills them with longing for Him, and encourages them to obey Him. This is not like the attribute of anger, had He mentioned it instead of mercy, since anger grieves men, excites fear, depresses the mind, and does not delight it.

The words of God, "All types of perfect praise belong to God alone, the Lord of all the worlds" (الْحَمْدُ لِلَّهِ رَبِّ الْعَالَمِينَ), include two things. One is the basis of praise which is gratitude. This gratitude is the beginning of the straight path and, as it were, a half of it, since practical faith (*al-Īmān al-ʿamalī*) has two halves—half is patience and half is gratitude.[132] The real meaning of this you will know with certainty, if you wish to do so, from the work. *The Revival of the Religious Sciences,* especially from the 'Book of Gratitude and Patience'.[133]

131. Sūrah 1.

132. Unidentified.

133. This is the second 'book' (*supra* p. 26, n. 67) of the fourth part of *the Revival.* This 'book' consists of eighty-two large pages. For the gist of the contents of this 'book' see Quasem, *Ethics,* pp. 155-161, 147-152.

The superiority of gratitude to patience is like the superiority of mercy to anger, because gratitude proceeds from joy, whereas patience under God's decree proceeds from fear and awe, and is not free from distress and sorrow. To walk along the straight path to God by way of love and to perform actions of love are much better than to walk along the path of fear. The secret of this will assuredly be known from 'the Book of Love and Yearning'[134] taken from the work, *The Revival.* That is why the Messenger of God (may He bless him and greet him!) said, "The first of those who will be called to Paradise are those who praise God in every condition."[135] [In addition to this] the words of God (may He be exalted!), "The Lord of all the worlds," indicate all His works and their relation to Him. The phrase which is most concise and which most perfectly encompasses the various types of divine works is "the Lord of all the worlds." Lordship is the best description of the relation of God to His works, since it is more complete and more perfect in magnifying Him than your words 'the Highest of all the worlds and the Creator of all the worlds'.

The words of God, "Most Gracious, Ever Merciful" (الرَّحْمَٰنِ الرَّحِيمِ), the second time, indicate His attribute once again. Do you imagine that this is a repetition? There is no repetition in the Qur'an, for repetition is defined as that which does not contain any additional benefit. The mention of mercy after the mention of "all the worlds" and before the mention of "the Master of the Day of Judgement," has two great benefits in expounding the channels of mercy. One pays attention to creation by the Lord of all the worlds—He has created every one of these according to the most perfect and best of its kind and has given it everything it needs.

Thus one of the worlds God has created is the world of animals, the smallest of which are the mosquito, the fly, the spider, and the bees. Look at the mosquito, how God has

---

134. This forms the sixth 'book' of *The Revival* and consists of sixty-nine large pages. The substance of this 'book' is to be found in Quasem, *Ethics,* pp. 181-189, 147-152.

135. Aḥmad ibn Ḥanbal, *Musnad,* IV, 434.

created its limbs. He has created in it every limb which He has created in the elephant; even He has created for it a long proboscis attached to its head. Thus He has guided it to its food, to suck man's blood. You see it prick its proboscis into him and suck its food from that hole. He has created two wings for it in order that they may be the instrument of fleeing when it is repelled. Look at the fly, how God has created its limbs. He has created its two pupils of the eye open without eyelids, since its head is too small to contain eyelids. Eyelids are needed for cleansing the pupils from the dirt and dust which reach them. Look how in exchange for the eyelids He has created for it two superfluous hands so that, besides four legs, it has two superfluous hands. When, as you see, it falls on the earth, it always wipes its two pupils with its two hands cleansing them from dust. Look at the spider, how God has created its limbs and has taught it the device of weaving and how He has taught it the tricks of hunting without two wings, for He has created for it sticky saliva by which it connects itself with a corner lying in wait for the passing of a mosquito close to itself. It throws itself onto the mosquito, catches it, shackles it with its threads composed from its saliva, and thus disables it from escaping until it eats it or puts it in store. Look at the spider's [methods of] weaving its house, how God has guided it in its weaving according to geometrical proportion in the order of warp and woof. Look at the bee and the innumerable wonders of its gathering honey and [producing] bees-wax. We [should like to] make you aware of the geometry of its hive. It is built on the figure of the hexagon in order that space may not be narrow for its companies who become crowded in one place in a great number. If it should build its hive circular, there would remain, outside the circular hive, an empty space since circles are not contiguous to one another. Likewise are all other figures. As to squares, they are contiguous to one another, but the shape of the bee is inclined to roundness and so inside the hive there would remain empty corners as, in a circular house, there would remain an empty corner outside the house. Thus none of the figures other than the hexagon approaches the circular figure in contiguity, and this is known by geometrical proof. Consider, then, how God has guided the bee to the characteristic of this figure.

This is a sample from the wonders of God's works and His kindness and mercy to His creation, for the lowest constitutes an evidence of the highest. [Even] in the long lifetimes of many men it is impossible thoroughly to study these strange events, i.e. that part of them which is revealed to man, and that is surely small in relation to that part which is not revealed. This knowledge is exclusively appropriate to God and the angels. Sometimes you will find remarks of this kind in 'the Book of Gratitude'[136] and 'the Book of Love'[137] [from the work, *The Revival]*. Seek them if you are fit for them, otherwise close your eyes to the signs of God's mercy, and do not look at them, do not graze in the field of the knowledge of His works, and do not be a spectator of it, but be occupied with the poems of al-Mutanabbī,[138] wonders of the syntax of grammar of Sībawayh,[139] consequences of Ibn al-Ḥaddād in the rare matters of divorce, and tricks of argument in theology. These are more suitable to you, for your worth is according to the worth of your ambition. "Were I intended to counsel you my counsel would not profit you, if God willed to pervert you," and "Whatsoever of mercy God bestows upon men may be withheld

---

136. See *supra,* p. 11, n. 33.
137. See *supra,* p. 11, n. 34.
138. Al-Mutanabbī (905-965 AD) was the greatest Arabic poet of medieval times. Even now Arab children are required to memorize verses of his poetry.
139. Abū Bishr 'Amr Ibn 'Uthmān Sībawayh was a celebrated grammarian of the Baṣrah school of Arabic grammar. He really proved to be a genius for comprehensiveness, if not so much for originality. His *Kitāb* (book) has throughout the ages been regarded as the final word on Arabic grammar and has become proverbial for its unique position in the field. Those who followed him right down to the present time could only comment upon, remove obscurities from, and arrange and rearrange the material furnished in the *Kitāb* without adding much to it. Sībawayh, a native of Shiraj, died at the young age of about forty years in the last quarter of the second century of the Hijrah.

by none and whatsoever He withholds may not be released by any after that."

Let us return to the [main] aim, for our motive [here] is to make you aware of a sample of divine mercy in the creation of all the worlds. Its connection with His words, "Master of the Day of Judgement," is that it indicates His mercy on the Day of Recompense at the time of granting the favour of perpetual kingdom [i.e. Paradise] in exchange for [belief in] the sentence [of testimony] and for worship.[140] Its explanation would take a long time. What we intend to say is that [really] there is no repetition in the Qur'an. If you see anything that appears to be repeated in it, look at what precedes it and what follows it so that the additional benefit of its [apparent] repetition may be revealed to you.

The words of God, "Master of the Day of Judgement" (مَالِكِ يَوْمِ الدِّينِ), are an indication of the life to come, which is the concern of one of the fundamental divisions [of Qur'anic verses],[141] together with an indication of the meaning of kingdom and the Master which belongs to the attributes of divine glory. The words of God, "You alone we worship" (إِيَّاكَ نَعْبُدُ), comprise two great parts. One is worship with sincerity in relation to Him especially, and this is the spirit of the straight path, as you will know it from 'the Book of Vice of Influence and Ostentation'[142] from the work, *The Revival.* The second is the belief that none other than God deserves worship, and this is the essence of belief in divine unity. This is achieved by the abandonment of belief in [man's] ability and power, and by the knowledge that God is alone in [the

140. The sentence of testimony *(kalimah al-shahādah)* is: There is no god but God (*lā ilāha illā Allāh*). Worship here means ritual prayer, fasting, divine tax and pilgrimage to Makkah. Thus belief in the sentence of testimony and worship taken together refer to the well known prophetic tradition (al-Bukhārī, *Ṣaḥīḥ*, Īmān, 2; Muslim, *Ṣaḥīḥ,* Īmān, 21) in which Islam is described as built on five pillars.

141. See *supra*, chaps. 2, 3.

142. This is the eighth 'book' of the third part of *The Revival.* It consists of sixty-two large pages. The substance of this 'book' is briefly given in Quasem, *Ethics,* pp. 131-136, 105-108.

execution of] all works and that man is not independent by himself and without His help. Thus His words, "You alone we worship," are an indication of making the soul beautiful by worship and sincerity, while His words, "You alone we implore for help" (وَإِيَّاكَ نَسْتَعِينُ), are an indication of its purification from belief in partnership and from paying attention to [man's] ability and power; we have already mentioned[143] that traversing the straight path is supported by two things: One is purification of the soul by the denial of that which is not befitting, and the other is making it beautiful by the achievement of that which should be achieved, and these two are comprised in these two sentences from the sum total of the sentences of the Sūrah of Opening.

The words of God, "Guide us along the straight path" (اهْدِنَا الصِّرَاطَ الْمُسْتَقِيمَ), are a prayer which is the marrow of worship, as you will know it from ['the Book of] Mention of God and Invocations'[144] from the 'books' of *The Revival.* These words of His make man aware of the need for entreaty and supplication to Him (may He be exalted!) which form the spirit of servitude and [also] make man aware that the most important of his needs is guidance along the straight path, for it is by [following] this path that advancement towards God (may He be exalted!) is, as already mentioned,[145] accomplished.

God's words, "The path of those on whom You have bestowed Your favours..." (to the end of the sūrah) (صِرَاطَ الَّذِينَ أَنْعَمْتَ عَلَيْهِمْ غَيْرِ الْمَغْضُوبِ عَلَيْهِمْ وَلَا الضَّالِّينَ), are a reminder of His favour to His friends and His revenge upon, and anger towards, His enemies, in order that encouragement may be given and awe may be excited from the depth of the hearts [of people]. We have already mentioned[146] that the stories of prophets and [God's] enemies [related in the Qur'an] form two great divisions of [Qur'anic verses].

---

143. *Supra,* pp. 9-10.
144. This forms the ninth 'book' of the first part of *The Revival* and consists of thirty-five large pages divided into five chapters which are sub-divided into sections.
145. *Supra,* pp. 9-11.
146. *Supra,* pp. 12-13.

Thus the Sūrah of Opening has comprised eight of the ten divisions [of the Qur'an]—divine essence, attributes and works, description of the life to come and of the straight path together with both its sides, i.e. purification [of the soul] and making it beautiful, description of [God's] favour to His friends and of His anger towards His enemies, and [finally] description of the resurrection. Only two divisions [of the Qur'an] fall outside this sūrah, namely, [God's] argument with infidels and judgements of jurists—two subjects from which the sciences of theology and jurisprudence stem off.[147] From this it becomes clear that [in reality] these two subjects fall into the lowest of the grades of religious sciences. It is only the love of wealth and influence [obtainable by them] which has raised them to a higher status.

147. *Supra*, pp. 22-27.

13

Sūrah al-Fātiḥah—key to doors of Paradise

سُورَةُ الفَاتِحَةِ مِفْتَاحُ الجَنَّةِ.

The Sūrah of Opening is the key to Paradise. (Prophet Muḥammad (ṣ))

At this point we [should like to] make you aware of a subtle matter. So we say that this sūrah[148] is the opening of the Book [i.e. the Qur'an] and the key to Paradise. It is the key only because the doors of Paradise are eight, and the meanings of the Sūrah of Opening [too] amount to eight. So know with certainty that each of these is a key to one of the doors of Paradise. This is testified to by Tradition.[149]

If you are such a one whose mind by chance does not have a belief in this [i.e. that the Sūrah of Opening is the key to Paradise] and yet you seek to understand the relationship [between the two], then abandon what you understood about the outward aspect of Paradise. [Should you do so] it will not be hidden from you that each meaning [of the Sūrah of Opening] will open the door of one of the gardens of gnosis (*ma'rifah*), as we have indicated[150] in [our discussion of] the signs of God's mercy (may He be exalted!), the wonders of His works, and so on. Do not imagine that the repose of a Gnostic [which proceeds] from delight in the watery meadows of gnosis and its gardens is less than the repose of the one who will enter the Paradise which he knows and in which he will satisfy his desires for food, drink and sex. How can they be equal? On the contrary, it cannot be denied that among the gnostics there may be one whose desire for opening the door of gnosis in order to behold the kingdom of the heavens and the earth and the glory of their Creator and Disposer is more intense than

148. Sūrah 1.
149. Unidentified.
150. *Supra*, pp. 50-54.

his desire for women, food and clothing. How cannot the former be predominating in the discerning gnostic when it is shared with the angels in the highest Paradise, since they have no enjoyment in food, drink, women and clothing? Perhaps the enjoyment of animals in food, drink and copulation exceeds the enjoyment of men. If you consider the sharing with animals and their pleasures as more necessary to seek than sharing with the angels in their joy and delight in the study of the beauty of Lordly Excellency, then how great are your error, ignorance and stupidity, and how lowly is your ambition! Your worth is in accordance with the worth of your ambition.

As to the gnostic, when eight of the doors of the Paradise of gnosis are opened to him and he [enters and] secludes himself in it, he will never pay heed to the Paradise of the fools, since most of the people of Paradise are fools and the 'Illiyyūn[151] are indeed the possessors of intelligence, as is held in a Tradition.

O you who fall short [of the highest stage], your ambition for pleasures is also excessive and oscillating like that of animals! Do not deny that stages in Paradise are obtained by different kinds of gnosis. If the watery meadows of gnosis do not themselves deserve to he named Paradise, they [at least] deserve to be the means of obtainment of Paradise, and thus they will be the key to Paradise. Do not, therefore, deny that in the Sūrah of Opening are to be found the keys to all doors of Paradise.

151.Qur'an, 83:19-22.

14

The Verse of the Throne

آيَةُ الْكُرْسِيِّ سَيِّدَةُ آيِ الْقُرْآنِ.

The Verse of the Throne is the chief of Qur'anic verses. (Prophet Muḥammad (ṣ))

Concerning the Verse of the Throne[152] I should ask you: Do you have the ability to think of the reason why the Verse of the Throne is named the chief of the Qur'anic verses?[153] If you are unable to discover it by your independent thought turn back to the divisions [of Qur'anic verses] which we have already discussed and to their grades which we have already set in order.[154] We have mentioned to you that knowledge of God, His essence and attributes is that which is the ultimate aim of the Qur'anic sciences, and that all other divisions are sought because of it, while it is sought for itself and not for anything other than itself. Thus this knowledge is that which is sought, and all other things are its followers. This knowledge is the chief form of cognition which comes first and towards which the faces of the followers and their hearts are directed; so they imagine it and follow the example of it and the aim of it. The Verse of the Throne [is named the chief of Qur'anic verses because it] is concerned with the divine essence, attributes and works only; it contains nothing other than these.

Thus the word 'God' (اللَّهُ) [occurring in the Verse of the Throne] indicates His essence. His words, "There is no god but He" (لَا إِلَٰهَ إِلَّا هُوَ), are an indication of the unity of His essence. God's words, "The Ever Living, the Self-subsisting and All-sustaining" (الْحَيُّ الْقَيُّومُ), indicate the attribute of His essence and His glory, for the meaning of Self-subsisting and All-sustaining is One Who sustains Himself, while all other things

152. Qur'an, 2:255.

153. Unidentified.

154. *Supra*, chaps. 2, 3.

are sustained by Him; so His normal state is not connected with anything, and the state of everything is connected with Him; this is the ultimate [state] of glory and greatness. God's words, "Neither slumber nor sleep seizes Him" (لَا تَأْخُذُهُ سِنَةٌ وَلَا نَوْمٌ), describe His freedom from the attributes of accidents which are impossible in His case. Freedom from what is impossible in His case is not one of the obscure divisions of knowledge [of Him]; rather it is the clearest of them.

God's words, "To Him belong whatsoever is in the heavens and whatsoever is in the earth" (لَهُ مَا فِي السَّمَاوَاتِ وَمَا فِي الْأَرْضِ), indicate all His works, and that all of these have their origin in Him and return to Him. The words of God, "Who is he that will [be able to] intercede with Him except by His permission"? indicate His being alone in sovereignty, authority and command and that whoever will have the right of intercession will possess it only because God ennobles him and permits him—a thing which is the negation of partnership with Him in sovereignty and command. God's words, "He knows what lies before them [i.e. men] and what is after them and they cannot comprehend anything of His knowledge except that which He pleases," are an indication of His attribute of knowledge, of the detailing of some of the things known, and of His being alone in knowledge so that no one other than Him has any knowledge by himself—if he has any knowledge it is through God's gift and according to the measure of His will. God's words, "His throne comprises the heavens and the earth," indicate the greatness of His sovereignty and the perfection of His power. In this lies a secret the disclosure of which is not made possible by its condition, since knowledge of the throne [of God], of its attributes and of the wideness of the heavens and the earth is a noble and obscure knowledge with which many other forms of knowledge are bound up. The words of God, "The preserving of them [i.e. the heavens and the earth] does not weary Him" (وَلَا يَئُودُهُ حِفْظُهُمَا), indicate the divine attributes of power and its perfection, and freedom from weakness and imperfection. God's words, "He is the Most High, the Most Great" (وَهُوَ الْعَلِيُّ الْعَظِيمُ), indicate two great principles of divine attributes. The explanation of these two attributes would take a long time. That part of them which is possible to explain we have explained in the work *The Supreme Aim in the Beautiful Names of God.*[155]. Seek it from that book.

Now when you reflect on all these meanings [contained in the Verse of the Throne] and then recite all other verses of the Qur'an, you will not find all these meanings—divine unity, sanctification, and explanation of high attributes—gathered together in a single one of them. This is the reason why the Prophet (ṣ) said, "The Verse of the Throne is the chief of the verses of the Qur'an."[156] In the verse beginning with "God bears witness"[157] (شَهِدَ اللَّهُ) there is only the mention of divine unity. In the sūrah[158] beginning with "Say: He is God, the Single" (قُلْ هُوَ اللَّهُ أَحَدٌ), there is only the mention of divine unity and sanctification. In the verses beginning with "Say: O God, Lord of sovereignty"[159] (قُلِ اللَّهُمَّ مَالِكَ الْمُلْكِ), there is only the mention of divine works and perfection of His power. In the Sūrah of Opening[160] (الفَاتِحَة) there are hints of all these attributes without their explanation, whereas these are explained in the Verse of the Throne. What approaches this verse in all these meanings is the end of the Sūrah of Gathering[161] (أَوَّلُ الحَشْرِ) and the beginning of the Sūrah of Iron[162] (أَوَّلُ الحَدِيدِ), since these two include many divine names and attributes, but these are verses and not one verse, whereas the Verse of the Throne is one verse. When you have compared this verse with one of these verses, you will find it more comprehensive of the aims of the Qur'an, and this is the reason why it deserves headship over all other verses. The Prophet (ṣ) said, "That [i.e. the Verse of the Throne] is the chief of the verses."[163] How can it not be so when in it occurs [the

155.*Al-Maqṣad al-Asnā fi Asmā' Allāh al-Ḥusnā,* trans, by Robert Stade, Ibadan, Nigeria, 1970, pp. 68-69, 72-75.
156.Al-Tirmidhī, *Sunan,* Thawāb al-Qur'an, 2.
157.Qur'an, 3:18-19.
158.Sūrah 112.
159.Qur'an, 3:26-27.
160.Sūrah 1.
161.Qur'an, 59:22-24.
162.Qur'an, 57:1-6.
163.Al-Tirmidhī, *Sunan*, Thawāb al-Qur'ān, 2.

phrase,] "the Ever Living, the Self-subsisting and All-sustaining," which is the greatest divine name (*al-ism al-aʿẓam*) and which contains a secret. This is evident from the Tradition[164] that the greatest divine name lies in the Verse of the Throne, in the beginning of the Sūrah of the House of ʿImrān[165] (آل عِمْرَان) and [also] in the words of God, "All faces shall be humbled before the Ever Living, the Self-subsisting and All-sustaining"[166] (وَعَنَتِ الْوُجُوهُ لِلْحَيِّ الْقَيُّومِ).

164.Cf. Abū Dāwūd, *Sunan,* Witr, 23.
165.Sūrah 14.
166.Qur'an, 20:111.

15

Sūrah al-Ikhlāṣ—a third of the Qur'an

قُلْ هُوَ اللهُ أَحَدٌ تَعْدِلُ ثُلُثَ الْقُرْآنِ.

[The sūrah beginning with] 'Proclaim: He is God, the Single' is equal to a third part of the Qur'an. (Prophet Muḥammad (ṣ))

I do not find that you comprehend the reason for the words of the Prophet (ṣ), "[The Sūrah[167] beginning with] 'Say: He is God, the Single' is equal to a third part of the Qur'an [in respect of value]".[168] Sometimes you say, "He mentioned this for encouragement in the recitation [of this sūrah], and what is meant by it is not its valuation." This is far from the status of prophethood! Sometimes you say, "This [statement of him] is remote from understanding and interpretation; since the Qur'anic verses are more than six thousands, how can this amount be their third part?" This question of you is because of your small knowledge of the realities of the Qur'an and your observance of its outward expressions, so that you think that verses become numerous by the length of expressions and small by their shortness. This [way of your thinking] resembles the conception of a man who prefers many silver coins to one jewel, seeing their great number.

Know that the Sūrah of Sincerity is assuredly equal to a third part of the Qur'an [in respect of value], and return to the three divisions which we have mentioned as dealing with the important matters of the Qur'an[169]. They are knowledge of God (may He be exalted!) knowledge of the Hereafter, and knowledge of the straight path; these three forms of knowledge are

167.Sūrah 112.
168.Muslim, *Ṣaḥīḥ,* Musāfirīn, 260; al-Tirmidhī, *Sunan,* Ḥajj, 95.
169.*Supra,* chaps. 2, 3.

the important concerns, and the remainder are those which follow them. The Sūrah of Sincerity comprises one of these three, namely, knowledge of God, His unity and His purification from partnership in genus and species. This purification is what is meant by the negation of origin, branch and equality [in the case of God]. His attribute of "Self-existing and Besought of all" informs man that in existence there is no one other than Him who can be sought for the fulfilment of [men's] needs. True, in this sūrah there is no talk of the future life or of the straight path, whereas we have already mentioned that the basic important concerns of the Qur'an are knowledge of God (may He be exalted!), knowledge of the future life, and knowledge of the straight path. This is why it is equal to a third part of the Qur'an, i.e. a third part of the basic concerns of the Qur'an, as the Prophet (ṣ) said, "[Halting at] 'Arafah is the pilgrimage" (الْحَجُّ عَرَفَةُ), i.e. it is the basis and the remaining activities of pilgrimage [only] follow it.

16

Sūrah Yā Sīn—heart of the Qur'an

قَالَ صَلَّى اللهُ عَلَيْهِ وَسَلَّمَ: يس قَلْبُ الْقُرْآنِ.

The Prophet (ṣ) said, The Sūrah of Yā Sīn is the heart of the Qur'an.

Perhaps you now long to know the meaning of the statement of the Prophet (ṣ), "[The Sūrah of] Yā Sīn[170] is the heart of the Qur'an."[171] I consider it proper to entrust it to your understanding in order that you may discover it for yourself on the analogy of that of which I have [just] made you aware in similar statements [of the Prophet (ṣ)][172]. It may be that you will know [by yourself] the reason for the Sūrah of Yā Sīn being the heart of the Qur'an. Energy and awakening on your own account is greater than the joy achieved by awakening caused by others. Awareness by one's own effort increases energy more than awakening [by others]. I hope that when you become aware of the secret [of the Qur'an] by yourself, your motive will be prepared for, and your energy will hasten to, the continuance of reflection coveting investigation and knowledge of [more] secrets. It is by this reflection that there will be opened to you the real meanings of those Qur'anic verses which are striking and which we shall soon gather for you in order that consideration of them and [thereby] discovering of their secrets may be easy for you.

---

170. Sūrah 36.
171. Aḥmad ibn Ḥanbal, *Musnad,* V, 26; al-Tirmidhī, *Sunan,* Thawāb al-Qur'ān, 7.
172. *Supra,* chap. 15.

17

Merits of Verse of the Throne and Sūrah al-Fātiḥah

فَاتِحَةُ الْكِتَابِ أَفْضَلُ الْقُرْآنِ.

The Sūrah of Opening is the best of all Qur'anic sūrahs. (Prophet Muḥammad (ṣ))

Perhaps you will ask me, "Why is the Verse of the Throne[173] distinguished as the chief [of Qur'anic verses] and the Sūrah of Opening[174] as the best [of the Qur'anic sūrahs]? Is there any secret in this? Or is it just by chance, as in praising a person the tongue passes to one expression and in praising a similar person it passes to another?"

So I say: The truth is far from this [latter alternative], for this befits me, you and him who all speak from passion and not him [i.e. the Prophet (ṣ)] who speaks from revelation. Do not, therefore, imagine that a single sentence proceeded from the Prophet (ṣ) in his different states such as anger and pleasure, except its being right and true. The secret of this specification [of the Verse of the Throne and the Sūrah of Opening] is that that which unites many kinds of excellence is called excellent: so that that which unites even more kinds is named the most excellent, for excellence is excess and the most excellent is the greatest excess. As to the headship it means the stability of the meaning of nobility which necessitates following by others but itself refuses to follow any other. When you review the meanings we have already mentioned[175] in the two sūrahs, you will know that

173.Qur'an, 2:255.
174.Sūrah 1.
175.*Supra,* chaps. 14, 15.

the Sūrah of Opening comprises remarks on many and different meanings, and hence it is the most excellent, and that the Verse of the Throne comprises the greatest knowledge which is the one followed and intended by all other forms of knowledge, and so the name of headship befits it best.

Then be mindful of this kind of freedom in dealing with the striking verses of the Qur'an and of what will follow this, in order that your knowledge may be abundant and your mind opened, in which case you will see wonders and signs and be delighted in the Paradise of different kinds of gnosis. This is the Paradise the bounds of which are limitless, because knowledge of God's glory and works (may He be exalted!) has no bounds. [But] the Paradise you know consists of bodies, and is, therefore, limited although its bounds are wide, since the creation of body without limit is impossible. Take care not to accept the lowest in exchange for the best, in which case you will be among the fools although you will be among the people of Paradise. The Prophet (ṣ) said, "Most of the people of Paradise are fools, and the 'Illiyyūn[176] are indeed the possessors of intelligence."[177]

---

176. Qur'an, 83:19-22.
177. Unidentified.

18

The condition of the gnostics

Know that if the yearning to encounter God, and if such a desire for knowing His glory which is truer and stronger than your desire for eating and sexual intercourse had been created in you, then you would have preferred the Paradise of different kinds of gnosis, its watery meadows and its gardens, to the Paradise in which the sensuous desires will be satisfied. Know [further] that this desire is created in the gnostics and not in you, as desire for worldly influence *(jāh)* is created [in young men] and not in children who have only the desire for play. You are surprised at children for their addiction to the pleasure of play and their being without the pleasure of domination, whereas the gnostic is surprised at you for your addiction to the pleasure of worldly influence and domination because the world on all sides is [a mere] play to him. When this desire is created in the gnostics, their delight in knowledge is in proportion to the measure of their desire. This desire has no relationship to the pleasure of [satisfaction of] sensuous desires, for the former is a pleasure which does not pass away and which is not changed by weariness, [whereas the latter does]. On the contrary, that pleasure, unlike all other pleasures, is always multiplying, continuing and increasing with increase in knowledge and yearning for it. That desire, moreover, is only created in man after maturity, I mean, after reaching the limit of [the full] man. The man in whom this desire is not created is either [like] a boy whose natural disposition is not perfected to receive this desire, or [like] an impotent person whose original natural disposition is corrupted by the troubles of the world and its desires. When the gnostics are provided with the desire of gnosis and the pleasure of beholding God's glory, they, in their study of the beauty of the Lordly Excellency, are in a Paradise the breadth of which is as the heavens and the earth[178] (وَجَنَّةٍ عَرْضُهَا السَّمَاوَاتُ وَالأَرْضُ أُعِدَّتْ لِلْمُتَّقِينَ), indeed even more. That is a lofty Paradise the clusters of fruits of which are near to gather[179] (فِي جَنَّةٍ عَالِيَةٍ ۞ قُطُوفُهَا دَانِيَةٌ), for its fruits are the qualities of the gnostics themselves and are unfailing and unforbidden[180] (وَفَاكِهَةٍ كَثِيرَةٍ ۞ لَا مَقْطُوعَةٍ وَلَا مَمْنُوعَةٍ) since there is no weariness in gnosis.

The gnostics look at those addicted to the base desires just as intelligent men look at children at the time of their addiction to the pleasure of play. This is why you find them to have a disliking for people, and to prefer life in retirement and solitude which are the best loved things to them; they flee away from worldly influence and wealth, because these divert them from the pleasure of conversation with God; they shun wife and child avoiding being diverted by these from God (may He be exalted!). So you see that people deride them. They say in the case of anyone of these gnostics whom they see, "He is a man to whom wicked things are suggested by Satan; rather he is a fugitive in whom the beginnings of insanity have appeared." The gnostics, [for their part], laugh at them for their contentment in the goods of this world and say, 'If you mock at us, we will mock at you, even as you mock at us; and you shall then know [which party is afflicted with humiliating punishment]'.[181] The gnostics are preoccupied with the preparation of the ship of salvation (*najāh*) for others and for themselves, because they know the danger of the life to come. So they laugh at the heedless just as an intelligent man laughs at children when they are occupied with play and when a victorious sovereign has drawn near to the city intending to make a raid in it so that he may kill some people and clothe others with robes of honour.

178.Qur'an, 3:133.
179.Qur'an, 69:22-23.
180.Qur'an, 56:32-33.
181.Qur'an, 11:38-39.

O poor man occupied with your great worldly influence which embitters life and with little wealth which causes disorder, you arouse astonishment when you are content with these, [neglecting] to look at the beauty of the Lordly Excellency and its glory despite its luminosity and appearance, for it is so apparent that it need not be sought and so obvious that it does not require reflection. After the purification of the soul from the base desires of the world nothing bars the soul from occupation with that beauty, except its strong luminosity together with the weakness in the pupils of the eye. Glory be to Him Who has disappeared from the sight of men's eyes by His dazzling light, and become veiled from them by His great appearance!

19

Stringing the jewels and pearls of the Qur'an

We shall now string the jewels of the Qur'an on one thread and its pearls on another. Both may sometime be found strung in one verse by chance, and since it is impossible to divide it we shall consider the greater part of its meaning. The first half of the Sūrah of Opening[182] (سُورَةُ الفَاتِحَةِ) belongs to the jewels, and the second half[183] to the pearls, and this is why God (may He be exalted!) said, "I have divided the Sūrah of Opening between Me and My servants ...." (to the end of the Tradition)[184] (قَسَمْتُ الفَاتِحَةَ بَيْنِي وَبَيْنَ عَبْدِي ، وَلِعَبْدِي ... الحَدِيث) We [should like to] remind you that the purpose of the string of jewels is only to gather the light of knowledge [of God, His attributes and His works], and the purpose of the pearls is steadfastness on the straight path by action. Thus the first is cognitive and the second is practical, and the basis of faith (*īmān*) lies in both cognition and action.

---

182. Qur'an, 1:1-5.
183. Qur'an, 1:6-7.
184. This Tradition (*ḥadīth*) in its full form is as follows. "The Messenger of God (ṣ) has declared that God (may He be exalted!) said, "I have divided ritual prayer [in which the Opening Sūrah is read] into two halves between Me and My servant, and My servant will receive what he asks". When the servant says, 'All types of perfect praise belong to God alone, the Lord of all the worlds', God (may He be exalted!) says, 'My servant has praised Me'. When he says, 'The Most Gracious. Ever Merciful', God (may He be exalted!) says, 'My servant has lauded Me', When he says, 'Master of the Day of Judgement'. God says, 'My servant has glorified Me'. When he says, 'You alone do we worship and You alone do we implore for help', God says, 'This is between Me and My servant, and My servant will receive what he asks'. Then when he says, 'Guide us along the straight path-the path of those on whom You have bestowed Your favours, those who have not incurred Your displeasure, and those who have not gone astray'. God says, 'This is for My servant, and My servant will receive what he asks'." See Muslim, *Ṣaḥīḥ*, Ṣalāh, 38.

Part Two
The Aims

This part deals with the aims. It comprises the pith of those Qur'anic verses which are regarded by al-Ghazālī as jewels and pearls. The jewels are those verses which especially concern the essence of God, His attributes and His works. This is the cognitive part. The pearls are the verses which describe the straight path and the verses which urge man to follow it. This is the practical part.

1

The jewels of the Qur'an

The jewels of the Qur'an are seven hundred and sixty-three verses

They Start with the Opening Sūrah of the Qur'an (*al-Fātiḥah*)

"In the name of God, Most Gracious, Ever Merciful. All praises belong to God, the Lord of all the worlds, Most Gracious, Ever Merciful, Master of the Day of Judgement. You alone we worship and You alone we ask for help. Guide us along the straight path[1]—the path of those on whom You have bestowed Your favours, those who have not aroused Your anger, and those who have not gone astray." (1:1-7)[2]

Fourteen Verses from the Sūrah of the Cow (*al-Baqarah*)

"[Your Lord is He[3]] Who has spread out the earth like a bed for

---

1. The straight path means the path of the truth (*ṭarīq al-ḥaqq*), i.e. the religion of Islam. See al-Zamakhsharī, *Op. Cit.*, I. 68.
2. These seven verses contain the gist of eight of the ten divisions of Qur'anic verses made by al-Ghazālī. They constitute the key to all doors of Paradise. This sūrah is distinguished as the best of all Qur'anic sūrahs. See *supra*, chaps. 12, 13, 17.
3. In the Qur'an it is God Who speaks. So the pronouns, I, We, My, Our and the like refer to the divine, but often He, His, Him, Himself are also used to indicate to the divine, and there is constantly a transition from the first person to the third and vice versa. [There are reasons for this transition; see al-Zamakhsharī, *Op. Cit.*, I, 62-64]. The English usage of employing the capital letter for the purpose of indicating that the pronoun has reference to the divine should be helpful to the reader. Another important point is: God is One, but He often speaks in the plural number: hence the pronouns We, Us, Our, Ourselves, and the like.

you and has made the heaven like a canopy, and has caused water to come down from the heaven and has therewith brought forth fruits as provision for you. Do not, therefore, knowingly set up equals with God." (2:22)

"He it is Who created all that is in the earth for your benefit; then He turned towards the heavens and fashioned them seven heavens. He has the fullest knowledge of everything." (2:29)

"They [i.e. the angels] said: Glory be to You! We have no knowledge save that which You have taught us. Surely You alone are the All-knowing, the All-wise." (2:32)

"Do you not know that to God belongs the Kingdom of the heavens and the earth, and that there is no protector nor any helper for you besides Him?" (2:107)

"To God belong the East and the West; so wherever you turn, there is the face of God; surely God is All-embracing, All-knowing. They [i.e. Christians, Jews and pagans[4]] say, 'God has taken to Himself offspring (*walad*)'[5]. May He be exalted! To Him belongs all that is in the heavens and the earth; all are obedient[6] to Him. The Originator of the heavens and the earth, He, when He determines the coming into being of a thing, only says concerning it 'be', and it becomes".[7] (2:115-117)

---

4. All these categories of people are charged here; see al-Zamakhsharī, *Op. Cit.*, I, 307.
5. In those verses where the term *walad*, not *ibn* (son), occurs what is meant is not merely son but child, offspring which includes daughter as well. For Christians Jesus is the son of God; for Jews Ezra is the son of God (Qur'an 9:30); pagan Arabs of pre-Islamic Arabia believed that their deities were angels whom they considered as daughters of God. From the context of the verse in which '*walad*' occurs one should determine who are charged in it—Christians or Jews or pagans—and what is meant by this word—son or daughter or both.
6. This means that nothing can refuse God's creation, predetermination and will. See al-Zamakhsharī, *Op. Cit.*, I, 307.
7. "'be' and it becomes" is a metaphorical expression; in reality God does not utter the word 'be'. The real meaning of this expression is that anything concerning which God decrees and intends that it should come into existence does come into being without any refusal or hesitation. See al-Zamakhsharī, *Op. Cit.*, I, 307.

"God will suffice you [for defence] against them [i.e. the disbelievers]; He is the All-hearing, the All-knowing. [Proclaim: We take our religious] colour from God, and who is better than God at colouring?[8] We are worshipping Him." (2:137-138)

"Your God is one God; there is no god but He, the Most Gracious, the Ever Merciful. In the creation of the heavens and the earth, in the alternation of night and day, in the vessels that sail in the sea carrying that which profits people, in the water that God sends down from the heaven reviving therewith the earth after its death and scattering therein all kinds of crawling things, and in the course of the winds and the clouds pressed into service between the heaven and the earth—are indeed signs [of God's existence] for a people who understand." (2:163-164)

"When My servants [i.e. men] question you concerning Me, then [tell them:] Surely I am near. I respond to the call of the caller when he calls to Me; so they should respond to Me and have belief in Me, that they may be rightly guided." (2:186)

"God! There is no god but He, the Ever Living, the Self-subsisting and All-sustaining. Neither slumber nor sleep seizes Him. To Him belong whatever is in the heavens and whatever is in the earth. Who is he that will [be able to] intercede with Him except by His permission? He knows what lies before them [i.e. men] and what is after them, and they cannot comprehend anything of His knowledge except that which He pleases. His throne comprises the heavens and earth; the preservation of them does not weary Him. He is the Most High, the Most Great."[9] (2:255)

"No compulsion is there in religion, [for] right direction has become clear from error; then anyone who rejects Satan [or idols] and believes in God, has taken hold of the strongest

---

8. For this meaning of the verse see al-Zamakhsharī, *Op. Cit.*, I, 316.
9. This is the well known Verse of the Throne (*Āyah al-Kursī*) regarded as the chief of Qur'anic verses. It is greatly admired by Muslims and frequently recited. For a brief discussion of its excellence and glorious meaning see *supra*, chaps. 14, 17.

and most dependable support which will never break. God is All-hearing, All-knowing." (2:256)

Thirteen Verses from the Sūrah of the House of 'Imrān (*Āl 'Imrān*)

"*Alif lām mīm.*[10] God! There is no god but He, the Ever Living, the Self-subsisting and All-sustaining. He has sent down to you the Book [i.e. the Qur'an] in accordance with the requirements of truth and wisdom,[11] confirming the revelation that preceded it; He sent down the Torah and the Gospel before this as a guidance for the people; He sent down that [Qur'an] which distinguished [between truth and falsehood]. Those who have disbelieved in God's revelations shall certainly receive a severe punishment; God is All-mighty, Possessor of power to requite. Nothing is hidden from God in the earth or in the heaven. He it is Who fashions you in the wombs as He wills there is no god but He, the All-mighty, the All-wise." (3:1-6)

"God bears witness that there is no god but He—and so do the angels as well as those who possess knowledge—maintaining justice. There is no god but He, the All-mighty, the All-wise. Surely the [true] religion in the estimation of God is Islam." (3:18-19)

"Say: O God, Lord of sovereignty, You give sovereignty to whomever You please, and You take away sovereignty from whomever You please; You exalt whomever You please, and you abase whomever You please; in Your hand is all good; surely You are powerful over everything. You make the night pass into the day and make the day pass into the night; You bring forth the living from the dead and bring forth the dead from the living; You give sustenance to whomever You please

10. These are names of three Arabic letters. In the beginning of many other sūrahs also Arabic letters occur. No satisfactory explanation has been given of their occurrence and significance. It is better not to translate them.

11. This meaning of the word *bi al-ḥaqq* is given by al-Zamakhsharī in his *Op. Cit.*, II, 29, 226. This word occurs many times in the Qur'an.

without measure." (3:26-29)

"Say: Surely all bounty is in the hand of God; He gives it to whomever He pleases; God is Lord of vast bounty, All-knowing. He singles out for His mercy whomever He pleases; God is of great bounty." (3:73-74)

"To God belongs the Kingdom of the heavens and the earth; God is powerful over everything. In the creation of the heavens and the earth, and in the alternation of the night and the day are indeed signs [of God's existence, power and wisdom] for people of understanding, who remember God [while they are] standing, sitting and [lying] on their sides and ponder over the creation of the heavens and the earth, [which impels them to supplicate:] Our Lord, You have not created all this without purpose;[12] glory be to You; shield us, then, from the torment of Hell-fire. Our Lord, you have surely humiliated him whom You do condemn to enter Hell-fire, and there is no helper for the evildoers." (3:189-192)

Two Verses from the Sūrah of Women (*al-Nisā'*)

"O people of the Book [i.e. Christians], do not exceed the limits in [the matter of] your religion, and do not say of God anything but the truth. Surely the Messiah, Jesus son of Mary, was only a messenger of God, and His word that He conveyed to Mary, and a spirit (*rūḥ*) from Him. So believe in God and His messengers, and do not say: There are three gods. Desist, [it will be] better for you. Indeed God is the only one God. Far is it removed from His glory that should have a son. To Him belong whatever is in the heavens and whatever is in the earth; sufficient is God as a guardian. The Messiah would never disdain to be accounted a servant of God, nor would [even] those angels who are near to Him. Those who disdain to worship Him and wax proud, He will gather all together before Him." (4:171-172)

---

12. The Prophet (ṣ) said, "Woe to him who has recited this verse but has not reflected on it!" He himself used to look at the sky at midnight, recite this verse and reflect on it. See al-Zamakhsharī, *Op. Cit.*, I, 487-488.

Ten Verses from the Sūrah of the Table (*al-Mā'idah*)

"They are indeed disbelievers who say: God is the Messiah, son of Mary. Say [to them]: Who can have any power against God if He should desire to destroy the Messiah son of Mary and his mother and all those that are in the earth? To God belongs the Kingdom of the heavens and the earth and of all that which exists between them; He creates what He pleases. God is Most Powerful over everything." (5:17)

"Do you not know that God is He to Whom belongs the Kingdom of the heavens and the earth? He punishes whom He pleases and forgives whom He pleases; God is Most Powerful over everything." (5:40)

"God has made the Ka'bah,[13] the Holy House, a permanent means of support and uplift for mankind, as also the Holy month, the offerings and the animals with collars designed for sacrifice. That is so that you may know that God knows whatever is in the heavens and whatever is in the earth and that God has fullest knowledge of everything. Know that God is severe in punishment and that God is [also] Most Forgiving, Ever Merciful." (5:97-98)

"The duty of the Messenger of God is only to convey the message. God knows what you do openly and what you hide." (5:99)

["Keep in mind] when God shall say [on the Day of Judgement]: O Jesus son of Mary, did you say to the people, 'Take me and my mother for two gods apart from God'? He shall answer: Glory be to You! It is not proper for me to have said that to which I have no right. Had I said it, You would surely have known it. You know what is in my mind, and I do not know what is in Your mind. It is only You Who possess the fullest knowledge of all that is hidden. I said nothing to them

---

13. The Holy Ka'bah is the house of God (*bayt Allāh*) situated under the sky, in the open courtyard of the Sacred Mosque (*al-Masjid al-Ḥarām*) in Makkah. It is to the direction of this Ka'bah that a Muslim must turn his face when performing ritual prayer. A pilgrim too is required to circumambulate this Ka'bah as a rite of pilgrimage to Makkah.

except that which You commanded me. that is:[14] Worship God, my Lord and your Lord. I was a witness over them as long as I was present among them, but since You took me to Yourself, You have been the One to watch over them; and You are witness over all things. If You punish them, surely they are Your servants; if You forgive them, You surely are the All-mighty, the All-wise. God shall say: This day the truthful will profit by their truthfulness. For them are Gardens beneath which rivers flow; therein they shall dwell forever; God is well-pleased with them and they are well-pleased with Him; that is the great triumph. To God belongs the Kingdom of the heavens and the earth and of whatever is in them; He has the fullest power over everything." (5:116-120)

Forty-five Verses from the Sūrah of the Cattle (*al-An'ām*)

"All praise is due to God, Who created the heavens and the earth and made darkness and light; yet those who disbelieve set up equals with their Lord. It is He Who created you from clay, and then decreed a term [i.e. the day of death]; a term is fixed with Him; yet you entertain doubt. He alone is God in the heavens and in the earth; He knows, your secret [thoughts] and your outward [acts] and [also] knows whatever you acquire." (6:1-3)

"To Him belongs all that exists in the night and the day; He is the All-hearing, the All-knowing. Say [to the disbelievers]: Shall I take as protector someone other than God, Originator of the heavens and the earth, Who feeds [all] and is not fed? Tell [them]: I have surely been commanded to surrender to God completely. [I have also been commanded:] Never be of those who associate partners with God. Tell [them also]: Assuredly, I fear, if I were to disobey my Lord, the punishment of an awful day [i.e. the Day of Judgement]. He from whom the punishment is averted on that day will have been shown mercy by God; that is the manifest triumph." (6:13-16)

14. Cf. John 17:3, 12.

"If God were to afflict you, there is none that can remove the affliction but He; if He were to bestow upon you some good, He has the fullest power over everything. He is Supreme over His servants; He is the All-wise, the All-aware." (6:17-18)

"There is not an animal that moves about in the earth, nor a bird that flies on its two wings, but forms communities like you. We have neglected nothing in the Book [i.e. the Qur'an]; then to their Lord they will be gathered together." (6:38)

"Say [to the disbelievers]: Tell me, if God were to take away your hearing and your sight, and to seal up your minds, who is the god, other than God, who could bring them back to you? Observe, how We expound the signs [in diverse ways], yet they turn away [from the truth]. Say: Tell me, if God's punishment came upon you suddenly or openly, will any be destroyed, except the wrongdoing people?" (6:46-47)

"With Him are the keys of the unseen; none knows it but He. He knows whatever is in the land and in the sea; not a leaf falls but He knows it; nor is there a grain in the darkness of the earth, nor anything green or dry, but is [recorded] in a clear Book, [i.e. the Preserved Tablet.[15]] (*Lawḥ Maḥfūẓ*)" (6:59)

"He it is Who takes your souls into custody by night and knows whatever you do by day; then He raises you up during the day that a term that has been appointed may be completed; then to Him is your return; then He will inform you of that which you used to do." (6:60)

"He is Irresistible over His servants [i.e. men], and sends guardian [angels][16] to watch over you until, when death comes to any of you, Our deputed [angels of death] take his soul and

15. The Preserved Tablet is commonly understood to be in heaven. It contains the originals of all revealed Books including the Qur'an (Qur'an 13:39). Everything which God has decreed to bring into being from the beginning of creation to Doomsday is recorded in it (Qur'an 22:52). It is referred to sometimes as the Tablet, sometimes as a clear Book, and sometimes as a clear Imām. See al-Zamakhsharī, *Op. Cit.*, II, 363, 539; al-Ghazālī, *Iḥyā'*, IV, 504-505.

16. They are those angels who record whatever a man says or does. In the Qur'an 82:11 they are called honoured recorders (*Kirām Kātibīn*).

they do not fail in the discharge of their duty in any respect. Then they are returned to God, their true Protector. Take notice, His is the judgement and He is the swiftest of reckoners." (6:61-62)

"Tell [the polytheists]: Who is it who delivers you from the darkness [i.e. calamities] of the land and the sea, when you call upon God humbly and secretly [saying], 'If He delivers us from this, we will surely be among the grateful'? Tell [them]: It is God Who delivers you from them and from every [other] distress; yet you associate partners with Him:" (6:63-64)

"Tell [the polytheists]: He [i.e. God] is able to send on you punishment from above you or from beneath your feet or to throw you into confusion, [making you] of different parties and involve you with each other in violence. See, how We expound the signs [in diverse ways] that they may understand." (6:65)

"He it is Who created the heavens and the earth in accordance with the requirements of truth and wisdom; the day He says [concerning a thing] 'be', it becomes[17]. His words shall be fulfilled. His will be the Kingdom on the day when the trumpet will be blown. He is knower of the unseen and the visible; He is All-wise, the All-aware." (6:73)

["Call to mind] when Abraham said to his father Āzar: Do you take idols for gods? I see you and your people in manifest error. Thus We were showing Abraham [Our] Kingdom over the heavens and the earth so that he might be of those who have sure faith. When the darkness of night outspread over him he saw a star and exclaimed, 'This is my Lord'. But when it set he said: I do not like those that set. Then when he saw the moon rising, he said, 'This is my Lord'. But when it set he said: Had my Lord not guided me I would most surely have been of those who go astray. [Finally] when he saw the sun rising, he said, 'This is my Lord; this is the biggest'! But when that [too] set he said, 'O my people, certainly I am free from that which you associate with God. I have wholly turned myself to Him Who originated the heavens and the earth, as a man of

17. See *supra*, pp. 78. n. 11, 76. n. 7.

pure faith, and I am not of those who associate partners with God'." (6:74-79)

"It is God Who causes the grain of corn and the date-stones to sprout. He brings forth the living from the dead, and it is He Who brings forth the dead from the living. That is your God; how, then, are you turned back? He causes the break of day, and has made the night for rest, and the sun and the moon the means for reckoning time. That is the measure determined by the All-mighty, the All-knowing. He it is Who has made for you the stars, that you may follow the right direction in the darkness of the land and sea. We have explained the signs [of Our existence, power and wisdom] in detail for a people who know. He it is Who has produced you from a single self [i.e. Adam] and [has appointed for you] a place of temporary resort and a more permanent abode. We have expounded the signs in detail for a people who understand." (6:95-98)

"It is He Who sends down water from the sky; with it We bring forth the buds of every kind; then We bring forth from it green [foliage] from which We produce clustered grain; from the date palm, out of its spathe, spring bunches hanging low. [We also produce] gardens of grapes, the olives, and the pomegranate, some similar and some dissimilar. Observe the fruit of every kind of tree when it bears fruit and the process of its ripening. Surely in this are indeed signs [of Our existence, power and wisdom] for a people who believe." (6:99)

"They [i.e. polytheists] have appointed partners of God out of jinn's[18], whereas He has created them; and they falsely attribute to Him sons and daughters without any knowledge.

18. Jinn constitute a class of intelligent beings created by God. They are bodies (*ajsām*) composed of vapour or flames, intelligent, imperceptible to our senses, capable of appearing in different forms and of carrying out heavy labours. They are created of smokeless flame (Qur'an 55:15). They are capable of salvation; they fall under religious obligations (Qur'an 51:56, 55:39, 60:128, 6:130); some jinn will enter Paradise while others will be cast into Hell (Qur'an 7:38, 179). They can mix with men. There are stories of love between jinn and human beings. There are many stories too of relations

Glory be to Him! High be He exalted above that which they I describe [of Him]! The Originator of the heavens and the earth! How can He have a child when He has no consort, and He has created everything and has the fullest knowledge of all things? That is God, your Lord: there is no god but He, the Creator of everything; so worship Him; He is Guardian over everything. Eyes cannot comprehend Him, but He comprehends [all] eyes; He is the All-subtle, the All-aware. Clear proofs have indeed come to you from your Lord; so he who sees things clearly, it is for his own benefit; and he who ignores, it is to his own loss; I am not a keeper over you." (6:100-104)

"The word of your Lord shall be fulfilled in truth and justice; there is nothing that can change His words; He is the All-hearing, the All-knowing." (6:115)

"Your Lord is Self-sufficient, Merciful. He can do away with you if He pleases and cause to succeed you anything He pleases even as He raised you from the offspring of another people." (6:133)

"He it is Who has produced trellised and untrellised gardens, date-palms, crops, all varying in taste, the olive and the pomegranate, similar and dissimilar. Eat of the fruit of each when it bears fruit, pay His due on the day of harvesting, but do not be extravagant;[19] surely He does not love the extravagant. Of the cattle [He produces] some for burden and some for slaughter. Eat of that which God has provided for

---

between saints and jinn; see Ibn al-Nadīm, *Kitāb al-Fihrist*, trans. by Bayard Dodge, New York, 1970, pp. 209, 291, 539, 728-729, 756-757, 760, 823; D.B. Macdonald, *Development of Religious Attitude and life in Islam*, Beyrouth, 1965, pp. 144 ff.; *idem*, H. Masse *et al.*, "Djinn," *EI* 2 II, 546-550.

19. In the Qur'an extravagance and miserliness are both condemned and the harmfulness of both is set out; moderation or the mean is prescribed as the right course for the believers (Qur'an 25:67, 17:29, 70:31, 48:29). The Prophet (ṣ) also emphasized the middle course; his statement, "The best of all things is their mean," is well known and often quoted. The concept of moderation is taught in Islamic jurisprudence, in philosophy and in Sufism; see Quasem, *Ethics*, pp. 81-85.

you, and do not follow in the footsteps of Satan; surely he is a manifest enemy of you." (6:141-142)

"Say: My ritual prayer, my ritual sacrifices, my living, and my dying—are all for God, the Lord of the worlds. No partner He has. Thus I am commanded, and I am the foremost of Muslims. Tell [the worshippers of idols]: Shall I seek someone other than God as Lord, while He is the Lord of all things? Everyone must bear the consequences of that which he does; no bearer of a burden can bear the burden of another. Then to your Lord will be your return, and He will inform you of that on which you used to differ." (6:162-164)

"He it is Who has made you take the place of others on the earth, and has exalted some of you over others in rank, that He may try you by that which He has bestowed upon you. Surely your Lord is swift in punishment; surely He is Most Forgiving, Ever Merciful." (6:165)

Ten Verses from the Sūrah of the Heights (*al-A'rāf*)

"Indeed We established you in the earth and provided for you therein the means of livelihood. But little gratitude you express. We did create you; then We gave you shape; then We said to the angels: Fall prostrate before Adam. So they fell prostrate; but not Iblīs—he was not of those who made prostration." (7:10-11)

"They [i.e. the people of Paradise] shall say: All praises belong to God Who has guided us to this; if God had not guided us, we could not have found guidance. The messengers of our Lord did indeed bring us the truth. It shall be proclaimed to them: This is your Paradise; it has been bestowed upon you because of that which you used to do." (7:43)

"Surely your Lord is God Who created the heavens and the earth in six days; then He set Himself up on the throne; He makes the night cover the day pursuing it swiftly; He has created the sun, the moon and the stars, all made subservient by His command. Take notice, His are the creation and the command. Blessed be God, the Lord of the worlds!" (7:54)

"Call on your Lord humbly and secretly; He does not love those who exceed the limit. Do not create disorder in the earth after it has been set in order, and call upon Him fearfully and in hope; surely the mercy of God is near to the good-doers." (7:55-56)

"He it is Who sends the winds as glad tidings in advance of mercy, till when they bear cloud, We drive it to a dead land; then We send down water from it and We bring forth with water fruits of every kind. Thus We bring forth the dead that you may take heed. Good land brings forth its vegetation by the permission of its Lord, and that land which is bad brings forth poor crops scantily. Thus We expound the signs [in diverse ways] for a people who are grateful." (7:57-58)

"When Moses arrived at the tryst at Our appointed time and his Lord spoke to him, he said: O my Lord, show Yourself to me that I may behold You. He replied: You can by no means behold Me, but look towards the mountain—if it remains firm in its place, You will soon see Me. When his Lord manifested Himself on the mountain He broke it into bits, and Moses fell into a faint. When he recovered, he said: Glory be to You! I turn wholly to You, and I am the foremost among the believers." (7:143)

"Do they not observe the Kingdom of the heavens and the earth and whatever thing God has created? [Do they not reflect that] the time appointed [for their destruction] may be drawing near? Then in what report will they believe after that?" (7:185)

Four Verses from the Sūrah of Repentance (*al-Tawbah*)

"They [i.e. Jews and Christians] had only been commanded to worship the one God. There is no god but He. Glory be to Him above that which they associate with Him! They desire to extinguish the light of God by blowing through their mouths, but God utterly rejects everything except that He will perfect His light even though the disbelievers may dislike it. He it is

Who has sent His Messenger with guidance and the religion of truth [i.e. Islam], that He may make it prevail over every other religion, even though those who associate partners with Him may dislike it." (9:31-33)

"Surely it is God to Whom belongs the Kingdom of the heavens and the earth. He gives life, and causes death; you have no friend nor helper besides God." (9:116)

Eighteen Verses from the Sūrah of Jonah (*Yūnus*)

"Surely your Lord is God, Who created the heavens and the earth in six days; then He set Himself upon the throne, regulating the affair. No one may intercede with Him save with His permission. That is your god, your Lord; so worship Him. Will you not, then, be admonished? To Him is the return of all of you. This is God's promise in Truth. Surely He originates the creation, then He repeats it that He may justly reward those who believe and do good deeds. Those who disbelieve shall have a drink of boiling water, and a painful chastisement, because they disbelieved." (10:3-4)

"He it is Who has made the sun a source of light, and the moon shedding lustre, and ordained it for stages, that you may learn the method of calculating the years and determining the time. God did not create this system save with the requirements of truth and wisdom; He expounds the signs [of His existence, power and wisdom] in detail for a people who know. In the alternation of the night and the day, and in all that God has created in the heavens and the earth, there are indeed [many] signs for a people who fear God." (10:5-6)

"Say [to them]: Who provides sustenance for you from the heaven and the earth? Or who is it that controls the ears and the eyes? Who brings forth the living from the dead and brings forth the dead from the living? Who regulates the affairs [of the universe?] They will surely say: It is God. Then ask them: Will you not then do your duty to Him? That is your God, your true Lord. So what is there after discarding the truth but error? How then are you being turned away?" (10:31-32)

"Whatever you may be engaged in, whatever portion of the Qur'an you may recite, and whatever work all of you may do, We indeed are witness of whatever in which you may be engaged. Not the smallest particle in the earth or heaven is hidden from your Lord; there is nothing smaller or bigger but is [recorded] in a clear Book (i.e. the Preserved Tablet)."[20] (10:61)

"He it is Who has made the night so that you may rest in it, and has made the day bright. Surely in this are indeed signs [of His existence, power and wisdom] for a people who listen [to the truth and seek to derive benefit from it]. They [i.e. Christians, Jews and pagans] say, 'God has taken to Himself offspring'.[21] Glory be to Him! He is Self-sufficient. To Him belong whatsoever is in the heavens and whatsoever is in the earth. You have no authority in support of that which you allege. Do you say concerning God that which you do not know?" (10:67-68)

"If your Lord had enforced His will, surely all those in the earth would have believed without exception. Will you then force people until they become believers? No one can believe except by the permission of God; He lays uncleanness upon those who do not use their understanding. Say [to them]: Observe what is happening in the heavens and the earth. Signs and warnings do not avail a people who do not believe." (10:99-101)

"Say: O people, if you are in doubt concerning my religion, then [let me make it clear to you that] I do not worship those whom you worship apart from God. Rather I worship God Who will cause you to die, and I have been commanded to be of the believers. [I have also been commanded thus:] Devote yourself to the religion as a man of pure faith, and never be of those who associate partners with God; do not call, apart from God, on anything which neither profits you nor harms you, for if you do so, you will surely be of the wrongdoers. If God afflicts you with distress there is none who can relieve you of it

20. See *supra*, p. 82, n. 15.
21. See *supra*, p. 76, n. 5.

but He; if He desires any good for you, there is none who can repel His bounty. He bestows it upon whomsoever of his servants [i.e. men] He wills. He is the Most Forgiving, Ever Merciful." (10:104-107)

"Say: O people, the truth has indeed come to you from your Lord. Then anyone who follows the guidance follows it only for the good of his own self, and anyone who errs does so only to his own detriment. I am not appointed a keeper over you. Follow that which is revealed to you; be patient until God gives judgement; He is the best of judges." (10:108-109)

Eleven Verses from the Sūrah of Hūd

"To God is your return; He has the fullest power over everything. Take notice, they [i.e. the hypocrites] surely fold up their breasts that they may hide [their thoughts] from Him. Take notice, even when they cover themselves up with their garments, He knows what they conceal and what they disclose; certainly He has the fullest knowledge of what is in their minds. There is no creature that moves in the earth but it is for God to provide it with sustenance, and He knows its temporary lodging and its permanent house. All this is recorded in a clear Book (i.e. the Preserved Tablet)."[22] (11:4-6)

"It was commanded [after the deluge]: O earth, swallow up your water; O sky, desist. The water subsided, the affair was accomplished, the ark [of Noah] came to rest on Jūdī, and it was said: A far removal [from God][23] is for the wrong doing people!" (11:44)

"[The prophet Hūd said to his people:] Surely, I have put my trust in God, my Lord and your Lord; there is no creature that moves on the earth but He holds it completely in His power;

---

22. See *supra*, p. 82, n. 15.
23. Removal from God has become an important concept in Sufism. The Sufis are very afraid of removal from their Beloved and of veil (*ḥijāb*) from Him. They are strongly influenced by this and similar verses of the Qur'an, e.g. 11:60, 68, 95, 23:41, 44.

surely my Lord is on the straight path; if now you turn away, I have already conveyed to you that with which I have been sent to you, and my Lord will make another people your successors, and you can not do any harm to Him; surely, my Lord is Guardian over everything." (11:56-57)

"Had your Lord enforced His will He would surely have made mankind one community; as it is, they will not cause to differ, except those on whom your Lord has bestowed mercy, and for this had He created them. But the word of your Lord shall be fulfilled: Surely, I will fill Hell with jinn[24] and men, all together." (11:118-119)

"All that We relate to you of the tidings of [Our] messengers is such that thereby We make your heart firm; in that have come to you the truth, and an exhortation and a reminder for the believers." (11:120)

"Say to those who do not believe: Act according to your station; We, too, are acting. Wait; we are also waiting." (11:121-122)

"To God alone belongs [knowledge of the] unseen [matters] of the heavens and the earth, and to Him will all matters be returned. So worship Him and put your trust in Him. Your Lord is not heedless of that which you do." (11:123)

Nineteen Verses from the Sūrah of Thunder (*al-Ra'd*)

"*Alif lām mīm rā.*[25] These are verses of the Book [i.e. the Qur'an]. That which has been revealed to you from your Lord is the truth, but most men do not believe." (13:1)

"God is He Who raised up the heavens without any pillars that you can see. Then He set Himself upon the throne, and constrained the sun and the moon to serve you; each of them pursues its course during an appointed term. He regulates the affair, and expounds the signs [of His existence, power and wisdom], that you may have firm belief in the meeting with your Lord. He it is Who spread out the earth and made

24. See *supra*, p. 84, n. 18.
25. See *supra*, p. 78, n. 10.

therein firmly fixed mountains and rivers, and of fruits of every kind He has made pairs. He causes the night to cover the day. In all this are indeed signs for a people who reflect. In the earth are diverse tracts adjoining one another, vineyards, corn-fields and date-palms, some growing from one root and others from separate roots, which are irrigated by the same water, and [yet] We make some of them excel others in the quality of their fruits. In all this [also] are indeed signs for a people who understand." (13:2-4)

"God knows that which every female bears, that which the wombs reject as defective and that which they foster. With Him is everything in proper measure. He is the Knower of the unseen and the visible, Great above all, Most exalted. He among you who talks in secret and he who talks openly are equally within His ken; and so also he who seeks to hide himself by night and he who goes forth openly by day." (13:8-10)

"Surely God does not change the good condition of a people unless they [first] change the good condition of themselves.[26] When God desires punishment for a people, there is no repelling it; nor can they have any helper apart from Him." (13:11)

"He it is Who shows you the lightning to inspire fear and hope, and raises heavy clouds. The thunder proclaims His praise, and [so do] the angels for awe of Him. He directs the thunderbolts and smites with them whom He wills, yet they dispute concerning God, and He is mighty in wrath. To Him should be the true prayer. Those on whom they call, apart from Him, do not respond to them at all. Their case is like that of one who stretches forth his hands towards water that it may reach his mouth, but it does not reach. The prayer of the disbelievers goes only astray. To God submits whosoever is in the heavens and in the earth willingly or unwillingly, and [so do] their shadows in the mornings and the evenings." (13:12-15)

"Say [to the idolaters]: Who is the Lord of the heavens and the

26. The Sufis often quote this verse in support of the strong emphasis they lay upon the improvement of man's inward self (*bāṭin*).

earth? Then tell them: It is God. [Again] ask them: Have you, then, taken beside Him helpers who have no power to acquire benefit or to repel harm even in respect of their own selves? Ask them: Can the blind and the seeing be equal? Or, can darkness and light be the same? Or, have they assigned to God partners who have created the like of His creation so that the two creations appear indistinguishable to them? Tell [them]: God alone is the Creator of everything, and He is the Single, the Most Irresistible. He sends down water from the sky so that valleys begin to flow according to their capacity, and the flood carries swelling foam [on its surface]. A foam like it comes up from that which they heat up in the fire for the purpose of making ornaments or articles of domestic use. Thus God illustrates truth and falsehood. The foam vanishes like froth, while that which benefits men stays on the earth. Thus God sets forth similitudes." (13:16-17)

"For those who respond to their Lord is the best [reward i.e. Paradise]; those who do not respond to Him, if they had all that is in the earth and the like of it added to it, they would seek to ransom themselves with all these. They will have an evil reckoning, and their abode is Hell. A wretched resting place it is!" (13:18)

"It was not possible for any messenger of God to bring a sign except by God's permission. For each period there is a Book. God effaces what He wills and establishes [what He wills]; with Him is the source of the Book (which is the Preserved Tablet in which everything is recorded)."[27] (13:38-39)

"Whether We do bring to pass during your lifetime some of that which We have promised them [i.e. disbelievers] or We do cause you to die before its happening, your part is only to convey the message; it is for Us to make the reckoning. Do they not see that We are approaching from the borders of the land, reducing it as We proceed? God judges; no one has power to reverse His judgement; He is swift in reckoning." (13:40-41)

"Those who were before them [also] devised plans, [but these came to nothing]. All planning belongs to God. He knows what

---

27. See *supra*, p. 82, n. 15.

everyone acquires. The disbelievers will soon know to whom belongs the true recompense of the ultimate resort. Those who disbelieve say: You [i.e. Muḥammad] are not a messenger of God. Say [to them]: Sufficient is God as a witness between you and me, and so also is he who possesses knowledge of the Book." (13:42-43)

Nine Verses from the Sūrah of Abraham (*Ibrāhīm*)

"*Alif lām rā*[28]. This is a Book which We have sent down to you that you may bring mankind out of darkness into the light, by the permission of their Lord, to the path of All-mighty, the All-laudable God to Whom belong whatsoever is in the heavens and whatsoever is in the earth. Woe to the disbelievers for a severe chastisement!" (14:1-2)

"God is He Who created the heavens and the earth, and caused water to come down from the sky and brought forth with it fruits for your sustenance. He has constrained for you the vessels so that they may sail through the sea by His command, and the rivers also He has constrained to your service. He has also constrained to your service the sun and the moon, both constant upon their courses; He has subjected to you the night and the day. He has given you of all that you asked of Him; if you try to count God's favours, you will not be able to count them; surely man is very unjust and ungrateful." (14:32-34)

"The day [will come] when the earth will be changed into another earth, and the heavens [will also be changed], and they [i.e. man, jinn, Satan, lower animal, and so on] will all appear before God, the Single, the Most Irresistible. You shall see the guilty ones secured in chains on that day; their garments will be of pitch, and the fire shall envelop their faces; this will be in the course of God's requital of each soul for what it has earned. Surely God is swift at reckoning. This is a message for mankind that they may be warned thereby, that they may know that He is the only one God, and that those possessed of minds may take heed." (14:48-52)

---

28. See *supra*, p. 78, n. 10.

Nine Verses from the Sūrah of the Rocky Track (*al-Ḥijr*)

"We[29] have spread out the earth, set in it firm mountains, and caused every appropriate article to grow therein. We have provided in it means of livelihood for you and for such of Our creation as you are not able to provide for. There is not a thing but We have [unbounded] stores of it, but only send it down in a regulated measure." (15:19-21)

"We[30] send winds carrying moisture; then We send down water from the sky; with it We provide you with drink. You could not have stored it up [for yourselves]. Surely, it is We Who give life and cause death, and it is We Who are the [sole] inheritors [of all]. We know well those of you who go ahead, and We know well those of you who lag behind. Surely your Lord is He Who will gather them all together; He is All-wise, All-knowing." (15:22-25)

"Indeed We created man from dry ringing clay which was wrought from black mud, and the jinn We had created before from the fire of a glowing blast." (15:26-27)

Forty-nine Verses from the Sūrah of the Bee (*al-Naḥl*)

"God's command [of punishment] comes; so do not seek to hasten it. Glory be to Him! High be He exalted above that which they [i.e. polytheists] associate with Him! He sends down the angels [with revelation] by His command on whomsoever of His servants [i.e. men] He pleases, [directing:] Warn people that there is no god but I; so keep your duty to Me." (16:1-2)

"He [i.e. God] has created the heavens and the earth in accordance with the requirements of truth and wisdom. High be He exalted above that which they [i.e. polytheists] associate with Him! He has created man from sperm and lo, he becomes a manifest adversary![31] He has created cattle; they are a source of warmth and benefit for you, and you [also] eat

29. See *supra*, p. 75, n. 3.
30. See *ibid.*
31. This verse was revealed in connection with Ubayy Ibn Khalaf, who

of their flesh; there is beauty in them for you in the evening and in the morning; they carry your loads to a place which you could not reach without great hardship to yourselves. Surely your Lord is Compassionate, Ever Merciful. [He has created] horses, mules and asses that you may ride them, and [also] as an adornment; and He will create [for that purpose other means] which you do not [yet] know." (16:3-8)

"God points out the right way; some ways are devious. Had He enforced His will, He would have guided you all." (16:9)

"He it is Who sends down water from the sky for you; you drink from it and with it grows trees [i.e. shrubs] on which you pasture your cattle. With it He grows for you corn, the olive, the date-palm, the grape and all other kinds of fruits. In that is indeed a sign [of His existence, power and wisdom] for a people who reflect. He has constrained to your service the night and the day and the sun and the moon; the stars [too] are constrained to your service by His command. In all this there are indeed signs for a people who understand. In that which He has created for you in the earth of diverse types of articles, there is indeed a sign for a people who take heed. He it is Who constrained the sea to your service that you may eat fresh flesh from it and may take out from it articles that you wear as ornaments. You see the vessel ploughing through it that you may [voyage across the ocean] seeking His bounty [by commerce] and that you may be grateful. He has set in the earth firm mountains lest it shake with you, and [has made] rivers and tracts that you may find your way. [He has set other] marks; [by these] and by the stars they [i.e. people] find their ways. Is He, then, Who creates like he who does not? Will you not, then, take heed? If you try to count God's favours, you will not be able to number them. Most surely, God is Most Forgiving, Ever Merciful." (16:10-18)

"God knows all that you conceal and all that you disclose. Those on whom they call apart from God, create nothing, but

brought arguments against the possibility of Resurrection. See al-Zamakhsharī, *Op. Cit.*, II, 401.

are themselves created. [They are] lifeless, not living; they are not aware when they will be raised up. Your God is one God. The minds of those who do not believe in the world to come are strangers to truth and they are arrogant. Without any doubt whatever God knows that which they conceal and that which they disclose ." (16:19-23)

"Have they [i.e. the disbelievers] not observed that the shadows of all things that God has created move from the right and from the left in prostration to God? Whatever is in the heavens and whatever creature is in the earth, and the angels [also] all humbly prostrate to God, and they do not behave proudly. They fear their Lord above them and do that which they are commanded."(16:48-50)

"God has commanded: Do not take two gods; there is only one God; so fear Me alone. To Him belongs whatsoever is in the heavens and in the earth, and His is the [true] religion for ever. Will you, then, keep duty to any being other than God? Whatsoever bounty you have is from God; then when distress afflicts you it is to Him that you cry for help. Then, when He removes the distress from you, lo, some of you ascribe partners to their[32] Lord, thus denying that which We have bestowed upon them. Well then enjoy yourselves for a while; you will soon realize [the consequences of what you do.]" (16: 51-55)

"God has sent down water from heaven and has quickened with it the earth after its death. Most surely in that is a sign [of His existence, power and wisdom] for a people who listen [to the truth]. There is indeed a lesson for you in the cattle. We provide you with a drink out of that which is in their bellies; that is, from between the faeces and the blood [We provide] milk pure and pleasant for those who drink it. Of the fruits of date-palms and the grapes you obtain an intoxicating drink as well as a good provision. Most surely in that is a sign for a people who make use of their understanding. Your Lord

32. Here transition is made from the second person to the third—a transition which forms one of the special characteristics of God's style of speaking in the Qur'an. In an ordinary human speech the possessive pronoun in this case should be 'your', not 'their'. Also see *supra*, p. 75, n. 3.

inspired the bee: Prepare hives in the hills, in the trees and in the trellises which they [i.e. men] put up, and eat of every kind of fruit and follow the ways appointed for you by your Lord which have been made easy [for you]. There comes out of the bellies of the bees a drink of diverse hues [i.e. honey], possessing healing qualities for people. In that is indeed a sign for a people who reflect." (16:65-69)

"God has created you; then He will cause you to die; there are some among you who are made to a decrepit old age in which they loose all knowledge after having acquired it. Surely God is All-knowing, All-powerful." (16:70)

"God has favoured some of you over others in [the matter of] provision; those more favoured will by no means hand over [a portion of] their provision to those under control so that they may be equal sharers therein. Will they then deny God's favour? God has made for you wives of your own kind, has produced for you sons and grandsons from your wives, and has provided for you all kinds of wholesome things. Will they then believe in falsehood and deny God's favour?" (16:71-72)

"To God belongs [knowledge of the] unseen of the heavens and the earth; the coming of the Hour [of the Doom] is only like the twinkling of an eye, or even quicker. Surely God has the fullest power over everything." (16:77)

"God brought you forth from the wombs of your mothers, when you knew nothing, and gave you ears, eyes and hearts, that you may be grateful." (16:78)

"Do they not see the birds held under control in the vault of heaven? It is only God Who keeps them back from swooping down. In that are indeed signs [of His power and wisdom] for a people who believe." (16:79)

"God has made your homes your places of rest and has made for you, of the skins of cattle, houses [i.e. tents] which are easy for you to transport and easy to set up; He provides for you from the wool, furs and hair of cattle, household goods and articles for use over a period. God has made for you, of that which He has created, trees and other means of shade; He has made for you places of shelter in the mountains; He has made for you garments which protect you from heat, and coats of mail which protect you in battle. Thus He completes His bounty upon you, that you may wholly submit [to Him]." (16:80-81)

"Had God enforced His will, He would surely have made you [all] one religious community, but He leads astray whom He pleases and guides whom He pleases; you will certainly be asked about what you are doing." (16:93)

Nine Verses from the Sūrah of the Children of Isrā'īl (*Banī Isrā'īl*)

"We have made the night and the day two signs; the sign of the night We obliterate and the sign of the day We make sight-giving that you may seek the bounty of your Lord, and that you may know the computation of years and the method of reckoning. We have expounded everything in great detail." (17:12)

"Every person's doing we have fastened firmly to his neck; on the Day of Judgement We shall bring forth for him a book which he will find wide open, and [he will be told:] Read your record; you are sufficient as a reckoner against yourself this day. He who follows the right way, only follows it to his own good, and he who goes astray, only does it to his own loss; no one laden bears the load of another. We do not punish [a people] until after We have sent a messenger to them." (17:13-15)

"Tell [the polytheists]: Had there been other gods with God, as they allege, they would surely have sought a way to the Lord of the throne. Glory be to Him! High indeed be He exalted above that which they allege! The seven heavens and the earth and those that are in them glorify Him with His praise; there is not a thing but glorifies His praise [through the language in action][33], but you do not comprehend their glorification. Surely He is Forbearing, Most Forgiving." (17:42-44)

---

33. For an explanation of this see *supra*, p. 41; al-Zamakhsharī, *Op. Cit.*, II. 451.

"We have indeed honoured the children of Adam, provided for them means of transportation in land and sea, given them wholesome food, and exalted them high above the greater part of Our creation." (17:70)

"Say: All praises belong to God Who has taken to Himself no child[34] and Who has no partner in His Kingdom, nor has He any protecting friend through dependence. Proclaim His greatness very much."[35] (17:111)

Three Verses from the Sūrah of Mary (*Maryam*)

"There is none in the heavens and the earth but he shall come to the All-gracious as a slave. He has indeed counted them [all] and has numbered them exactly. Every one of them shall come to Him singly on the Day of Judgement." (19:93-95)

Nine Verses from the Sūrah of Ta Ha (*Ṭā Hā*)

"*Ṭā hā.*[36] We have not sent down the Qur'an to you that you may be distressed, but as an exhortation for him who fears God. It is a revelation from Him Who created the earth and the high heaven, the All-gracious One Who set Himself upon the throne. To Him belong whatever is in the heavens and whatever is in the earth, and whatever is between them, and whatever is beneath the moist subsoil. If you speak aloud [He hears it]; surely He knows all that is secret and all that is most hidden. God is He besides Whom there is no god. His are the most beautiful names."[37] (20:1-8)

"He [i.e. Pharaoh] asked: Who, then, is the Lord of you both,

---

34. See *supra*, p. 76, n. 5.
35. A Muslim who calls people to ritual prayer (*mu'adhdhin*) usually recites this verse when starting the call (*adhān*), on the grounds that the essence of the sentences repeated in the call is identical with that of the verse.
36. See *supra*, p. 78, n. 10.
37. The Qur'anic verses 59:22-24, 7:180 also speak of the most beautiful names of God. In the verse 7:180 the believers are commanded to call on

Moses? He answered: Our Lord is He Who has given everything its creation and then guided it. Pharaoh asked: What, then, is the state of the former generations? Moses replied: The knowledge of that is with my Lord, [all recorded] in a Book [i.e. the Preserved Tablet][38]; My Lord neither errs nor forgets. [Moses added: My Lord is He] Who has made the earth a cradle for you, and caused pathways to run through it for your benefit, and Who sent down rain from the sky. [My Lord says:] Thereby We bring forth diverse kinds of vegetation; so eat [of them] and [also] pasture your cattle. Surely in that are indeed signs [of His existence, power, wisdom, and so on] for those who are endowed with reason. From the earth We have created you, into it We shall cause you to return, and from it We shall bring you forth once more. We did show Pharaoh all Our signs, but he regarded them as false and refused to believe them." (20:49-56)

"On that day [i.e. the Day of Judgement] people will [all] follow the caller in whose teaching there will be no deviation; all voices shall be hushed before the Most Gracious One, and nothing you will hear except a subdued murmur. On that day no intercession will avail except on the part of one to whom permission is granted by the Most Gracious One and with whose word He is pleased. He knows all that is ahead of them and all that is behind them, and they cannot encompass Him with their knowledge. [On that day] faces shall be humbled before the Ever Living, Self-subsisting and All-sustaining One, and he who

---

God by His most beautiful names. There is, moreover, a Tradition that the Prophet (ṣ) said, "God has ninety-nine names, one hundred minus one. He is the Odd and loves the odd number. The one who enumerates them in meditation will enter Paradise." Pious Muslims repeat them and meditate on them on completion of every ritual prayer, and the ṣūfis, in addition, recite them in their *dhikr* (remembrance of God). Theological discussion of divine attributes is also connected with God's names. Al-Ghazālī first mentions the ninety-nine names of God, together with the Tradition just quoted, in his book *al-Maqṣad al-Asnā Sharḥ Asmā' Allāh al-Ḥusnā* and then explains their meanings one after another. Also see L. Gardet, "Al-Asmā' al-Ḥusnā," *EI*[2], 1, 714-717.

38. See *supra*, p. 82, n. 15.

bears [the burden of] evildoing shall be ruined." (20:108-111)

Twenty-one Verses from the Sūrah of the Prophets (*al-Anbiyā'*)

"We[39] did not create the heaven and the earth and whatever is between the two in sport. Had We wished to find a pastime We would surely have found it in that which is with Us if at all We would have been inclined in that way. On the contrary, We hurl the truth at falsehood and it crushes it and it disappears. Woe to you for that which you describe of Us!" (21:16-18)

"To Him belongs whatsoever is in the heavens and in the earth. Those who are in His presence [i.e. the angels] are not too proud to worship Him, nor do they weary of it; they glorify Him night and day, and do not flag." (21:19-20)

"Have they [i.e. the idolaters] taken gods from the earth who can raise the dead? If there had been in the heavens and the earth other gods besides God, then surely both would have gone to ruin? Then glorified be God, the Lord of the throne, above that which they describe of Him! He cannot be questioned concerning what He does, but they will be questioned. Have they taken gods apart from Him? Say [to them]: Bring your proof. This [Qur'an] is the reminder of those who are [contemporary] with me and the reminder of those who were before me. But most of them do not know the truth, and so they turn away from it." (21:21-24)

"We[40] sent no messenger before you [i.e. Muḥammad] but We revealed to him that there is no god but I; so worship Me alone[41]. But they [i.e. pagans, Christians and Jews][42] say, 'The Most Gracious One has taken to Himself offspring'. Glory be to Him! Those [whom they so designate] are only His honoured servants. They do not utter a word more than He directs, and they only carry out His command. He knows what is ahead of them and what is left behind them; they cannot intercede

39. See *supra*, p. 75, n. 3.
40. See *ibid.*
41. Cf. John 17:3, 12.
42. See *supra*, p. 76, nn. 4, 5.

except for him with whom He is pleased, and they tremble with fear of Him." (21:25-28)

"Whosoever of them should say: I am a god apart from Him, We shall requite him with Hell; thus We requite the wrongdoers." (21:29)

"Do the disbelievers not realize that the heavens and the earth were a solid mass, then We split them asunder, and We made from water every living thing? Will they not, then, believe? We have placed in the earth firm mountains lest it should shake with them, and We have made wide pathways in the earth that they may thereby journey from place to place. We have made the heavens a guarded and protected roof; yet they turn away from its signs. He it is Who created the night and the day, and the sun and the moon each gliding freely in its orbit." (21:30-53)

"We have not granted everlasting life to any human being before you. Then if you should die will they [i.e. disbelievers who desire your death] live on forever? Everyone shall suffer death; We try you [i.e. human beings] with good and evil for a testing, and to Us you will be returned." (21:34-35)

Sixteen Verses from the Sūrah of the Pilgrimage (*al-Ḥajj*)

"O mankind, if you are in doubt concerning being raised up again, then [let Us make it clear to you that] surely We created you from dust, then from a sperm-drop, then from clotted blood, then from a lump of flesh, formed and unformed, that We may make it clear to you. We cause that which We will to stay in the wombs for an appointed term, then We bring you forth as babes, then [We cause you to grow] that you attain your full strength. Then some of you die [at that age] and some of you are kept alive to the most extreme old age, when they do not know a thing after once having had knowledge of it. You observe the earth lose all its productive capacity; then when We send down water on it, it stirs, swells and grows every kind of lovely vegetation. This shows that it is God Who is the Truth, that He brings the dead to life, that He has the fullest power over everything, that the Hour [of the Doom] will undoubtedly come, and that God will raise up those who are within the graves."[43] (22:5-7)

"Have you not seen that to God submit whatsoever is in the heavens, whatsoever is in the earth, the sun, the moon, the stars, the mountains, the trees, the beasts, and many of mankind? There are many who have been condemned to punishment. Whomsoever God disgraces, none can raise him to honour. Verily God does what He wants." (22: 8)

"That proves that God causes the night to enter into the day, and causes the day to enter into the night, and that God is All-hearing, All-seeing. That is because it is God Who is True, while that which they [i.e. the idolaters] call apart from Him is false and because iris God Who is the High, the Great. Have you not seen that God sends down water from the sky, and the earth thereby becomes green? God is All-subtle, All-aware. To Him belong whatever is in the heavens and whatever is in the earth. Surely it is God Who is All-sufficient, All-laudable. Have you not seen that God has subjected to you whatever is in the earth, that the vessels sail in the sea by His command, and that He holds back heaven lest it should fall upon the earth except by His permission? Surely, God is Compassionate and Ever Merciful towards mankind. He it is Who gave you life, then He will cause you to die, then He will give you life again. Surely man is most ungrateful." (22:61-66)

"Do you not know that God knows whatever is in the heaven and the earth? Surely that is [all preserved] in a Book [i.e. the Preserved Tablet][44] and that is certainly easy for God." (22:70)

"O people, carefully listen to this similitude: Surely those whom you call, apart from God, can never create [even] a fly,

43. These verses form the argument for God's power to raise the dead. First His power to give life to man is determined; then His power to revive vegetation is shown. This proves that He has power raising the dead.

44. See *supra*, p. 82, n. 15.

although they should all combine together for this purpose; if a fly should snatch away anything from them, they cannot recover it from the fly. How weak is he who calls on them and how weak are those on whom he calls! They have not estimated God as He should be estimated. Surely God is Powerful, All-mighty." (22:73-74)

"God chooses His messengers from among angels and from among men. Surely God is All-hearing, All-seeing. He knows what lies ahead of them and what is left behind them; to God all affairs are returned." (22:75-76)

Twenty-nine Verses from the Sūrah of the Believers (*al-Mu'minūn*)

"Verily, We created man from an extract of clay; then We placed him as a sperm-drop in a safe depository [i.e. the womb], then We made the sperm-drop a clot; then We made the clot a shapeless lump, then We made this shapeless lump bones, then We clothed the bones with flesh; after that We produced him as another creature. So blessed be God, the Best of creators! After this you will surely die; then on the Day of Judgement. You will certainly be raised up." (23:12-16)

"Verily, We have created above you seven ways[45], and We were not neglectful of Our creation. We send down water from the clouds according to measure, and We cause it to stay in the earth; We are certainly able to take it away. With water [which We send down from the clouds] We produce for you gardens of date-palms and vineyards, in which there are abundant fruits for you, and of them you eat. [With water We also produce] the tree [i.e. the olive] which springs forth from Mount Sinai containing with it oil and relish for those who eat it. In the cattle there is indeed a lesson for you. We provide for you drink out of that which is in their bellies, and you derive many other benefits from them; the flesh of some of them you eat; on

---

45. Seven ways refer to the seven heavens. They may also refer to the paths of the planets. See al- Zamakhsharī, *Op. Cit.*, III, 28.

them and on ships you are borne." (23:17-22)

"He it is Who has made for you ears, eyes and hearts; little gratitude you show. He it is Who has multiplied you in the earth, and to Him you will be gathered. He it is Who gives life and causes death, and He controls the alternation of night and day. Will you not, then, understand?" (23:78-80)

"Rather they [i.e. those who believe in a superior deity but deny the future life] say like that which the former people said: They said: Is it that when we are dead and have become dust and bones, we shall surely be raised up again? This is what we and our fathers have been promised before; this is nothing but the fairy tales of the ancients. Ask them: To whom do the earth and all that is in it belong, if you really know? They will soon say: To God. Say [to them]: Will you not then be admonished? Ask them: Who is the Lord of the seven heavens and the Lord of the great throne? They will soon say: These belong to God. Say to them: Will you not then observe your duty to Him? Ask them: In whose hand is the dominion over everything and who grants protection, but against whom no protection is available[46], if you really know? They will soon say: All this belongs to God. Say to them: How are you then bewitched? Rather, We have brought them the truth and they reject it. God has not taken to Himself any child, nor is there any god along with Him; in that case each God would have walked away with that which He had created, and some of them would surely have dominated over others. Glory be to God, above all that which they describe [of Him]! He is the knower of the unseen and the seen. May He be exalted above that which they associate with Him!" (23:81-92)

"Did you imagine that We had created you for nothing, and that you would not be brought back to Us? Then high exalted be God, the Real King! There is no god but He, the Lord of the noble throne. He who calls upon other god than God, along with God, for which he has no proof, shall render an account of it to his Lord. Surely, the

46. This means that in God's strength He can guarantee protection to others, but none is strong enough to guarantee protection against Him.

disbelievers will not be successful. Pray: My Lord, forgive and have mercy, for You are the Best of those who are merciful." (23:115-118)

Nine Verses from the Sūrah of the Light (*al-Nūr*)

"God is the light of the heavens and the earth. His light is as if there were a niche, in which is a lamp contained in a crystal globe; the globe is as bright as a glittering star. [The lamp is] lit with [the oil of] a blessed tree, an olive, neither of the East nor of the West. The oil would very near glow forth even though no fire were to touch it. Light upon light! God guides to His light whomever He wills. God sets forth similitudes for man, and He has the fullest knowledge of everything, [The light illumines] the houses which God has ordained that they be exalted and in which His name is commemorated. In them is He glorified, in the mornings and the evenings, by men whom neither trade nor traffic diverts from remembrance of God, performance of ritual prayer, and payment of divine tax; they fear a day [i.e. the Day of Judgement] on which hearts and eyes will be agitated."[47] (24:35-37)

"Do you not see that all who are in the heavens and the earth celebrate the praises of God, and also the birds in rows upon rows? Each one knows his own mode of prayer and praise, and God knows fully well that which they do. To God belongs the Kingdom of the heavens and the earth, and to God is the return." (24:41-42)

"Do you not see that God gently wafts the clouds, then joins them together, then piles them up so that you see the rain issue forth from the midst of that? He sends down from the heaven mountain masses [of clouds] in which is hail; He smites with it whom He pleases and turns it away from whom He pleases. The flash of His lightning is very near to take away the sight of

---

47. These are known as the light-verses (*āyāt al-nūr*). They have been given various Sufi interpretations; al-Ghazālī wrote a complete book, *Mishkāh al-Anwār*, on them.

some eyes. God alternates the night and the day; in all this is indeed a lesson for those who have intelligence. God has created every animal from water. Some of them move on their bellies, some of them on two feet and some on four. God creates what He pleases. Surely God has the fullest power over everything." (24:43-45)

"Take notice, Surely to God belongs whatever is in the heaven and in the earth. He knows well what condition you are in. On the day when they will be returned to him, He will inform them of that which they did. God has the fullest knowledge of everything." (24:64)

Fourteen Verses from the Sūrah of the Criterion (*al-Furqān*)

"Blessed is He Who has sent down the discriminating Book [i.e. the Qur'an] to His servant, that he may be a warner to all beings. He it is to Whom belongs the Kingdom of the heavens and the earth. He has not taken to Himself any child. He has no partner in the Kingdom of the heavens and the earth. He has created everything and has determined its measure very exactly." (25:1-2)

"Do you not see how your Lord spreads out the shadow [at the sunrise]? Had He willed, He could have made it stationary [i.e. of the same length]. Then [as the day proceeds] We make the sun an indicator of the length of the shadow. Then We draw it in towards Ourselves slowly [i.e. We cause it gradually to get shorter]. He it is Who has made the night a covering for you, and sleep [a source of] rest; He has made the day for rising again. He it is Who sends the breezes as heralds of His mercy [in the form of rain] and We send down pure water from the clouds, that We may thereby revive a dead land, and give it for drink to some of that which We have created—cattle and men in great numbers." (25:45-49)

"He it is Who has let forth the two seas;[48] [the water of] one

48. The two seas refer to the large body of fresh water and the large body of salt water. See al-Zamakhsharī, *Op. Cit.*, III. 96.

is sweet and palatable and [that of] the other is salt and bitter; between them He has placed as a barrier a system that keeps them separate. He it is Who has created man from water and has made for him kindred by descend and kindred by marriage. Your Lord is All-powerful." (25:53-54)

"Put your trust in the One Who is Ever Living Who does not die, and glorify Him with His praise. Sufficiently is He Aware of the sins of His servants [i.e. men]. [He it is] Who created the heavens and the earth and that which is between them in six days, then set Himself on the throne—the Most Gracious One. Ask, concerning Him, one who is aware." (25:58-59)

"When it is said to them [i.e. the disbelievers]: Prostrate yourselves before the Most Gracious One, they ask: And what is the Most Gracious One? Shall we prostrate ourselves before whatever you bid us? It increases their aversion." (25:60)

"Blessed be He Who made constellations in the heaven and has placed in it an illuminating lamp and a moon giving light! He it is Who has made the night and the day to follow each other, for him who desires to take heed or desires to be grateful." (25:61-62)

Twelve Verses from the Sūrah of the Poets (*al-Shu'arā'*)

["Abraham said to his father and to his people: The Lord of the worlds is He] Who has created me and then Himself guides me, Who Himself gives me to eat and drink, and Who Himself heals me when I fall ill, Who will cause me to die and then bring me to life again, and Who, I am eager, will forgive me my offence on the Day of Judgement. My Lord, bestow a [right] judgement upon me and join me with the righteous, give me a true appreciation in later generations, include me among the inheritors of the Paradise of delight, forgive my father who is surely one of those who are astray, do not disgrace me on the day when they [i.e. all people] will be raised up, the day when neither wealth nor sons will profit, and he alone [will be saved] who comes to God with a pure soul." (26:78-89)

Thirteen Verses from the Sūrah of the Ant (*al-Naml*)

["Satan has turned the people of Sheba from the right path] so that they do not prostrate themselves before God Who brings to light what is hidden in the heavens and the earth, and He knows that which you conceal and that which you disclose. God! There is no god but He, the Lord of the great throne." (27:25-26)

["Is God better or that which the idolaters associate with Him?] Or, He Who created the heavens and the earth, and sent down for you water from the clouds with which We caused to grow joyous orchards? It is not in your power to grow the trees of them [yourselves].Then is there a god with God? Rather, they are a people who set up equals with Him. Or is not He [better] Who made the earth a fixed place, placed rivers in the midst of it, placed upon it firm mountains, and put a barrier between the two seas?[49] Then is there a god with God? Rather, most of them [i.e. the idolaters] do not know [the truth]." (27:60-61)

"Or is He [not better] Who responds to the distressed person when he calls upon Him, and removes the evil, and makes you successors of the earth? Then, is there a god with Him? Little is it that you heed! Or is He [not better] Who guides you in the darkness of the land and the sea, and Who sends the breezes as heralds of His mercy [in the form of rain]? Then, is there a god with Him? High exalted be God above that which they [i.e. the idolaters] associate with Him! Or is He [not better] Who originates creation and then repeats it, and Who provides for you from the heavens and the earth? Then, is there a god with God? Ask them: Bring forward your proof, if you are truthful [in your belief that there are gods with God."] (27:62-64)

"Tell them: None in the heavens and the earth, except God, knows the unseen, nor are they aware when they will be raised up." (27:65)

"Surely your Lord is bountiful towards mankind; but most men are not grateful. Surely your Lord knows well that which

49. See *supra*, p. 108, n. 48.

they conceal in their minds and that which they disclose. There is nothing hidden in the heaven and the earth, but is [recorded] in a clear Book (i.e. the Preserved Tablet)."[50] (27:73-75)

"Surely your [i.e. Muḥammad's] Lord will decide between them [i.e. the children of Isrā'īl] by His judgement [set forth in the Qur'an]. He is the All-mighty, the All-knowing. So put your trust in God; surely you [stand] on manifest truth." (27:78-79)

Seven Verses from the Sūrah of the Story (*al-Qaṣaṣ*)

"Your Lord creates what He pleases and chooses; they have no choice. Glory be to God! High be He exalted above that which they [i.e. the idolaters] associate with Him! Your Lord knows that which they conceal in their minds and that which they disclose. He is God, there is no god but He. To Him belong all praises in this world (*al-ūlā*) and in the Hereafter (*al-ākhirah*);[51] His is the Judgement, and to Him you will be returned." (28:68-70)

"Ask [the idolaters]: Have you thought, if God were to extend the night over you until the Day of Resurrection, what god other than God is there who could bring you light? Will you not, then, hear? Ask [them also]: Tell me, if God were to extend the day over you until the Day of Resurrection, what god other than God is there who could bring you night in which you could rest? Will you not, then see? Of His mercy He has made for you the night and the day, that you may rest therein, that you may seek of His bounty and that you may be grateful." (28:71-73)

"Do not call on another god with God. There is no god but He. Everything will perish except Himself. His is the Judgement, and to Him you will be returned." (28:88)

---

50. See *supra*, p. 82, n. 15.
51. The phrase '*fī al-ūlā wa al-ākhirah*' must be translated as 'in this world and in the Hereafter', not as 'in the beginning and in the end' as is done by a recent translator of the Qur'an. Praise in the Hereafter is explicitely stated in

Nine Verses from the Sūrah of the Spider (*al-'Ankabūt*)

"Have they not seen how God originates creation, and then repeats it?[52] That indeed is easy for God. Tell them: Travel in the earth and observe how He originated the creation and then He provides the second creation. Surely God has the fullest power over everything. He punishes whom He pleases and grants mercy to whom He pleases, and to Him you will be returned. You cannot make Him unable in the earth or in the heaven, nor have you any friend or helper apart from Him." (29:19-22)

"How many an animal there is that does not carry about its own sustenance! God provides for it and for you. He is the All-hearing, the All-knowing." (29:60)

"If you were to ask them [i.e. those idolaters who admitted the existence of a supreme deity, God], 'Who has created the heavens and the earth and has constrained the sun and the moon into service?, they would surely answer: God. How then are they perverted? God enlarges the provision for such of His servants [i.e. men] as He pleases, and straightens it for whom He pleases. Surely God has the fullest knowledge of everything. If you were to ask them, 'Who sends down water from the clouds, and with it revives the earth after its death?', they would surely answer: God. Say: All praises belong to God. But most of them do not understand." (29:61-63)

"This life of this world is nothing but sport and pastime, and the abode of the Hereafter is surely the real life, if they but know." (29:64)

---

verses 35:34, 39:74. It is also spoken of in prophetic tradition. See al-Zamakhsharī, *Op. Cit.*, III, 189.

52. The reference here is to the death and revival of vegetation; the same is true of the phrase 'provides the second creation' occurring in a latter sentence. All this however, is also a sign of resurrection. This sort of proof for resurrection is employed many times in the Qur'an because it is understandable to all people. Very subtle and more abstract logical arguments are avoided on the grounds that these are beyond the understanding of common men. The message of the Qur'an is directed towards all people, intellectually higher and lower.

Seventeen Verses from the Sūrah of the Romans (*al-Rūm*)

"Glory be to God in the evening and in the morning. To Him belong all praises in the heavens and the earth, in the afternoon and when the sun begins to decline."[53] (30:17-18)

"He brings forth the living from the dead, and He brings forth the dead from the living; He revives the earth after its death. In this manner you will be brought forth. Of His signs it is that He created you from dust, and then lo! you are human beings spread over the earth. One of His signs is that He has created spouses for you from yourselves, that you may live with them, and He has put love and mercy between you. In that are indeed signs [of His power and wisdom] for a people who reflect. One of His signs is the creation of the heavens and the earth, and the diversity of your tongues and colours. In that are indeed signs for those who have knowledge." (30:19-22)

"Of His signs is your sleep by night and by day, and your seeking of His bounty. In that are indeed signs for a people who listen. Of His signs is that He shows you the lightning to inspire fear and hope, and He sends down water from the clouds and with it quickens the earth after its death. In that are indeed signs for a people who understand. Of His signs is that the heaven and the earth stand firm by His command. Then when He calls you to come forth from the earth [i.e. grave] at once, lot you will come forth." (30:23-25)

"To Him belongs whoever is in the heavens and the earth. All are obedient to Him. He it is Who originates the creation and then repeats it,[54] and it is easiest for Him. His is the most exalted similitude in the heavens and the earth; He is the All-mighty, the All-wise." (30:26-27)

"God is He Who created you, then He provided for you, then He will cause you to die, then He will bring you to life. Is there any of your [alleged] partners of God who can do any of

---

53. In these two verses reference is made to all five ritual prayers. See al-Zamakhsharī, *Op. Cit.*, III, 217.

54. See *supra*, p. 112, n. 52.

these things? Glory be to Him! High be He exalted above that which they associate with Him!" (30:40)

"Of His signs it is that He sends the breezes as heralds of good fortune, that He may grant you of His mercy, that vessels may sail at His command, that you may seek of His bounty, and that you may be grateful." (30:46)

"God is He Who sends the winds that stir up clouds which He spreads in the sky as He pleases and which He shatters; then you see the rain issuing forth from their midst. When He causes it to fall on whom He pleases of His servants [i.e. men] lo! they rejoice at it, although before its coming down on them, just before that, they were surely in despair. Observe, then, the token of God's mercy, how He quickens the earth after its death. Surely He is the One Who will quicken the dead [on the Day of Judgement], and He has the fullest power over everything." (30:48-50)

"God is He Who created you in a state of weakness, and after weakness He gave you strength; then after strength He caused weakness and old age. He creates what He pleases. He is the All-knowing, the All-powerful." (30:54)

Eight Verses from the Sūrah of Luqmān

"He [i.e. God] has created the heavens without any pillar that you can see, has placed in the earth firm mountains lest it shake with you, and has spread in it all kinds of creatures. We[55] have sent down water from the clouds, and have caused every goodly species to grow on the earth." (31:10)

"Have you not seen that God has constrained for your service whatever is in the heavens and whatever is in the earth, and has lavished on you His visible and invisible favours? Yet there are some among men who dispute concerning God without knowledge, or guidance, or an illuminating book." (31:20)

"To God belongs whatsoever is in the heavens and the earth. Surely God is the Self-sufficient, the All-laudable. If all the trees in the earth became pens, and the ocean, reinforced by seven

55. See *supra*, p. 75, n. 3.

oceans, [became ink for writing down the words of God], His words would not be exhausted. Surely God is All-mighty, All-wise." (31:26-27)

"Your creation and your being raised up [on the Day of Judgement] are only like that of a single person. Surely God is All-hearing, All-seeing. Do you not see that God makes the night pass into the day and makes the day pass into the night, and has constrained the sun and the moon into service, each pursuing its course during an appointed term, and that God is fully aware of what you do? That is because it is God Who is True, and that which they [i.e. the idolaters] call apart from Him is false, and because it is God Who is the All-high, All-great. Do you not see the vessels sail on the sea by the grace of God, that He may show you of His signs? In that are indeed signs for every steadfast grateful person." (31:28-31)

Seven Verses from the Sūrah of Prostration (*al-Sajdah*)

"God is He Who has created the heavens and the earth and that which is between the two, in six days; then He seated Himself on the throne. Apart from Him you have no protector or intercessor. Will you not, then, take heed? He directs the affair from the heaven to the earth; then it ascends to Him in a day, the measure of ehich is a thousand years of your reckoning. Such is the Knower of the unseen and the seen, the All-mighty, the Ever Merciful, Who has created everything in the best condition and Who began the creation of man from clay. Then He made his progeny from an extract of insignificant fluid. Then He shaped him in due proportion, and breathed into him of His spirit. He made for you hearing, sight, and hearts. Little gratitude you show!" (32:4-9)

"Have they [i.e. men] not seen that We drive the water to the dry land and produce thereby crops of which their cattle and they themselves eat? Do they not observe?" (32:27)

Five Verses from the Sūrah of Sheba (*Saba'*)

"All praises are due to God to Whom belong whatever is in the heavens and whatsoever is in the earth. To Him belongs praise in the Hereafter [also]. He is the All-wise, the All-aware. He knows whatever penetrates into the earth and whatever comes forth from it, and whatever descends from the heaven [i.e. angels, revelation and rain] and whatever ascends into it [i.e. angels, men's words and smoke]. He is Ever Merciful, Most Forgiving." (34:1-2)

"The disbelievers say: The Hour [of the Doom] will not come upon us. Tell them: Yes, by my Lord, the Knower of the unseen, it will most surely come upon you. Not the smallest particle in the heavens or the earth, or anything less than that or greater escapes Him, but all is [recorded] in a clear Book (i.e. the Preserved Tablet)."[56] (34:3)

"Do they not observe that which lies before them and that which lies behind them of the heaven and the earth? We could, if We please, cause the earth to swallow them up, or cause the clouds to fall upon them in a deluge. Surely, in that is indeed a sign for every servant [of Ours] who turns to Us." (34:9)

"Say: Surely my Lord enlarges the provision to whomever He pleases and straightens it for whomever He pleases. But most people do not know it." (34:36)

Thirteen Verses from the Sūrah of the Originator (*Fāṭir*)

"All praises belong to God Who is the Originator of the heavens and the earth, Who appoints the angels His messengers, having two, three and four wings. He adds to His creation whatever He pleases. Surely God has the fullest power over everything." (35:1)

"Whatever of mercy God bestows upon men may be withheld by none, and whatever He withholds may not be released by any after that. He is the All-mighty, the All-wise. O mankind, remember God's favour to you. Is there any creator apart from God Who provides for you from the heaven and the

56. See *supra*, p. 82, n. 15.

earth? There is no god but He. How then are you turned away?" (35:2-3)

"God it is Who sends down the winds which stir up the clouds; then We drive them to a dead land and thereby quicken the earth after its death. Likewise is the raising of the dead [on the Day of Resurrection]." (35:9)

"Anyone who seeks honour [should realize that] all honour belongs to God. To Him ascend good words, and righteous deed exalts them. Those who devise evil deeds will suffer severe chastisement, and their devising will come to nothing." (35:10)

"God created you from dust, then from a sperm-drop, then He made you pairs. No female conceives nor does she give birth, except with His knowledge; no one who is given long life is given it nor is anything diminished of his long life, but it is [recorded] in a Book [i.e. the Protected Tablet in which is written down all that happens][57]. Surely that is easy for God." (35:11)

"The two seas[58] are not alike. One is sweet, palatable and pleasant to drink, and the other is salt and bitter. From each you eat fresh meat, and bring forth articles that you wear as ornaments. You see the vessels ploughing through them that you may seek of His bounty, and that you may be grateful." (35:12)

"He [i.e. God] merges the night into the day and merges the day into the night; and He has constrained the sun and the moon into services each running its course for an appointed term. Such is God, your Lord; His is the Kingdom. Those whom you call upon apart from God, possess no power whatever." (35:13)

"Do you not see that God sends down water from the clouds, and with it We bring forth fruits of diverse colours; of the mountains some are streaks white and red, of diverse colours, others raven black; in the same way men, beast and cattle [too] are of diverse colours? Of the servants of God [i.e. men] it is only those who have knowledge [of God] that fear Him. Surely God is All-mighty, Most Forgiving." (35:27-28)

---

57. See *supra*, p. 82, n. 15.
58. See *supra*, p. 108, n. 48.

"Surely God holds the heavens and the earth, lest they should deviate [from their places]. If they did deviate, none could keep them from that after it. Surely He is Forbearing, Most Forgiving." (35:41)

"Have they not travelled in the earth and seen what was the end of those before them and they were stronger than these in power? Nothing is in the heavens or the earth that could frustrate His designs. Surely He is All-knowing, All-powerful." (35:44)

"If God were to catch [i.e. punish] people for that which they do, He would not leave a living creature on the surface of the earth; but He defers them to an appointed term, and when their term comes, verily [they will find that] God was watching His servants [i.e. men]." (35:45)

Twenty-five Verses from the Sūrah of Yā Sīn

"A sign for them [i.e. men] is the dead land. We quicken it [by rain] and bring forth from it grain of which they eat. We have made in it gardens of date-palms and vines, and We have caused fountains to gush forth in them, that they may eat of the fruits of them. It was not their hands that made them. Will they not then be grateful? Glory be to Him Who created all things in pairs, of that which the earth grows, of [human beings] themselves, and of that which they do not know." (36:33-36)

"A sign for them is night. We strip off the day from it, and lo! they are left in darkness. The sun moves to an appointed goal. That is the ordaining of the All-mighty, the All-knowing. We have appointed stages for the moon, till it waves into the shape of an old dry branch of a palm-tree. It is not proper for the sun to approach the moon, nor does the night outstrip the day. All glide along in an orbit." (36:37-40)

"A sign for them is [also] that We carried their offspring in laden ships, and We have created for them other similar means of transportation on which they ride. If We willed We could drown them; then they would have none to cry to for help, nor would they be rescued except by Our mercy, and as comfort for a time." (36:41-44)

"Do they [i.e. the idolaters] not see that, among Our handiwork, We have created for them cattle of which they then become owners? We have subjected cattle to them, so that they ride some of them and eat of [the flesh of] others. They derive [other] benefits from them and [also] obtain drink from them. Will they not, then, be grateful? They have taken, apart from God, gods, that they might be helped [by these]. These [gods] are not able to help them, though they be hosts made ready for them. So let not their words grieve you. Assuredly We know that which they conceal and that which they disclose." (36:71-76)

"Does not man consider that surely We have created him from a sperm-drop? Then lo! he becomes an open disputer; he sets for Us a similitude and forgets [the fact of] his creation; he says: Who will quicken the bones when they are decayed? Tell him: He Who created them the first time will quicken them. He has the fullest knowledge of every creation. He is the One Who produces fire for you out of the green tree, and lo! you kindle from it. Is not He Who created the heavens and the earth able to create the like of them? Yes, He is indeed the Supreme Creator, the All-knowing. His affair is such that when He desires a thing, He says concerning it 'be', and it is.[59] So glory be to Him in Whose hand is the dominion of everything, and to Whom you will be brought back!" (36:77-83)

Fourteen Verses from the Sūrah of the Rangers (*al-Ṣāffāt*)

"By those who range themselves in close ranks,[60] by those who restrain very sternly, by those who are constant in reciting the

---

59. See *supra*, p. 76, n. 7.
60. The commonly held view is that angels standing in rank are meant here. A few other meanings are also possible. See al-Zamakhsharī, *Op. Cit.*, III, 333-334.

Reminder [i.e. revealed book], most surely your God is One, the Lord of the heavens and the earth and all that exists between them and the Lord of the different points of the East [at which the sun rises according to the season of the year]. We have adorned the lowest heaven with the adornment of the stars which also preserve it against every rebellious Satan. They cannot listen to the Assembly on High and are pelted from every direction and repulsed; and for them is an everlasting chastisement. But if any of them snatches away something [by stealth] he is pursued by a piercing flame. So ask them [i.e. the disbelievers] whether it is they who are stronger as a creation or those whom We have created? We created them of clinging clay." (37:1-11)

"Glory be to your Lord, the Lord of honour, above that which they [i.e. the idolaters] describe of Him! Peace be upon the messengers of God! All praises belong to God, the Lord of the worlds." (37:180-182)

Four Verses from the Sūrah of Ṣād

"Say [to the disbelievers]: I am only a warner. There is no god but God, the One, the Most Irresistible, the Lord of the heavens and the earth and of all that which is between the two, the All-mighty, the Most Forgiving. Tell [them]: This is a great announcement from which you are turning away." (38:65-68)

Sixteen Verses from the Sūrah of the Companies (*al-Zumar*)

"If God had desired to take to Himself a child, He could have chosen whom He pleased out of His creation. Glory be to Him! He is God, the One, the Most Irresistible. He created the heavens and the earth in accordance with the requirements of truth and wisdom. He makes the night overspread the day, and makes the day overspread the night. He has constrained the sun and the moon into service, each moving until an appointed term. Take notice, He is the All-mighty, the Most Forgiving. He created you from a single self [i.e. Adam]; then from that self He made his mate [i.e. Eve]. He has provided for you eight head of cattle in pairs [i.e. sheep, goats, camels, and oxen]. He creates you, in the wombs of your mothers, creation after creation [i.e. in several stages] in a three-fold darkness [i.e. that of the belly, the womb, and the membranes enclosing the foetus]. That is God your Lord. To Him belongs the Kingdom. There is no god but He. How then are you turned away [from God to idols]?" (39:4-6)

"Have you not seen that God sends down water from the clouds, then causes it to flow in the earth in streams, and then brings forth thereby herbage, different in hues; then it withers, and you see it turn yellow; then He reduces it to broken straw? Surely in that is indeed a reminder for those who have understanding." (39:21)

"Is he whose mind God has expanded for the acceptance of Islam so that he possesses a light from his Lord, [like him who is not in this condition]?[61] Woe then to those whose minds are hardened against the remembrance of God![62] They are in manifest error." (39:22)

"Is not God sufficient for His servant? Yet they [i.e. the disbelievers] frighten you with those who are apart from Him? There is no one to guide him whom God leads astray, and no one can lead astray him whom God guides. Is not God All-mighty, Revengeful?" (39:36-37)

---

61. The Sufis often quote this verse and explain it by a Tradition that the Prophet (ṣ), when he recited this verse, was asked, "How is the expansion of the mind, O messenger of God?" He replied, "The mind is expanded and widened when light [from God] enters into it." He was asked again, "What is the sign of this, O messenger of God"? He replied, "The sign is that the person turns to the Eternal Abode [i.e. the Hereafter] and flees away from the Abode of Deception [i.e. the blameworthy aspect of this world], and prepares for death before it overtakes him." The commentators of the Qur'an also cite this Tradition when explaining this verse. See al-Zamakhsharī, *Op. Cit.*, III, 394.
62. This and other Qur'anic verses in which hardness of the mind (*qasāwah al-qalb*) is condemned are often quoted by the Sufis as justification of their strong fear of hardness of the mind when traversing the mystic path.

"If you were to ask them [i.e. the pagans who believed in a Supreme deity, God]: Who created the heavens and the earth?, they will most surely answer: God. Then ask them: Have you considered that if God desires affliction for me can those [pagan deities] whom you call upon apart from God remove His affliction? Or, if He desires mercy for me, can they withhold His mercy from me? Tell them: God is enough for me; in Him trust those who trust." (39:38)

"God takes charge of souls at the time of death and of those not yet dead during their sleep. Then He retains those in respect of which He has decreed death, and sends back the others for an appointed term. Most surely in that are signs [of His power and knowledge] for a people who reflect." (39:42)

"Say: O God, Originator of the heavens and the earth, Knower of the unseen and the seen, You will judge between Your servants [i.e. men] concerning that in which they differ." (39:46)

"They [i.e. men] have not estimated God as He should be estimated. The whole earth shall be His handful on the Day of Resurrection, and the heavens shall be rolled up in His right hand. Glory be to Him! High be He exalted above that which they associate with Him! The trumpet shall be blown, and whosoever is in the heavens and whosoever is in the earth shall be struck senseless, save those whom God pleases. Then it shall be blown a second time, and lo! they shall be standing, beholding. The earth shall be lit up with the light of its Lord, the Book [i.e. the original of the revealed scriptures] shall be set in place, the prophets and the witnesses shall be brought, and judgement shall be given between them with justice, and no wrong will be done to them. Everyone shall be paid in full for what he did; He has the fullest knowledge of what they do." (39:67-70)

"They [i.e. the dwellers of Paradise] shall say: All praises belong to God, Who has been true in His promise to us, and has bestowed upon us this vast region as an inheritance to make our abode in Paradise wherever We please. How excellent, then, is the reward of those who do good deeds!

You shall see the angels circling the throne [of God], glorifying their Lord with His praise. Judgement shall be made between them with justice, and it shall be announced: All praises belong to God, the Lord of all the worlds." (39:74-75)

Nineteen Verses from the Sūrah of the Believer (*al-Mu'min*)[63]

"*Ḥā mīm.*[64] The revelation of this Book [i.e. the Qur'an] is from God, the All-mighty, the All-knowing, the Forgiver of sin, the Accepter of penitence, the Severe in punishment, the Bountiful. There is no god but He. To Him is the final return." (40:1-3)

"Those [angels] who bear the throne [of God] and those who are around it, glorify their Lord with His praise, believing [fully] in Him, and pray for forgiveness for those who believe [saying]: Our Lord, You do embrace everything in Your mercy and knowledge; so forgive those who have repented and followed your way, and safeguard them against the punishment of Hell." (40:7)

"It is He Who shows you His signs and sends down provision for you from heaven; but none pays heed save he who turns to Him. So call on Him with [perfect] sincerity of religion although the disbelievers may be averse." (40:13-14)

"He [i.e. God] is the most exalted of ranks, the Possessor of the throne. He casts the Spirit of His bidding upon whomsoever of His servants [i.e. men] He pleases, that he may warn [people] of the Day of Meeting, the Day when they [all] will come forth; nothing concerning them will be hidden from God. Whose is the Kingdom this Day? Of God, the One, the Most Irresistible. This Day every one will be recompensed for that which he has earned; no injustice will be done this Day. Surely God is swift at reckoning." (40:15-17)

---

63. This sūrah is also called *Ghāfir* (the Forgiver).
64. See *supra*, p. 78, n. 10.

"God is He Who has made the night that you may seek repose in it, and the day illuminating. Most surely God is bountiful towards mankind, but most people are not grateful. Such is your God, your Lord, the Creator of everything. There is no god but He. How then are you being turned away [from Him]? Thus indeed are turned away those who stubbornly deny the signs of God." (40:61-62)

"God is He Who has made the earth a fixed place and the heaven a canopy; He has shaped you and shaped you well, and has provided you with the good things. Such is your God, your Lord. Blessed be God, the Lord of the worlds! He is Ever Living. There is no god but He. So call on Him in [perfect] sincerity of religion. All praises belong to God, the Lord of the worlds." (40:63-65)

"He it is Who created you from dust, then from a sperm-drop, then from a clot; then He brings you forth a child; then He lets you attain your full strength; then He lets you become old—some of you are given death before—that you may reach an appointed term and that [through all this] you may understand. It is He Who gives life and causes death. When He decrees a thing, He only says concerning it 'be', and it is."[65] (40:67-68)

"God is He Who created cattle for you, that you may ride some of them, and eat [of the flesh] of some—you have [other] uses for them—and that through them you may attain your mental desires; on them and on vessels you are borne. He shows you His signs; then which of God's signs will you deny?" (40:79-80)

Twelve Verses from the Sūrah of Ḥā Mīm al-Sajdah[66]

"Ask [the idolaters]: Do you indeed disbelieve in Him Who created the earth in two days,[67] and set up equals to Him? He

65. See *supra*, p. 76, n. 7.
66. This sūrah is also known as *Fuṣṣilat* (the Distinguished).
67. cf. Genesis 1:9-19.

is the Lord of the worlds. He placed in the earth firm mountains, rising above its surface, blessed it, and provided it nurture for its dwellers in proper measure, equally for [all] seekers, in four days[68]. Then He turned to the heaven which was mist,[69] and said to it and to the earth: Come [i.e. submit] both of you willingly or unwillingly. They said [through their language in action]:[70] We have come willingly. He ordained them seven heavens in two days, and revealed in each heaven its affair; We adorned the lowest heaven with lights and for protection [from demons]. This is the decree of the All-mighty, the All-knowing." (41:9-12)

"Do not prostrate yourselves before the sun, nor before the moon, but prostrate yourselves before God, Who created them, if it is He Whom you [really] worship. If they wax proud, yet those who are with your Lord glorify Him night and day, and are never wearied. One of His signs is that you see the earth humble [i.e. with its vegetation withered and no life on it], but when We send down water on it, it stirs and swells with verdure. He Who quickens it will most surely quicken the dead [on the Day of Resurrection]. Certainly He has the fullest power over everything." (41:37-39)

["The people of Moses differed concerning the Book revealed to him.] Had it not been for a word [i.e. for the decision to leave the differences to be settled on the Day of Judgement], the matter would have been decided between them. They are certainly in a disquieting doubt concerning it." (41:45)

"Anyone who performs righteous acts, it is for the good of his own self; anyone who does evil, it is against the good of his own self. Your Lord is not in the least unjust to His creatures." (41:46)

"Knowledge of the Hour [of Doom] rests entirely with God. No fruit comes forth from its spathes, nor does any female conceive, nor give birth to a child, but it is within His knowledge. On the Day [of Judgement] when He will call to them [i.e. the idolaters], 'Where are My partners'? they will

---

68. cf. *ibid.*, 1:20-31
69. cf. *ibid.*, 1:2.
70. See *supra*, p. 41-42.

reply: We declare it to You, not one of us is a witness of it." (41:47)

"We will show them [i.e. the disbelievers] Our signs in the universe and [also] among their own selves, until it becomes manifest to them that the Qur'an is the truth. Is it not enough that your Lord is witness over everything? Take notice, they are in doubt concerning the meeting with their Lord. Take notice, He certainly encompasses everything." (41:53-54)

Sixteen Verses from the Sūrah of Counsel (*al-Shūrā*)

"*Ḥā mīm. 'Ayn sīn qāf.* [71] Thus God, the All-mighty, the All-wise, has sent revelations to you and to those who were before you. To Him belong whatever is in the heavens and whatever is in the earth. He is the High, the Great. The heavens are about to rend asunder from above them, while the angels glorify their Lord with His praise and pray for the forgiveness of those on the earth. Behold, it is surely God Who is the Most Forgiving, the Ever Merciful." (42:1-5)

"He [i.e. God] is the Originator of the heavens and the earth. He has made for you spouses from yourselves, and of the cattle [also] He has made pairs. He multiplies you in the earth. There is nothing whatever like Him. He is All-hearing, All-seeing. To Him belong the keys of the heavens and the earth. He enlarges provision for whomsoever He pleases and straitens it for whomsoever He pleases. Surely He has the fullest knowledge of everything." (42:11-12)

"He [i.e. God] it is Who sends down rain after they [i.e. men] despair of it, and spreads out His mercy. He is the Protector, the All-laudable. One of His signs is the creation of the heavens and the earth, and of whatever living creatures He has spread out in both. He has the fullest power to gather them together when He pleases." (42:28-29)

"One of His signs consists in vessels sailing across the sea, like high banners. If He were so to will, He could cause the winds

71. See *supra*, p. 78, n. 10.

to drop so that they would become still upon its surface. In that, most surely, are signs [of His existence, power and mercy] for every steadfast grateful one." (42:32-33)

"To God belongs the Kingdom of the heavens and the earth. He creates what He pleases. He bestows females upon whom He pleases and He bestows males upon whom He pleases; or He mixes them, males and females; and He makes whom He pleases barren. Certainly He is All-knowing, All-powerful." (42:49-50)

"It is not possible for a man that God will speak to him except by revelation or from behind a veil or by sending a messenger to revel, by His permission, that which He pleases. Surely, He is All-high, All-wise. Thus We have revealed to you [i.e. Muḥammad] the revelation by Our command. You did not know what the Book was, nor what was the faith. But We have made that [revelation which We have sent to you] a light, by which We guide [mankind] to the straight path—the path of God to Whom belong whatsoever is in the heavens and whatsoever is in the earth. Take notice, to God all things do return." (42:51-53)

Sixteen Verses from the Sūrah of Ornament (*al-Zukhruf*)

"Were you to ask people, 'Who created the heavens and the earth?', they would most surely say: Created them the All-mighty, the All-knowing, Who has made the earth a cradle for you, and has made pathways in it for you, that you may be rightly guided, Who sends down water from the clouds in due measure, and We thereby quicken a dead land; likewise you will be brought forth [from the graves]. He it is Who has created everything in pairs, and has made vessels and cattle on which you ride, that you may settle yourselves firmly on their backs and when you are seated on them you may remember the favour of your Lord and say: Glory be to Him Who has subjected this to us, while we [ourselves] were not able to subdue it. Most surely to our Lord we shall return." (43:9-14)

"Do they [i.e. the disbelievers] imagine that We do not hear their secrets and their private counsels? Yea, Our envoys [from among angels] are with them recording everything." (43:80)

"Say [to Christians, Jews and pagans]: Had there been a child[72] of the Most Gracious One, I would have been the first of worshippers. Glory be to the Lord of the heavens and the earth, the Lord of the throne, above that which they describe of Him! Leave them alone to indulge in vain discourse and to amuse themselves until they come face to face with that Day of theirs which they have been promised. He it is Who is God in heaven and God on earth. He is the All-wise, the All-knowing. Blessed is He to Whom belongs the Kingdom of the heavens and the earth and of all that is between them; with Him is the knowledge of the Hour [of Doom] and to Him you will be returned." (43:81-85)

"Those on whom they [i.e. the idolaters who recognize a supreme deity, God] call, apart from God, have no power of intercession; but only he who bears witness to the truth [possesses this power], and they know it. Were you to ask them, 'Who created you'? they will most surely say: God. How then are they being turned away [from God to idols]? [Our Messenger's] saying is this: My Lord, surely these are a people who will not believe. [Our reply to him is:] Then pardon them and say: Peace. Soon they will know." (43:86-89)

Four Verses from the Sūrah of Smoke (*al-Dukhān*)

["Your Lord is the] Lord of the heavens and the earth and all that exists between them, if you would only have sure faith. There is no god but He. He gives life and causes death. He is your Lord and the Lord of your forefathers." (44:7-8)

"We did not create the heavens and the earth and all that exists between them in sport; We did not create them except

72. See *supra*, p. 76, nn. 4, 5.

for a real purpose, but most of them [i.e. people] do not know." (44:38-39)

Nine Verses from the Sūrah of Crouching (*al-Jāthiyah*)

"*Ḥā mīm.*[73] The revelation of this Book [i.e. the Qur'an] is from God, the All-mighty, the All-wise. In the heavens and the earth are indeed signs [of God's existence, power and wisdom] for the believers. In your [own] creation and in that of all the creatures that He spreads out in the earth, are signs for a people having sure faith. In the alternation of the night and the day, in the provision that God sends down from the clouds by which He quickens the earth after its death, and in the courses of the winds, are signs for a people who use their intelligence." (45:1-5)

"God is He Who has subjected the sea to you that vessels may sail thereon by His command, that you may seek of His bounty, and that you may be grateful. He has subjected to you whatever is in the heavens and whatever is in the earth, all of it. In that are indeed signs [of His existence, power, etc.] for a people who reflect." (45:12-13)

"Then to God belongs all praises. He is the Lord of the heavens and the Lord of the earth, Lord of all the worlds. His is the greatness in the heavens and the earth. He is the All-mighty, the All-wise." (45:36-37)

Four Verses from the Sūrah of the Sand-dunes (*al-Aḥqāf*)

"*Ḥā mīm.*[74] The revelation of this Book [i.e. the Qur'an] is from God, the All-mighty, the All-wise. We have not created the heavens and the earth and all that exists between them, except in accordance with the requirements of truth and wisdom and for an appointed time; but the disbelievers turn away from that of which they have been warned." (46:1-3)

---

73. See *supra*, p. 78, n. 10.
74. See *supra*, p. 78, n. 10.

"Do they [i.e. those who deny the future life] not realize that God Who created the heavens and the earth and was not wearied in creating them, is able to give life to the dead? Yes, surely He has the fullest power over everything." (46:33)

One Verse from the Sūrah of Victory (*al-Fatḥ*)

"To God belongs the Kingdom of the heavens and the earth. He forgives those whom He pleases, and He punishes those whom He pleases. He is Most Forgiving, Ever Merciful." (48:14)

Seven Verses from the Sūrah of Qāf

"Have they not looked at the sky above them, [and considered] how We have built it and adorned it and that there are no flaws in it? We have spread out the earth, placed therein firm mountains, and caused to grow therein every kind of beautiful species—a matter for contemplation and a reminder to every servant that turns [to Us]. We send down from the clouds blessed water, and We produce with it gardens, grain harvest and tall palm-trees with spathes piled one above the other as a provision for [Our] servants [i.e. men]; We quicken thereby a dead land. Even so will be the coming out [of the dead from their graves on the Day of Resurrection"]. (50:6-11)

"We indeed have created man, and We know what evil thought his mind produces. We are nearer to him than his jugular vein." (50:16)

Seven Verses from the Sūrah of the Scatterers (*al-Dhāriyāt*)

"In the earth are signs [of God's existence, power and wisdom] for those who have sure faith, and [also] in yourselves. Will you not, then, see? In the heavens is your sustenance[75], and [also]

75. The Sufis often quote this verse in support of their view that intuitive

that which you are promised. By the Lord of the heaven and the earth, it [i.e. the Qur'an] is as most surely true as that you speak." (51:22-23)

"We have built the heavens with might, and most surely We are makers of the vast extent of it. We have spread out the earth like a bed, and how excellently do We spread it out! Of everything We have created pairs that you may think." (51:47-49)

Eight Verses from the Sūrah of the Star (*al-Najm*)

"Surely the final decision [on the recompense of a man on the Day of Judgement] rests with your Lord. Surely it is He Who makes [man] laugh and makes [him] weep. Surely it is He Who causes death and gives life. Surely He created the two kinds, male and female, from a sperm-drop when it is poured forth. Surely it is for Him to effect the second creation [i.e. the raising of the dead]. Surely it is He Who gives wealth and riches. Surely it is He Who is the Lord of [the star] Sirius."[76] (53:42-49)

Seven Verses from the Sūrah of the Moon (*al-Qamar*)

"Surely We have created everything in due measure. Our command is only one word [i.e. 'be'][77] [and it operates as quickly] as the twinkling of an eye. Indeed We have destroyed people like you [before]; is there anyone who would take heed? Everything that they have done is recorded in the Scrolls. Every

(*kashfī*) knowledge is vouchsafed by God when the soul is prepared for it through mortification and self-discipline. They take the word 'sustenance' to mean intuitive knowledge.

76. This star was worshipped by some pagan Arabs of pre-Islamic Arabia. God says that He is the Lord of this star and as such it is He Who deserves worship.

77. See *supra*, p. 76, n. 7.

matter, small and great, is written down. Surely those who fear God will be in the midst of gardens and rivers [of Paradise] in the seat of truth with the Omnipotent King." (54:49-55)

Twenty-seven Verses from the Sūrah of the Most Gracious One (*al-Raḥmān*)

"The Most Gracious One has taught the Qur'an. He has created man and taught him the [art of] exposition. The sun and the moon [move] according to a fixed reckoning; the stars and trees submit to Him. He has raised the heaven high and has set up the measure (*mīzān*), that you may not transgress the measure. So weigh [all things] with justice and do not fall short of the measure. He has set the earth for [His] creatures; in it are fruits, palm-trees with sheaths, grain in the blade, and fragrant herbs. Then which of the bounties of your Lord will you both [jinn[78] and men] deny?" (55:1-13)

"He [i.e. God] created man from dry ringing clay like the potter's; the jinn[79] He created from a smokeless fire. Then which of the bounties of your Lord will you both deny? [He is the] Lord of the two Easts [i.e. the two points of sunrise at the winter and summer solstices] and the Lord of the two Wests [i.e. the two points of sunset at the winter and summer solstices]. Then which of the bounties of your Lord will you both deny? He has let forth the two seas[80] that meet together; there is a barrier between them [and so] they cannot encroach [one upon the other]. Then which of the bounties of your Lord will you both deny? Pearls and coral are taken out of both. Then which of the bounties of your Lord will you both deny? His are the vessels with lofty sail raised high on the ocean like banners. Then which of the bounties of your Lord will you both deny? All that is on the earth will perish. But your Lord [lit. the face of your Lord], the Master of glory and honour, will subsist."[81] (55:14-27)

---

78. See *supra*, p. 84, n. 18.
79. See *ibid.*
80. See *supra*, p. 108, n. 48.
81. This verse seems to be innocent of all but its apparent intention. It is

Seventeen Verses from the Sūrah of the Terror (*al-Wāqi'ah*)

"Have you considered the sperm-drop that you emit? Do you create it, or are We its creator? It is We Who have decreed death for [all of] you, and We are not to be prevented from replacing you with others like you and from making you to grow [again] in a fashion which you do not know. You have surely known the first creation; why then do you not take heed?" (56:58-62)

"Have you considered that which you cultivate? Is it you who foster it, or are We the fosterers? If We so pleased, We could surely reduce it all to broken particles; then you would start lamenting: Surely we are debt-loaded. Rather, we have been deprived [of the fruits of our labour]! Have you considered the water that you drink? Is it you who cause it to descend from the clouds, or do We? If We so pleased, We could make it bitter. Then why are you not grateful?" (56:63-70)

"Have you considered the fire that you kindle? Is it you who produce the tree for it, or are We the producers? We have made it a reminder, and a comfort to the dwellers of deserts. So glorify the name of your Lord, the Great." (56:71-74)

Six Verses from the Sūrah of Iron (*al-Ḥadīd*)

"Whatever is in the heavens and the earth glorifies God. He is the All-mighty, the All-wise. To Him belongs the Kingdom of the heavens and the earth; He gives life and causes death, and He has the fullest power over everything. He is the First and the Last, the Manifest and the Hidden,[82] and He has the fullest knowledge of everything."[83] (57:1-3)

---

taken by the ṣūfis as the peg upon which to hang their characteristic doctrine of passing away of everything (*fanā'*) except God Who alone remains subsistent (*bāqī*) in awareness.

82. This verse is often quoted by the Sufis and is interpreted by them in a special way.

83. These three verses together with those in the passage that follows them

"He it is Who created the heavens and the earth in six days; then He seated Himself upon the throne. He knows that which penetrates into the earth and that which comes out of it, and that which comes down from heaven and that which goes up to it. He is with you wherever you may be. God most fully sees all that you do. To Him belongs the Kingdom of the heavens and the earth, and to Him all affairs are returned. He causes the night to pass over into the day and causes the day to pass over into the night. He has the fullest knowledge of what is in men's minds." (57:4-6)

One Verse from the Sūrah of the Disputer (*al-Mujādilah*)

"Do you not know that God knows all that is in the heavens and all that is in the earth? There is no secret counsel of three, but He is the fourth of them, nor of five, but He is the sixth, nor of less than that, nor of more, but He is with them wherever they may be. Then on the Day of Judgement He will inform them of that which they did. Surely God has the fullest knowledge of everything." (58:7)

Four Verses from the Sūrah of the Gathering (*al-Ḥashr*)

"Had We sent down this Qur'an upon a mountain you would surely have seen it bend down in humility and rent asunder in awe of God. These are similitudes that We set forth for mankind, that they may reflect." (59:21)

"God is He apart from Whom there is no god; He is the Knower of the unseen and the seen; He is the Most Gracious, the Ever Merciful. God is He apart from Whom there is no

---

are generally known as 'the beginning of the Sūrah of Iron' (*awwal al-Ḥadīd*). They are often recited by pious Muslims, especially after each ritual prayer. The excellence of these verses lies in their comprehensive dealing with divine essence, attributes and works.

God; the Sovereign, the Most Holy, the Sound, the Bestower of security, the Protector, the All-mighty, the All-subduer, the Supreme in pride and greatness. Glory be to God, far above that which they [i.e. the idolaters] associate with Him! He is God, the Creator, the Maker, the Fashioner. His are the most beautiful names.[84] All that is in the heavens and the earth glorifies Him. He is the All-mighty, the All-wise."[85] (59:22-24)

Four Verses from the Sūrah of Congregation (*al-Jumuʿah*)

"Whatever is in the heavens and whatever is in the earth glorify God, the Sovereign, the Most Holy, the All-mighty, the All-wise. He it is Who raised among the unlettered people and among others from among them who have not yet joined them a Messenger [i.e. Muḥammad] from among themselves who recites to them His verses, purifies them and teaches them the Book [i.e. the Qur'an] and wisdom, though before that surely they had been in manifest error. He is the All-mighty, the All-wise. That is God's bounty; He bestows it on whom He pleases. God is the Possessor of great bounty." (62:1-4)

Four Verses from the Sūrah of Mutual Fraud (*al-Taghābun*)

"Whatever is in the heavens and whatever is in the earth glorify God. His is the Kingdom and His is the praise; He has the fullest power over everything. It is He Who has created you; then some of you are unbelievers and some are believers. God most fully sees all that you do. He has created the heavens and the earth with the requirements of truth and wisdom, and He

---

84. See *supra*, p. 100, n. 37.
85. The three verses comprised in this passage are generally known as 'the end of the Sūrah of Gathering' (*ākhir al-Ḥashr*). Pious Muslims recite them on completion of every ritual prayer and also in keeping vigil. These verses very emphatically assert the unity of God. His most beautiful names and His works.

shaped you and shaped you well. To Him is the final return. He knows whatever is in the heavens and in the earth, and He knows that which you conceal and that which you disclose. God has the fullest knowledge of that which is in your minds." (64:1-4)

One Verse from the Sūrah of Divorce (*al-Ṭalāq*)

"God is He Who created seven heavens, and of the earth the like of them. His command [concerning the details of creation] descends among them, [and He relates to you all this] that you may know that God has fullest power over everything, and that God encompasses everything in respect of knowledge." (65:12)

Thirteen Verses from the Sūrah of the Kingdom (*al-Mulk*)

"Blessed is He in Whose hand is the Kingdom—and He has the fullest power over everything—He Who has created death and life that He might try you which of you is best in conduct. He is the All-mighty, the Most Forgiving, Who created the seven heavens one upon another. You cannot see any flaw in the creation of the Most Gracious One. Then look again. Do you see any fissure? Then look again twice, sight will return to you frustrated and fatigued. Surely We have adorned the lowest heaven with lamps [of stars] and made them things to stone Satans. We have prepared for them the punishment of the Blazing Fire." (67:1-5)

"Whether you conceal that which you say or publish it abroad, [it is all the same to God;] surely He has the fullest knowledge of that which is in the minds [of men]. Would He Who created [you] not know? He is the All-subtle, the All-aware. He it is Who has made the earth submissive to you; so walk in its tracks, and eat of His provision. To Him will be the uprising [of the dead]." (67:13-15)

"Have they [i.e. the disbelievers] not observed the birds

above them, spreading their wings in flight and then drawing them in? None withholds them but the Most Gracious One. Surely He sees everything fully well." (67:19)

"Say [to people]: He it is Who produced you, and provided you with ears, eyes and hearts; [but] little gratitude you show. Say [also]: He it is Who has scattered you in the earth, and to Him you will be gathered." (67: 23-24)

"Say [to the disbelievers]: He is the Most Gracious One; in Him we have believed and in Him we have put our trust. Soon you will know who is in manifest error. Ask [them]: Have you considered if [all] your water were to disappear in the earth, then who will bring you flowing water?" (67:29-30)

Ten Verses from the Sūrah of Noah (*Nūḥ*)

"He [i.e. God] sends down rain on you abundantly, helps you with wealth and children, bestows gardens on you, and causes rivers to flow for you. What ails you that you do not look for dignity in God, seeing He has created you through stages? Have you not considered how God has created seven heavens one upon another, and has placed the moon in them as a light and the sun as a lamp? God has produced you from the earth fully, then He will return you to it, and will bring you forth completely [at the Resurrection]. God has made the earth a carpet for you, that you may traverse its spacious pathways." (71:11-20)

Five Verses from the Sūrah of the Jinn (*al-Jinn*)

"Surely our Lord—may His majesty be exalted!—has taken to Himself neither wife nor child." (72:3)

"Say [to those who disobey God and His Messenger]: I do not know whether that [punishment] which you are promised is near or whether my Lord has fixed a term for it. [He is] the Knower of the unseen, and He does not disclose His unseen to anyone, except to a Messenger whom He chooses. Then He dispatches an escort [of angels] to go before him and behind him, that He may know that the Messenger has delivered the messages of his Lord.[86] He encompasses all that is with them, and He keeps count of everything completely." (72:25-28)

Four Verses from the Sūrah of the Resurrection (*al-Qiyāmah*)

"Does man think that he is to be left purposeless? Was he not a sperm-drop emitted forth? Then he became a clot; then God created him and then proportioned him; and He made of him a pair, male and female. Is not such a One able to bring the dead to life?" (75:36-40)

Three Verses from the Sūrah of Man (*al-Insān*)

"Has not man passed through a space of time when he was not anything made mention of? Surely We have created man from a sperm-drop which is a mingling [of elements], that We may try him; so We made him hearing and seeing. Surely We have guided him the right way, and he is either grateful [and follows it] or ungrateful [and rejects it or neglects it]." (76:1-3)

Eight Verses from the Sūrah of the Loosed One (*al-Mursalāt*)

"Did We not create you from an insignificant fluid? We placed it in a secure repository. [i.e. the womb] for a fixed period. Thus We determined, and how excellently do We determine! Woe on that Day [i.e. the Day of Resurrection] to those who reject [this truth]! Did We not make the earth vast enough to gather the living and the dead? We placed on it high mountains, and provided for you sweet water to drink." (77:20-27)

Sixteen Verses from the Sūrah of the Tiding (*al-Naba'*)

"What do they [i.e. the disbelievers and the believers] question

86. Angels record whether the Messenger of God has fulfilled his task.

one another about? It is about the great tidings [of the Day of Judgement] concerning which they differ. No indeed; soon they will come to know. Again, no indeed, soon they will come to know." (78:1-5)

"Have We not made the earth a bed, and the mountains as pegs? We have created you in pairs, made your sleep a source of rest, made the night a covering, and made the day for livelihood. We have built above you seven strong [heavens], and We made a brightly burning lamp [i.e. the sun]. We send down from the rain-clouds water pouring forth abundantly, that We may bring forth thereby grains, vegetations, and luxuriant gardens." (78:6-16)

Sixteen Verses from the Sūrah of the Frowned (*'Abasa*)

"Ruin seize man how ungrateful he is! [He should reflect] of what did God create him? Out of a sperm-drop! He created him and set a measure for him; then He made the way easy for him [by sending guidance]; then He causes him to die and assigns a grave to him; then, when He pleases, He will raise him up again. Nay, man has not yet completed that which He prescribed for him." (80:17-23)

"Let man look at his food. We poured down water [from the clouds] abundantly, then We split the earth thoroughly and caused to grow in it grains, grapes, reeds, the olive, the date-palm, walled gardens thickly planted, fruits, and herbage—as provision for you and for your cattle." (80:24-32)

Three Verses from the Sūrah of the Splitting (*al-Infiṭār*)

"O man, what has deceived you against your Gracious Lord, Who created you, then fashioned you, and then wrought you in symmetry? He fashioned you in whatever form He pleased." (82:6-8)

Five Verses from the Sūrah of the Constellations (*al-Burūj*)

"Surely the assault of your Lord is severe. Surely it is He Who originates and repeats. He is the Most Forgiving, the Most Loving, Lord of the throne, the All-glorious, Who most fully performs whatever He wills." (85:12-16)

Six Verses from the Sūrah of the Night-star (*al-Ṭāriq*)

"Let man consider from what he is created. He is created from a fluid poured forth, which issues forth from between the loins and the breastbones. Surely He is able to bring him back [to life] on the Day [of Resurrection] when the secrets will be tried, and he will have neither strength nor helper." (86:5-10)

Five Verses from the Sūrah of the Most High (*al-A'lā*)

"Glorify the name of your Lord, the Most High, Who created and then shaped, Who determined [the species with their distinct qualities] and then guided [especially by revelation], Who brings forth the pasturage and then turns it into black stubble." (87:1-5)

Four Verses from the Sūrah of Envelope (*al-Ghāshiyah*)

"Do they [i.e. people] not look at the camel how it is created?, at the heaven how it is raised high?, at mountains how they are set up?, and at the earth how it is spread out?" (88:17-20)

Three Verses from the Sūrah of the City (*al-Balad*)

"Have We not given him [i.e. man] two eyes, a tongue, and two lips, and guided him on the two highways [of good and evil]"?[87] (90:8-10)

---

87. This means that God has bestowed favour upon man by granting him the knowledge of good and evil. Some people know about these by their

Eight Verses from the Sūrah of the Blood-clot (*al-'Alaq*)

"Read in the name of your Lord Who created [everything]. He created man from a clot of blood. Read,[88] since your Lord is the Most Beneficent, Who taught by the Pen, taught man that which he did not know. By no means, surely man does indeed transgress, for he considers himself self-sufficient. Surely to your Lord is the [final] return." (96:1-8)

---

intellect while others know by hearing from prophets. See al-Ghazālī, *Iḥyā'*, IV, 108.

88. This sūrah was the first revelation and hence the command of reading was very important. See al- Zamakhsharī, *Op. Cit.*, I, 30.

2
The pearls of the Qur'an

The pearls of the Qur'an are seven hundred and forty-one verses

Of Them Forty-six Verses are from the Sūrah of the Cow (*al-Baqarah*)

"In the name of God, Most Gracious, Ever Merciful. *Alif lām mīm.*[1] This [Qur'an] is the perfect Book;[2] there is no doubt in it; it is a guidance for those who fear God, who believe in the unseen,[3] observe ritual prayer and spend out of that which We[4] have given them as provision, who believe in that which has been revealed to you [Muḥammad] and in that which was revealed before you, and have firm faith in the Hereafter. These people are following the right guidance that has come from their Lord, and it is these who are the successful." (2:1-5)

"O mankind, worship your Lord Who has created you and created those who were before you, that you may be God-fearing." (2:21)

"O children of Isrā'īl, call to mind My favour which I bestowed upon you, and fulfil the covenant that you made with Me, I shall fulfil the covenant I made with you, and have awe of Me alone. Believe in the revelation which I have sent down, counting as true the revelation that was sent down to you and do not be the first to disbelieve in it. Do not barter my

---

1. See *supra*, p. 78, n. 10.
2. The translators of the Qur'an usually render the word '*al-kitāb*' as 'a Book'. A more accurate translation would be 'the perfect Book'. See al-Zamakhsharī, *Op. Cit.*, I, 111-112.
3. The term unseen (*al-ghayb*) here refers to God, angels, Last Judgement, Paradise, Hell, and other supernatural entities. It does not refer to the unseen in general.
4. See *supra*, p. 75, n. 3.

revelations for a paltry price, and fear Me alone. Do not mix the truth with falsehood nor hide the truth deliberately. Observe the ritual prayer, pay the divine tax, and bow your heads in worship along with those who bow. Do you admonish others to piety and forget your own selves, while you read the Book [i.e. the Torah?] Will you not then understand? Seek [God's] help with patience and ritual prayer; ritual prayer is indeed hard except for the humble in spirit." (2:40-45)

"Your [i.e. Jews'] minds became hardened after that and became like stones or even harder, for certainly of stones there are some out of which gush forth streams, there are some that cleave asunder and water flows out from them, and there are some that fall down for fear of God. God is not unmindful of that which you do. Do you [i.e. Muslims], then, expect that they [i.e. the Jews] will put faith in you, when a party of them are such that they hear the word of God, and then change it after they have comprehended it, knowingly well [the evil of what they do]?" (2:74-75)

["God took a covenant from the children of Isrā'īl:] You shall observe the ritual prayer and pay the divine tax. Then you turned away in aversion, except a small number of you." (2:83)

"The truth is that whoever completely submits himself to God and does good deeds shall have his reward with his Lord. No fear shall come upon him, nor shall he grieve." (2:112)

"Remember Me, and I shall remember you. Be grateful to Me—do not be ungrateful towards Me. O you who believe, seek the help [of God] through patience and ritual prayer; surely God is with the patient. Do not say of those who are killed in the path of God that they are dead; on the contrary, they are alive, but you are not aware of it. We will surely try you with some measure of fear and hunger, and loss of wealth, lives and fruits; then give glad tidings to the patient, who, when overtaken by misfortune, say: Surely to God we belong and to Him we shall return. It is these on whom are blessings from their Lord and mercy, and it is these who are rightly guided."(2:152-157)

"O mankind, eat of that which is lawful and wholesome in the earth, and do not follow in the footsteps of Satan; surely, he is your manifest enemy. He only enjoins you evil and turpitude, and that you should speak concerning God falsely that which you do not know." (2:168-169)

"Piety is not that you turn your faces to the East or the West; but pious are those who believe in God, the Last Day, the angels, the Book [i.e. the Qur'an] and the prophets, and who give their wealth, for love of Him, to the kindred, the orphans, the needy, the wayfarer, the beggars and for procuring the freedom of captives, observe the ritual prayer, pay the divine tax, fulfil their covenants whenever they make them, and are patient in adversity, under affliction and in battle. It is these who are true [in their faith], and it is these who are God-fearing."[5] (2:177)

"Observe your duty to God and know that God is with those who observe their duty to Him. Spend [your wealth] in the cause of God, and do not push yourselves into ruin with your own hands.[6] Do good; surely God loves those who do good." (2:194-195)

"Surely those who have believed and those who have emigrated and have fought in the cause of God are those who hope for His mercy. God is Most Forgiving, Most Merciful." (2:218)

"Know that God knows that which is in your minds; so beware of Him. Know also that God is Most Forgiving, Most Forbearing." (2:235)

"The case of those who spend their wealth in the path of God is like that of a grain of corn, which grows seven ears and in each ear there are a hundred grains. God multiplies it for whom He pleases; God is the Lord of vast bounty, All-knowing. Those who spend their wealth in the path of God

5. This verse is an important statement of man's chief duties in respect of belief and action. The part about belief is especially important and is often quoted.

6. This means that one should not spend so extravagantly that in consequence of it one would be dependent upon others and cause hardship to one's family. See al-Zamakhsharī, *Op. Cit.*, I, 343.

and then do not follow up that which they have spent with reproach or injury[7] have their reward with their Lord. They will have no fear nor will they grieve." (2:261-262)

"O you who believe, keep your duty to God and relinquish your claim to what remains of interest, if you are [truly] believers. If you do not do this, then take notice of war from the side of God and His Messenger. If you repent, you will [still] have your capital sums; thus you will commit no wrong, nor suffer any wrong yourselves. Should a debtor be in straitened circumstances, then grant him respite till [a time of] ease. But if [in such a case] you remit the capital sum as charity, it will be better for you, if you only knew. Guard against a day on which you will be brought back to God, and then everyone will be paid in full that which he has earned, and no wrong will be done to anyone." (2:278-281)

"To God belong whatever is in the heavens and whatever is in the earth. Whether you disclose that which is in your minds or keep it hidden, God will call you to account for it; then He will forgive whomever He wills and punish whomever He wills. God has the fullest power over everything." (2:283)

"The Messenger believes in that which has been sent down to him from his Lord, and [so do] the believers. All of them believe in God, His angels, His Books and His messengers, [affirming:] We make no distinction between any of His messengers. They [further] say: We have heard [the command of God] and obeyed it; so [we implore] Your forgiveness, Lord, and to You is [our] final return." (2:285)

"God does not charge anyone except with that which is within his capacity. Each shall have the benefit of the good he does and shall suffer punishment for the evil he commits. [Supplicate:] Lord, do not take us to task if we forget or make mistakes; Lord, do not place us under responsibility in the manner of those whom You did place under responsibility before us; Lord, do not burden us with that which we have not the strength to bear;

---

7. There is disagreement on the meaning of the terms *mann* and *adhā*, translated here as reproach and injury respectively. For a discussion of their meaning see al-Ghazālī, *Iḥyā'*, I, 216-218.

pardon us, forgive us and have mercy on us; You are our Protector, and so help us against those who are disbelievers." (2:286)

Thirty-four Verses from the Sūrah of the House of 'Imrān (*Āl 'Imrān*)

"He it is Who has sent down to you the Book [i.e. the Qur'an]; in it there are fundamental verses—they are the basis of the Book—and there are others which are allegories. As for those in whose minds perversity is present, they pursue that part of the Book which is allegoric, seeking to create confusion and to pervert its meaning, and none knows the meaning of that part except God and those who are firmly rooted in knowledge; these [latter] say: We believe in this [Book]; all of it is from our Lord. None takes heed except those possessed of understanding. [Those firmly rooted in knowledge also say:] Lord do not make our minds perverse after You have guided us; bestow upon us mercy from Yourself; surely You are the Greatest Bestower. Lord, surely You will assemble mankind together on the Day [of Judgement] concerning which there is no doubt. Surely God does not fail to keep His promise." (3:7-9)

"The love of desired objects—like women, children, stored-up reserves of gold and silver, pastured horses, cattle and tillage—is made attractive to people. All this is the enjoyment of the life of this world, and it is God with Whom is an excellent abode. Ask [people]: Shall I inform you of something better than all this? For those who keep from evil, there are gardens of Paradise with their Lord beneath which rivers flow, in which they will dwell forever, and pure spouses and [also] the pleasure of God. God sees well His servants, who supplicate: Lord, surely we have believed; so forgive us our sins and guard us against the punishment of Hell. [They are] the patient, the truthful, the obedient, those who spend [in the cause of God], and those who seek forgiveness of God just before dawn." (3:14-17)

"Let not the believers take the disbelievers for intimate

friends, rather than the believers. Whoever does that has no connection with God. Your only course is to keep away from them completely. God warns you against His punishment, and to God is your final return." (3:28)

"[O Muḥammad,] say [to mankind]: If you love God, then follow me, and God will then love you and forgive your sins; God is Most Forgiving, Ever Merciful. Say [also]: Obey God and the Messenger. If they turn away [let them know that] surely God does not love the disbelievers." (3:31-32)

"Do they seek a religion other than God's while to Him submits whoever is in the heavens and the earth, willingly or unwillingly,[8] and to Him they will be returned?" (3:83)

"You will never attain to [the highest degree of] piety unless you spend [in the cause of God] out of that which you love; whatever you spend, God surely knows it fully well." (3:92)

"O you who believe, observe your duty to God as it should be observed, and at the time of your death you must be Muslim.[9] Take fast hold all together of the rope of God, and do not be divided. Remember the favour of God which He bestowed upon you when you were at enmity with each other and He united your hearts in love, so that by His grace you became brethren.[10] You were upon the brink of a pit of Hell-fire [because of your disbelief] and He rescued you from it [by granting Islam to you]. Thus God explains to you His signs that you may be guided." (3:102-103)

"Let there be from among you a party whose business it should be to call to goodness, to enjoin right conduct and to forbid the wrong.[11] It is they who will be successful." (3:104)

---

8. See *supra*, p. 76, n. 6.
9. The Prophet (ṣ) said, "One whose last words [at death] are: 'There is no god but God and Muḥammad is His messenger' will enter Paradise." See al-Bukhārī, *Ṣaḥīḥ*, Janā'iz, 1.
10. This refers to the dissension, discord and enmity that existed among the Arabs of pre-Islamic time and to the subsequent harmony, mutual love and brotherhood that Islam brought among them. See al-Zamakhsharī, *Op. Cit.*, I, 451.
11. This verse has inspired the leaders of that Islamic missionary party which is known *Jamā'ah al-Tablīgh*. This party has, with perfect sincerity,

"They [i.e. the people of the Book—Jews and Christians] are not alike. Of the people of the Book there is a party[12] who stand [by their covenant]; they recite the revelations of God in the hours of night and prostrate themselves [before Him]. They believe in God and the Last Day, and enjoin right conduct and forbid wrong, and hasten to outdo each other in [different] forms of good. These are among the righteous. Whatever good they do will never be ignored. God has fullest knowledge of those who are righteous." (3:113-115)

"Surely those who disbelieve [will find that] their possessions and their children shall not avail them anything against God. They are the inmates of Hell; therein they will dwell forever. That which they spend in pursuit of the life of this world is like a biting frosty blast which smites the harvest of a people who have done wrong to themselves, and [utterly] destroys it. God does not do wrong to them, but they do wrong to themselves." (3:116-117)

"You are not concerned in the matter [of deciding about the wrongdoers]. God may turn to them in mercy, or punish them because they are wrongdoers. To God belong whatever is in the heavens and whatever is in the earth. He forgives whomever He pleases, and punishes whomever He pleases. God is Most Forgiving, Most Merciful." (3:128-129)

"Vie with one another in hastening to forgiveness from your Lord and to a Paradise, the breadth of which is [as] the heavens and the earth, prepared for those who are righteous—those who spend in prosperity and adversity, who repress their rage and who pardon the offences of people (and God loves those who do good to others), and those who, when they commit turpitude or do wrong to themselves, remember God, implore forgiveness for their sins (and who can forgive sins except God?), and do not persist knowingly in that wrong which they have done. It is these whose reward is forgiveness from their Lord and gardens of Paradise beneath which rivers flow, wherein they will dwell forever. How excellent is the

---

been working throughout the world to propagate Islam.

12. This refers to Jewish and Christian converts to Islam. See al-Zamakhsharī, *Op. Cit.*, I, 426.

reward of those who perform good actions!" (3:133 -136)

"No one can die except by the permission of God; that is a decree with a fixed term. Whoever desires the reward of this world, We shall give him of that; and whoever desires the reward of the Hereafter, We shall give him of that; We shall soon reward the grateful." (3:145)

"It is by the mercy of God that you [i.e. Muḥammad] are gentle with them [i.e. your companions] for if you had been harsh and hard-hearted they would surely have dispersed from around you. So pardon them, pray for forgiveness for them and take counsel with them in the conduct of affairs. Then when you have resolved [concerning any affair] put your trust in God; surely God loves those who put their trust in Him." (3:159)

"Never let those who are niggardly of that which God has bestowed upon them of His bounty, imagine that it is better for them. On the contrary, it is an evil for them. That of which they are niggardly shall be twisted as a collar round their necks on the Day of Resurrection. To God belongs the heritage of the heavens and the earth. God is fully aware of that which you do." (3:180)

"Never imagine that those who rejoice in their deeds and love to be praised for what they have not done are secure from chastisement. They will suffer a painful chastisement." (3:188)

"O you who believe, be patient, and vie with one another in patience; be on your guard; keep your duty to God, that you may be successful." (3:200)

Fifty-nine Verses from the Sūrah of the Women (*al-Nisā'*)

"O mankind, be careful of your duty to your Lord, Who created you from a single person [i.e. Adam] and from him created his mate [i.e. Eve], and from the two created and spread many men and women. Be careful of your duty towards God in Whose name you appeal to one another, and [observe your obligations in respect of] ties of kinship. Surely God watches over you." (4:1)

"God desires to make clear to you, and guide you to the ways of those before you and to turn to you [in mercy]; God is All-knowing, All-wise. God desires to turn to you in mercy, but those who follow their carnal desires want you to incline wholly [towards evil]. God desires to lighten your burden, for man has been created weak." (4:26-28)

"If you keep away from the more serious of the things that are forbidden to you, We shall acquit you of your [minor] evil deeds and shall admit you to a place of honour. Do not covet that by which God made some of you excel others. Men will have a share of that which they earn, and women will have a share of that which they earn. Ask God of His bounty. Surely God has the fullest knowledge of everything." (4:31-32)

"Worship God and associate nothing with Him. Do good to parents, kindred, orphans, the needy, the neighbour who is a kinsman, the neighbour who is not related to you, your associates, the wayfarer, and those whom you own [i.e. slaves]. Surely God does not love the proud and boastful [a] who are niggardly and enjoin others to be niggardly, and conceal that which God has given them of His bounty; (We have prepared for the disbelievers a humiliating chastisement), and [b] who spend of their wealth to show off to people and do not believe in God and the Last Day. Anyone who has Satan for his companion [should know] how evil a companion is he! What harm would befall them if they were to believe in God and the Last Day, and to spend out of that which God has given them as sustenance? God knows them best. Surely God does not do wrong, even by the weight of the smallest particle, and if there be a good deed He multiplies it and gives a great reward from Himself." (4:36-40)

"How then [will it be] when, [on the Day of Judgement], We shall bring a witness from every people, and shall bring you [i.e. Muḥammad] as a witness against them?" (4:41)

"Surely God will not forgive that any partner be associated with Him,[13] but will forgive any sin short of that to whomever

13. The one unforgiveable sin is *shirk*, associating god with God.

He pleases. Anyone who associates partner with God has indeed devised a tremendous sin." (4:48)

"Do you not know of those who consider themselves pure? The truth is that it is God Who purifies whomever He pleases, and they will not be wronged one whit." (4:49)

"Surely God commands you to make over the trusts to those best fitted to discharge them, and that when you judge between the people, you do it with justice. How excellent is that with which He admonishes you! Surely God is All-hearing, All-seeing." (4:58)

"O you who believe, obey God and obey the Messenger and those who are in authority among you. Then if you dispute over anything, refer it to God and the Messenger, if you [really] believe in God and the Last Day. That is the best and most commendable in the end." (4:59)

"We have sent no messenger but that he should be obeyed by the permission of God. If, when they had done wrong to themselves, they had come to you [i.e. Muḥammad] and prayed for forgiveness of God and the Messenger [i.e. Muḥammad] would [also] have prayed for forgiveness for them, they would surely have found God Most Returning [with compassion], Most Merciful. By your Lord, they will not [truly] believe until they make you judge in all that is in dispute between them and then do not find in their minds any demur concerning that which you decide, and submit with full submission." (4:64-65)

"Anyone who obeys God and the Messenger shall be among those upon whom God has bestowed his favours—the prophets, the most truthful men [in religion],[14] the martyrs, and the righteous. How excellent these companions are! That is God's grace, and God suffices as One Who is All-knowing." (4:69-70)

"Whatever of good comes to you is from God, and whatever of evil befalls you is from yourself. We have sent you [i.e. Muḥammad] as a messenger to mankind. Sufficient is God as a witness." (4:79)

---

14. The most truthful men (*ṣiddīqīn*) are the greatest companions of prophets. They preceded others in believing in them and were wholly true in their words and deeds. Abū Bakr al-Ṣiddīq was one of them. See al-Zamakhsharī, *Op. Cit.*, I, 540.

"Anyone who obeys the Messenger has indeed obeyed God; anyone who turns away, then We have not sent you as a keeper over them." (4:80)

"Put your trust in God. Sufficient is God as a Guardian." (4:81)

"Will they [i.e. people] not then ponder on the Qur'an [and thus understand its meanings]? Had it been from any other than God they would surely have found in it many contradictions." (4:82)

"When there comes to them any affair of security or fear, they noise it abroad, whereas if they were to refer it to the Messenger and to those in authority among them, surely those of them who are adept in discovering the truth would know it. Had it not been for the grace of God upon you and His mercy, you all, except a few, would surely have followed Satan." (4:83)

"Anyone who makes a good intercession will share in the good that ensues from it; anyone who makes an evil intercession will share in the evil that ensues in consequence of it. God has the fullest power over everything." (4:85)

"When you are greeted with a salutation, greet with a better salutation, or return the same. Surely God takes the fullest account of everything. God is He besides Whom there is no god. He will most certainly continue to gather you together till the Day of Resurrection, about which there is no doubt. Who is more truthful in his word than God?" (4:86-87)

"O you who believe, when you go forth in the cause of God make due investigation, and do not say to him who offers you the greeting of peace: 'You are not a believer', seeking the goods of the life of this world. God has abundant spoils [to grant you]. You too were like this before, but God has conferred His special favour on you. So do make due investigation. Surely God is well aware of what you do." (4:94)

"Those of the believers who remain at home, except those who are disabled, and those who fight in the cause of God with their belongings and their persons, are not equal. God has exalted in rank those who fight with their belongings and their persons above those who remain at home. To each [of these two groups] God has promised the best thing. God has exalted those who fight above those who remain at home with a promise of great reward, in the form of degrees of excellence [to be bestowed by Him], and forgiveness and mercy. God is Most Forgiving, Ever Merciful." (4:95-96)

"When you have finished the ritual prayer, remember God [while you are] standing, sitting and [lying] on your sides. When you feel secure, perform the ritual prayer. Surely the ritual prayer is an obligation on the believers to be performed at its appointed time." (4:103)

"Do not faint in seeking [non-Muslim] enemies. If you suffer [in the process], they surely too suffer even as you suffer, but you hope for, from God, what they do not; God is All-knowing, All-wise." (4:104)

"Surely We have sent down to you the Book [i.e. the Qur'an] comprising the truth, that you may judge between the people by that which God has shown you. Do not be a pleader on behalf of the treacherous ones, and pray for forgiveness of God; surely God is Most Forgiving, Ever Merciful. Do not plead on behalf of those who are treacherous to themselves. Surely God does not love those who are most treacherous and most sinful." (4:105-107)

"Anyone who does evil or does wrong to himself and then asks forgiveness of God will find God Most Forgiving, Ever Merciful. Anyone who commits a sin does so only against [the good of] himself; God is All-knowing, All-wise. Anyone who commits a fault or a sin, and then charges an innocent person with it, indeed takes on the burden of falsehood and a manifest sin." (4:110-112)

"But for the grace of God upon you [i.e. Muḥammad] and His mercy, a party of them would surely have resolved to lead you astray. They only lead themselves astray, and they cannot harm you in anything. God has sent down on you the Book [i.e. the Qur'an] and wisdom, and has taught you that which you did not know. God's grace on you is very great." (4:113)

"Most of their [i.e. people's] secret talks are devoid of good, except such as enjoin charity, or goodness, or making peace among the people. Anyone who does these, seeking the pleasure of God, will soon be given by Us a great reward." (4:114)

"Anyone who persists in his opposition to the Messenger after guidance has become clear to him and follows a way other than that of the believers, will be let by Us to pursue his course of action and will [in the end] be roasted by Us in Hell-fire. How evil a destination it is! Surely God does not forgive that anything should be associated with Him as His partner; but will forgive anything short of that to whomever He pleases.[15] Anyone who associates anything with God as His partner, has indeed strayed far away." (4:115-116)

"Who is better in respect of religion than one who submits himself wholly to God doing good deeds, follows the religion of Abraham, a man of pure faith? God took Abraham for a special friend.[16] To God belong all that is in the heavens and all that is in the earth, and God encompasses everything." (4:125-126)

"You will never be able to do [perfect] justice between your wives, however much you may desire it. So do not incline wholly [towards one], leaving the other in suspense. If you do good and fear God, surely God is Most Forgiving, Ever Merciful." (4:129)

["The hypocrites will certainly be in the lowest depth of Hell-fire], except such of them as repent, amend, hold fast to God, and do the religious duties sincerely for God. These are among the believers; God will soon give a great reward to the believers. Why should God punish you, if you would be grateful [to Him] and believe [in Him]? God is Appreciating, All-knowing." (4:146-147)

"God does not like the public avowal of evil, except on the part of one to whom injustice has been done. God is All-hearing, All-knowing. If you make public a good deed or do it

---

15. See *supra*, p. 150, n. 13.
16. Cf. 2 Chronicles 20:7; Isaiah 41:8; James 2:23; where Abraham is mentioned as a special friend of God.

secretly, or pardon an evil, God is surely Most Pardoning, All-powerful." (4:148-149)

["God has prepared a painful chastisement for the disbelievers among the Jews.] However those among them who are firmly grounded in knowledge and are believers, believing in that which has been sent down to you [i.e. Muḥammad] and that which was sent down before you, who observe the ritual prayer, pay the divine tax and believe in God and the Last Day will soon be given a great reward by Us." (4:162)

"O mankind, a proof has come to you from your Lord, and We have sent down to you a manifest light [i.e. the Qur'an]. Those who believe in God and hold fast to Him, He will soon admit them to His mercy and grace and guide to a straight path leading to Himself." (4:174-175)

Twelve Verses from the Sūrah of the Table (*al-Mā'idah*)

"Assist one another in piety and righteousness, and do not assist one another in sin and transgression; keep your duty to God; surely God's punishment is severe." (5:2)

"Forbidden to you are the flesh of a dead animal, blood, the flesh of swine, that on which the name of one other than God is invoked, the flesh of an animal that has been strangled or is beaten to death or is killed by a fall or is gored to death, the flesh of an animal of which a wild animal [including a beast of prey] has eaten—unless you have slaughtered it properly before its death—that which has been slaughtered at an alter, and [finally] to seek to draw lots by means of divining arrows. That [i.e. not to avoid these] is an act of disobedience to God. This day those who disbelieve have despaired of [causing harm to] your religion; so do not fear them, but fear Me alone. This day I have perfected your religion for your benefit, have completed My favour to you, and have chosen for you Islam as your religion.[17] Then anyone who is constrained by hunger [to eat

17. This verse is regarded by some authorities as the last revelation. It was

any of the above named forbidden things], without being wilfully inclined to sin, [in such a case] surely God is Most Forgiving, Ever Merciful." (5:3)

"O you who believe, be steadfast in the cause of God, bearing witness in justice. Let not the detestation for a people incite you not to do justice. Do justice; that is nearest to your duty. Observe your duty to God; surely God is fully aware of all that you do. God has promised to those who believe and do good deeds that they shall be granted forgiveness and a great reward." (5:8-9)

"O you who believe, observe your duty to God, seek out the means of approaching Him,[18] and strive hard in His cause that you may be successful." (5:35)

"Judge between them [i.e. people] by that which God has sent down [i.e. the Qur'an] and do not follow their passions; be on your guard against them lest they should involve you in trouble and lead you away from part of that which God revealed to you. If they should turn away, then know that God only intends to punish them for some of their sins. Indeed a large number of people are transgressors. Do they seek judgement in accordance with [the standards of the] time of ignorance? Who is better than God as a judge for a people having firm faith"?[19] (5:49-50)

"When they [i.e. the companions of Muḥammad] hear that which has been sent down to the Messenger, you see their eyes overflow with tears because of that which they recognized of the truth. They say: Lord, we have believed; so write us down among the witnesses. How should we not believe in God and in the truth which has come to us, when we earnestly desire that our Lord should include us among the righteous people? So God

---

revealed on Friday after the Late Afternoon Prayer at 'Arafah on the occasion of the Farewell Pilgrimage in 10 AH (al-Zamakhsharī, *Op. Cit.*, I, 593). It is chronicled that the revelation descended from the heights with so unearthly a force that the Prophet's camel collapsed to its knees.

18. The means to God consists in faith and action. See al-Zamakhsharī, *Op. Cit.*, I, 610. People, however, have formulated the theory that saints and Sufis may also be regarded as means to God.

19. These two verses insist that judgement in the Islamic community must be based on the Qur'an.

shall reward them, because of that which they said, with a Garden beneath which rivers flow; in them they will dwell forever. That is the recompense of those who do good." (5:83-85)

"There is no sin to those who believe and do good deeds, in respect of [those rich and delicious] foods which they eat, if they keep away [from that of these which is forbidden] and hold firmly to the faith and do good deeds, and keep marching forward in righteousness and in firmness of faith, and then go forward in righteousness and in doing good deeds. God loves those who do good deeds."[20] (5:93)

"O you who believe, be heedful of your own selves. He who has gone astray cannot harm you if you are rightly guided yourselves. To God all of you will return; then He will inform you of that which you used to do." (5:105)

Seventeen Verses from the Sūrah of the Cattle (*al-An'ām*)

"The life of this world is but sport and play, and surely the Abode of the Hereafter is better for those who keep their duty to God. Will you not then understand?" (6:32)

"When they [i.e. peoples of the previous prophets] forgot that with which they had been admonished, We opened to them the doors of everything, until when they were in a state of rejoicing for that which they had been given, We seized them suddenly and they were struck dumb with despair. Thus was cut off the last remnant of the people who did wrong. All praises belong to God, the Lord of all the worlds." (6:44-45)

"Do not drive away those who call upon their Lord morning and evening seeking His countenance. You are not at all accountable for them, nor are they at all accountable for you. If you drive them away you will be of the unjust. Thus We have tried some of them by others that they may ask: 'Are these [lowly

20. This meaning of the verse is mentioned by al-Zamakhsharī in his *Op. Cit.*, I, 643.

ones] those whom God has singled out for His favours from among us?' Does not God know best those who are grateful? When those who believe in Our signs come to you, tell them: Peace be upon you. Your Lord has charged Himself with mercy, so that anyone among you who does evil in ignorance and repents after that and amends, then surely He is Most Forgiving, Ever Merciful." (6:52-54)

"When you see those who are engaged in vain discourse concerning Our signs, keep away from them until they turn to some other talk. Should Satan cause you to forget, do not continue to sit with the unjust people after recollection. Those who are righteous are not at all accountable for them, but it is their duty to admonish them, that they [too] may be righteous." (6:68-69)

"For those who believe and do not debase their belief with injustice, is security, and they are rightly guided." (6:82)

"Forsake the outward sin and the inward. Surely those who commit sin will soon be requited for that which they do." (6:120)

"Whomever God wills to guide, He broadens his mind to the acceptance of Islam; whomever He wills to lead astray, He causes his mind to be constricted and oppressed [so that the entering of faith into it becomes as impossible] as his mounting up into the sky. Thus God lays abomination [of infidelity] upon [the minds of] those who do not believe. This [i.e. Islam] is the straight path leading to your Lord. We have explained the signs [of Our existence, power, wisdom, etc.] in detail for a people who take heed. For them is the Abode of Peace [i.e. Paradise] with their Lord and He is their Protector—because of that which they did." (6:125-127)

"Do not approach turpitude of any kind whether manifest or hidden. Do not kill anyone whose killing God has forbidden, except by right. That is what He has enjoined upon you, that you may understand. Do not approach the property of the orphan, except for the most beneficent purpose, until he is of age. Give full measure and weigh with justice. We charge anyone only with that which is in his capacity. When you speak be just, even if it be to a kinsman. Fulfil the covenant of God. That is what He has enjoined upon you, that you may take heed. Surely this is My straight path, so follow it. Do not follow diverse paths lest they lead you astray from His path. That is what He has enjoined upon you, that you may be righteous." (6:151-153)

"Anyone who does a good deed will have ten times as much, and anyone who does an evil deed will only be requited with the like of it; no wrong will be done to them." (6:160)

Eight Verses from the Sūrah of the Heights (*al-A'arāf*)

"Say [to people]: My Lord has enjoined justice and that you fix your attention [on Him] at every time and place of worship and that you call upon Him, making your religion purely for Him [alone]. As He originated you, so you will return [to Him]. A part of mankind He has guided, while error has been permitted to lead astray another part of men. They [i.e. the latter] have taken Satan for their friend, leaving aside God, and they imagine that they are rightly guided." (7:29-30)

"O children of Adam, take your adornment at every time and place of worship.[21] Eat and drink, but do not be prodigal; surely God does not love the prodigal." (7:31)

"If the people of the town [to whom the previous prophets were sent] had believed and had guarded against evil, We would surely have bestowed blessings upon them from heaven and earth; but they considered [the prophets] as false; so We seized them because of that which they did." (7:96)

"When they forgot that with which they had been admonished, We delivered those who were forbidding evil, and We afflicted the evildoers with a grievous chastisement because they were transgressors." (7:165)

21. Usually this is taken to mean best clothes. It is Sunnah to worship God in the most beautiful physical state. The verse is, of course, primarily intended to exclude the nudity of pagan worship. The pre-Islamic Arabs used to circumambulate the Ka'bah naked, believing that one must not worship God by wearing clothes which one wears when one commits sin. God has dis-

"When you [i.e. Muḥammad] do not bring them [i.e. disbelievers] a sign [in quick succession], they say: Why do you not choose one [from yourself]? Tell [them]: I follow only that which is revealed to me from my Lord; This [revelation] is replete with clear proofs from your Lord, a guidance and mercy for a people who believe." (7:203)

"When the Qur'an is recited, listen carefully to it and be silent, that God's mercy may be bestowed upon you." (7:204)

"Remember your Lord in your mind with humility and fear, in low tones, morning and evening, and do not be among the heedless. Surely those who are with your Lord [i.e. the angels] are not too proud to worship Him, but glorify Him and prostrate themselves before Him." (7:205-206)

Eleven Verses from the Sūrah of the Spoils of War (*al-Anfāl*)

"They [i.e. the believers] ask you concerning the spoils. Tell them: the spoils belong to God and the Messenger. So keep your duty to God, and try to promote accord between yourselves; obey God and His Messenger, if you are believers." (8:1)

"Believers are only those whose hearts are smitten with awe when [the name of] God is mentioned, whose faith is strengthened when His signs are recited to them, and who put their trust in their Lord, perform the ritual prayer and spend [in the cause of God] out of that which We have provided for them. These it is who are true believers. They have high ranks with their Lord, forgiveness and honourable provision." (8:2-11)

"O you who believe, respond to God and the Messenger when he calls you that he may bring you to life, and know that God stands [as guardian] between a man and his mind and that He it is to Whom you shall be gathered. Guard yourself against an affliction which shall not smite exclusively the wrongdoers among you. Know that God is severe in exacting retribution." (8:24-25)

"Remember the time when you were few in numbers, were

---

approved of this. See al-Zamakhsharī, *Op. Cit.*, II, 76. For nudity or partial nudity cf. 2 Samuel 6:20.

accounted weak in the land, and were afraid of being despoiled by people; but God gave you refuge, supported you with His help and gave you good things for sustenance, that you may be grateful." (8:26)

"O you who believe, do not betray God and the Messenger, and do not betray your trust knowingly. Know that your wealth and your children are but a trial and that surely it is God with Whom lies a great reward." (8:27-28)

["God's punishment visits the disbelievers]. That is because God would never withdraw a favour that He has conferred upon a people, until they change the condition of their souls. Surely God is All-hearing, All-knowing." (8:53)

Twelve Verses from the Sūrah of Repentance (*al-Tawbah*)

"He alone services the mosques of God who believes in God and the Last Day, observes the ritual prayer, pays divine tax, and fears none but God. It is these who are likely to be among those who are rightly guided." (9:18)

"Say [to the believers]: If your fathers, your sons, your brothers, your wives, your kinsfolk, the wealth you have acquired, the trade the dullness of which you fear and the dwellings that you fancy, are dearer to you than God and His Messenger and fighting in His cause, then wait until God declares His judgement [of punishment]. God does not guide the people who are transgressors." (9:24)

"O you who believe, what ails you that, when it is said to you: 'Go forth [to fight] in the cause of God', you are bowed down to the ground with heaviness? Is it that you prefer the life of this world to the Hereafter? [You should know that] the enjoyment of the life of this world is of very little value as compared to the Hereafter." (9:38)

"The believers, men and women, are friends one of another. They enjoin good and forbid evil, observe the ritual prayer and pay divine tax, and obey God and His Messenger. It is these on whom God will soon have mercy. Surely God is All-mighty,

All-wise." (9:71)

"God is well pleased with those who were foremost among the emigrants [from Makkah] and the helpers [in Madīnah], and those who followed them in doing good; and they are well pleased with Him. He has prepared for them Gardens beneath which rivers flow; in them they will dwell forever. That is the great success." (9:100)

"Do they [i.e. wrongdoers] not know that it is God Who accepts repentance from His servants [i.e. men] and takes alms, and that it is God Who is Oft-turning with compassion and is Ever Merciful? Tell [them]: Continue working. God will surely see your work and [also] His Messenger and the believers; you will soon be returned to Him Who knows the unseen and the seen; then He will tell you what you used to do." (9:104-105)

"God has surely purchased of the believers their selves and their possessions in return for the promise that they shall have Paradise, for they fight in the cause of God and they slay [the enemy] and are themselves slain. This is a promise that He has made incumbent upon Himself as set out in the Torah, the Gospel, and the Qur'an. Who fulfils his promise more than God? Rejoice, then, in the bargain that you have made with Him; that indeed is the supreme triumph." (9:111)

"[These believers are ones] who repent from sin, who worship God, who praise Him, who go about serving His cause, who bow down to Him, who prostrate themselves before Him, who enjoin good and forbid evil, and who safeguard the limits set by God. Give good tidings to such believers." (9:112)

"It is not proper for the believers to go forth all together. Why, then, does not a party from every section of them go forth that they may become learned in religion and that they may warn their people when they return to them so that they may guard against evil?"[22] (9:122)

"Surely a Messenger has come to you from yourselves; grievously heavy is it on him that you should suffer; He is

22. This is one of the two possible meanings of the verse. Both meanings are mentioned by al-Zamakhsharī in his *Op. Cit.*, II, 221.

ardently desirous of your welfare, compassionate and merciful towards the believers. Yet if they should turn away [from you, O Messenger], then say [to them]: Sufficient for me is God; there is no god but He; in Him I do put my trust; He is the Lord of the great throne." (9:128-129)

Eighteen Verses from the Sūrah of Jonah (*Yūnus*)

"Those who do not desire to meet Us and are pleased with the life of this world and feel at ease about it, and those who are heedless of Our signs will have their abode in Hell-fire because of what they used to do. Those who believe and do good deeds will certainly be guided by their Lord because of their faith. Rivers will be flowing beneath them in the Gardens of delight. Their prayer in them will be: Glory be to You, O God! Their greeting in them will be: Peace. The end of their prayer in them will be: All praises belong to God, the Lord of all the worlds." (10:7-10)

"He it is Who enables you to journey through the land and sea. When you have boarded the vessels and they sail with them [i.e. the inmates] with a fair wind and they rejoice in it, the vessels suddenly encounter a fierce gale and wave upon wave comes upon them from every side, and they think they are encompassed [and are about to perish]; then they call upon God, in complete sincerity of faith: If You deliver us from this we will certainly be among the grateful. But when He delivers them, lo! they revert to committing excesses in the earth wrongfully. O people, your committing excesses is certainly against [the benefit of] your souls. [You do this as] the enjoyment of the life of this world. Then to Us will be your return, and We shall inform you of that which you used to do." (10:22-23)

"The life of this world is assuredly like water that We send down from the clouds, then the vegetation of the earth, of which men and cattle eat, mingles with it and the earth is embellished and looks beautiful, and its owners think that they have power over it; then by night or by day, Our command comes and We make it as reaped corn, as if it had not existed there a day before. Thus We expound the signs [of Our existence, power and wisdom] to a people who reflect. God calls you to the Abode of Peace [i.e. Paradise] and guides whom He pleases to a straight path. For those who do good there will be a good reward and more besides.[23] Neither gloom nor ignominy will spread over their faces. It is these who are the inmates of Paradise; in it they will dwell forever." (10:24-26)

"Take notice, surely to God belongs whatever is in the heavens and the earth. Take notice, God's promise is true, but most people do not know. It is He Who gives life and causes death, and it is to Him that you will be brought back." (10:55-56)

"O mankind, there has come to you an exhortation from your Lord, a healing for all the ills which are in the minds, a guidance and a mercy for the believers. Tell [them]: All this is through the grace of God and His mercy. In it, therefore, let them rejoice. That is better than that which they hoard." (10:57-58)

"Take notice, the friends of God will have no fear nor will they grieve. They are those who believe and keep their duty to God. For them are good tidings in the life of this world and also in the Hereafter; there is no changing the words of God; that indeed is the great triumph." (10:62-64)

---

23. The word 'more' here refers to looking upon the glorious face of God in Paradise—a thing which will give so intense a pleasure to the dwellers of Paradise that they will forget all the other delights of Paradise. This explanation of the word 'more' is given by the Prophet (ṣ) himself. Once he recited this verse and said that when the dwellers of Paradise would enter into Paradise and the dwellers of Hell into Hell, a caller would call, "O dwellers of Paradise, God made a promise to you and He would like to fulfil it now." They will reply, "What is that promise? Did He not cause the balance of our good works to be heavy and our faces to be bright, and admit us into Paradise and save us from Hell?" Then the veil will be lifted up, and they will look on the glorious face of God. Nothing in Paradise will be more beloved to them than this sight. See al-Bukhārī, *Ṣaḥīḥ*, Īmān, 15; Muslim, *Ṣaḥīḥ*, Īmān, 304, Jannah, 41.

"Let not the [hostile] utterances of them [i.e. non-believers] grieve you. Surely all power belongs to God. He is the All-hearing, the All-knowing." (10:65)

Twenty Verses from the Sūrah of Hūd

"*Alif lām mīm.*[24] [This Qur'an is] a Book the verses of which have been firmly established and then expounded in detail. [It comes] from One All-wise, All-aware, [admonishing]: Worship none but God; surely I am to you a warner from Him and a bearer of good tidings. Seek forgiveness of your Lord and then turn to Him in repentance. He will give you a goodly provision till an appointed term, and will grant His bounty to every one who deserves it. If you turn away, then surely I will be fearful for you of the chastisement of a dreadful Day." (11:1-3)

"If We bestow upon a person a measure of Our grace, and then take it away from Him, truly he is despairing, ungrateful. But if We bestow upon him a bounty after he has experienced some distress, he will certainly say: Gone are all my ills; and surely He is joyous, boastful. Such are not those who are patient and do good deeds. It is these for whom there are forgiveness and a great reward." (11:10-11)

"If they [i.e. those who believe that Muḥammad forged the Qur'an himself] do not respond to your [demand that, if they are truthful, they should produce a chapter like the chapters of the Qur'an], then know that this [Qur'an] has surely been sent down with the knowledge of God, and that there is no god but He. Will you then not be Muslims?" (11:14)

"Those who desire the life of this world and its pomp will be fully paid by Us for their works in this life, and they will suffer no diminution in respect of that. Those are they who shall have nothing in the Hereafter save Hell-fire; that which they do [in this life] will have failed there, and their deeds will be of no avail to them." (11:15-16)

24. See *supra*, p. 78, n. 10.

"To [the tribe of] Thamūd [We sent] their brother Ṣāliḥ. He said: O my people, worship God; you have no god but Him. He produced you from the earth and has given you to live in it. So ask forgiveness of Him and turn wholly to Him. Surely my Lord is near, responsive [to prayer]." (11:61)

"To [the people of] Madyan [We sent] their brother Shu'ayb. He said: O my people, worship God; you have no god other than Him. Do not give short measure or short weight. Surely I see you in a good [economic condition], but certainly I am fearful for you of the punishment of an overpowering Day. O my people, give full measure and full weight with justice, and do not defraud people by making short delivery; nor commit inequity in the earth thereby creating disorder. If you are believers [you should realize that] the gains that God permits you to retain lawfully are better for you. [I am only to admonish you and] am not a keeper over you. They said: Shu'ayb, does your prayer bid you that we should forsake that which our fathers worshipped or that we should stop disposing of our belongings as we please? You must fancy yourself most forbearing, best guide to right conduct." (11:84-87)

"Do continue to stand upright, as you have been commanded, along with those who have turned wholly to God with you; do not exceed the bounds; surely God sees very well all that you do.[25] Do not incline towards those who do wrong lest Hell-fire should afflict you and then you will have no protectors apart from God, nor will you be helped. Observe the ritual prayer at the two ends of the day and in the early part of the night[26]. Surely good deeds drive away evil deeds. This is a reminder for those who would take heed. Be patient; for surely God does not leave to waste the reward of the gooddoers." (11:112-115)

---

25. This verse was the severest of all Qur'anic verses to the Prophet (ṣ), for in it he was commanded by God to be firm on the straight path, and this firmness was not an easy thing. He was so afraid of deviation from it that he said that it was this verse which caused his hair to grow white. See al-Zamakhsharī, *Op. Cit*, II, 295.
26. All five ritual prayers are referred to in this verse. See al-Zamakhsharī, *Op. Cit.*, II, 296-297.

Eight Verses from the Sūrah of the Thunder (*al-Ra'd*)

"Thus God sets forth similitudes. The best reward is for those who respond to their Lord. Those who do not respond to Him, if they possessed all that is in the earth and the like of it added to that, they would certainly seek to ransom themselves with this. They shall have an evil reckoning, and their abode will be Hell. How bad a resting place it is!" (13:17-18)

"Is he who knows that what is sent down to you from your Lord is the truth, like one who is blind? It is only those possessed of understanding who take heed. [They are] those who fulfil God's pact and do not break the covenant; who join together the ties of kinship that God has commanded to be joined, fear their Lord and dread the evil reckoning; who patiently endure, seeking the countenance of their Lord, observe the ritual prayer, spend secretly and openly out of that with which We have provided them, and avert evil with good. It is they for whom is the [reward of the] final [heavenly] Home." (13:19-22)

"God enlarges His provision or straitens it to whomever He pleases. They [i.e. the worldly] rejoice in the life of this world, whereas the life of this world is but a temporary provision when compared to the Hereafter. Those who disbelieve ask: Why has a sign [of God's existence] not been sent down to him [i.e. Muḥammad] by his Lord? Tell [them]: God surely lets go astray those whom He wills, and guides to Himself those who turn to Him—those who believe and whose minds find comfort in the remembrance of God. Take notice, in the remembrance of God minds do find comfort. Those who believe and do good deeds will have happiness and good retreat." (13:26-29)

Six Verses from the Sūrah of Abraham (*Ibrāhīm*)

"Do you not see how God sets forth a similitude—a good word is like a good tree whose roots are firm and whose branches reach into heaven; it brings forth fresh fruits at all times by the permission of its Lord. God sets forth similitudes for people, that they may take heed. The similitude of an evil word is an evil tree, which is uprooted from the earth and has no stability.[27] God strengthens the believers with the word that is firmly established, in the life of this world and in the Hereafter; God leads astray the evildoers. God does what He wills." (14:24-27)

["Abraham prayed:] Our Lord, You certainly know that which we conceal and that which we make known; nothing whatever is hidden from God, whether in the earth or in the heaven. All praise belongs to God Who has bestowed upon me, despite old age, Ishmael and Isaac. Most surely my Lord hears my prayer fully well. My Lord, make me constant in observing the ritual prayer and my offspring. Our Lord, accept my prayer. Our Lord, forgive me and my parents[28] and the believers on the Day when the reckoning will be held." (14:38-41)

Six Verses from the Sūrah of the Rocky Tract (*al-Ḥijr*)

"We[29] have created the heavens and the earth and all that is between these two, only in accordance with the requirements of truth and wisdom. The Hour [of Doom] is sure to come. So pardon generously. Truly it is your Lord Who is the Great Creator, the All-knowing. We have indeed given you the seven oft-repeated [verses] and the great Qur'an. Never lift your eyes towards that which We have bestowed upon some of them [i.e. disbelievers] of temporary provision and do not

---

27. By 'good word' is meant profession of God's oneness and by 'evil word' acknowledgement of partners of God (*shirk*). 'Good word' may also mean any good utterance, such as praise of God and invitation to Islam. Similarly 'evil word' may mean any evil utterance. See al-Zamakhsharī, *Op. Cit.*, II, 376.
28. This prayer of the prophet Abraham for his parents was before he realized that they were opposed to God (Qur'an 9:114). Prayer for disbelievers is forbidden.
29. See *supra*, p. 75, n. 3.

grieve over them; be kindly gracious towards the believers. Proclaim: I am indeed a manifest warner." (15:85-89)

"We already know that you are sorely grieved by that which they [i.e. disbelievers] say. But glorify your Lord with His praise and be of those who prostrate themselves before Him. Worship your Lord until death comes to you."[30] (15:97-99)

Fourteen Verses from the Sūrah of the Bee (*al-Naḥl*)

"If God were to punish people [instantly] for their wrongdoing, He would not spare a living creature on the earth, but He grants them respite till an appointed term; when their term arrives, they cannot put it back by a single hour nor put it forward." (16:61)

"We have only sent down the Book [i.e. the Qur'an] to you that you may expound to people that concerning which they differ and as a guidance and mercy to a people who believe." (16:64)

"We have sent down the Book [i.e. the Qur'an] to you as an exposition of everything, a guidance, a mercy, and glad tidings for the Muslims. Surely God enjoins justice, beneficence and giving to kinsmen, and forbids turpitude, wrong conduct and transgression; He admonishes you that you may take heed.[31]

---

30. Those Sufis whose thoughts and experiences are very close to the teachings of the Qur'an and the Sunnah often quote this verse in support of their emphasis upon the observance of the Sharī'ah (the revealed law) even after one has already reached the goal of mysticism. They condemn the false Sufis and the Shī'ites who both hold that when reality (*ḥaqīqah*) is revealed the Sharī'ah is no longer necessary.

31. With this verse the imam of the Friday Assembly Prayer concludes his sermon, for a perfect gradation of moral values has been prescribed in this verse. On the negative side, not only must every kind of trespass against person, property and honour be eschewed; but unmannerly behaviour and evil thoughts and desires must also be guarded against. On the positive side, there are two grades: Lower and higher. One at the lower grade of value must do justice, i.e. must return good for good and exact only proportionate retribution for a wrong suffered. But the man who is at the higher grade and

Fulfil the covenant of God when you have made one, and do not break your pledges after making them firm, having made God your surety. Surely God knows that which you do." (16:89-91)

"Whatever you have will pass away, but that which is with God is lasting. We will certainly reward those who patiently endure, according to the best of what they do. Of the believers, anyone who does good, whether male or female, We will certainly grant such a one an excellent life; and We will certainly reward him according to the best of what he does." (16:96-97)

"When you recite the Qur'an, seek the protection of God against Satan, the rejected. Surely he has no power over those who believe and put their trust in their Lord. He has power only over those who make friends with him and those who set up partners with God." (16:98-100)

"Call to the path of your Lord with wisdom and goodly exhortation, and contend with them in the best way. Surely your Lord knows best those who have strayed away from His path, and He knows best those who are rightly guided. If you desire to exact retribution, then chastise as you have been chastised, but if you patiently endure, that surely is better for those who are patient. [Try to] endure patiently, and you can do so only with [the help of] God. Do not grieve for them [i.e. wrongdoers] nor feel distressed because of their plottings. Surely God is with those who keep their duty to Him and those who do good [to others]." (16: 125-128)

Twenty-nine Verses from the Sūrah of the Children of Isrā'īl (*Banī Isrā'īl*)

---

who seeks the pleasure of God must be benevolent; that is, he must render good without any thought of return, and forgive wrongs and injuries till beneficence towards fellow-men becomes part of his nature and flows out of him as naturally as affection for close kindred. These two grades of values are in accordance with the two categories of the virtuous taught in the Qur'an, namely, the righteous and those drawn near to God; also see *infra*, p. 206, n. 66.

"Your Lord has commanded that you worship none but Him, and that you do beneficence towards your parents. Should either or both of them attain old age in your lifetime, do not say 'ugh' to them nor chide them, but speak gently to them. Be humbly tender with them and pray: Lord, have mercy on them as they nurtured me when I was little. Your Lord knows best that which is in your minds; if you are righteous, then surely He is Most Forgiving to those who turn constantly to Him."[32] (17:23-28)

"Give the kinsman his due and the needy and the wayfarer, and do not squander your wealth extravagantly. The extravagant are surely brothers of Satan[33] and Satan is ungrateful to his Lord. On occasions when you must turn away from any of those [who should be the objects of your benevolence], while seeking your Lord's mercy for which you hope, then speak kindly to them. Do not hold back altogether out of miserliness nor spend without any restraint, thus becoming blameworthy and reproached and denuded. Surely your Lord enlarges His provision for whom He wills, and straitens it [for whom He wills]. Surely He is aware of His servants [i.e. men] and sees them fully well. Do not destroy your offspring for fear of poverty; We provide for them and you; surely destroying them is a great sin." (17:26-31)

"Do not approach adultery; surely it is turpitude and an evil way. Do not destroy the life whose [destruction] God has forbidden, except by right. The heir of one who is killed wrongfully has Our authority [to demand retribution], but let him not transgress [the prescribed limits] in killing [in retribution]; [within the limits] he must be helped." (17:32-33)

"Do not approach the property of the orphan, except for the most beneficent purpose until he is of age. Fulfil every

32. These verses have commanded beneficence towards parents, kind behaviour with them and prayer for their well-being. The command is strengthened by joining it with the command of worship of God. In the previous revealed scriptures also, emphasis is laid upon respect for parents; see Matt. 15:4.

33. See *supra*, p. 85, n. 19.

covenant; you will surely be called to account for it [on the Day of Resurrection]. Give full measure when you measure out, and weigh out with a true balance, that is best and most commendable in the end. Do not follow that of which you have no knowledge; the ear, the eye and the heart shall all be called to account [on the Day of Judgement]. Do not walk haughtily on the earth, for thereby you can never tear the earth open nor can ever attain the mountain in height." (17:34-37)

"The evil of all this [mentioned above] is hateful in the sight of your Lord. This is [part] of the wisdom that your Lord has revealed to you. Do not set up with God another god, lest you be cast into Hell, reproached and rejected." (17:38-39)

"Perform the ritual prayer at different times between the declining of the sun and the deep darkness of the night, and [recite] the Qur'an at dawn. The [recitation of] the Qur'an at dawn is surely witnessed [by the angels]. At night also wake up for its recitation, a supererogatory act for you; it may be that thereby your Lord will raise you to a praiseworthy station. Pray [O Muḥammad]: My Lord, make my re-entry into Makkah a beneficent event, and make my going forth from Makkah [also] a beneficent event, and grant me from Yourself an authority and a helper. Announce: Truth has come and falsehood has disappeared; falsehood is bound to disappear."[34] (17:78-81)

"We reveal of the Qur'an that which is a [spiritual] healing and a mercy for the believers; but it only impels the wrongdoers into a great ruin. When We bestow a favour upon a person he turns arrogantly away and draws aside; and when evil afflicts him, he is in despair. Say: Everyone acts in his own way, and your Lord knows best who is the most rightly guided." (17:82-84)

"They [i.e. people] ask you concerning the soul. Tell [them]: The soul is of the affairs of my Lord, and you have been

---

34. When this verse was revealed on the day of the conquest of Makkah in January 630 the angel Gabriel asked the Prophet (ṣ) to break all 360 idols that were stationed inside and around the Ka'bah. When breaking each idol by himself the Prophet (ṣ) repeated this verse. See al-Zamakhsharī, *Op. Cit.*, II, 463.

granted but little knowledge [concerning it]." (17:85)

"Say [i.e. people]: Whether you believe in it. [i.e. the Qur'an] or not, those to whom knowledge has been given before it [i.e. Jews and Christians in their scriptures] fall down prostrate [in token of the complete submission] when it is recited to them, and say: Glory be to our Lord!; the promise of our Lord [that He would send a prophet] has surely been fulfilled. They fall down upon their faces weeping, and it adds to their humility." (17:107-109)

"Say [to people]: Call upon Him as God (*Allāh*) or call upon Him as the Most Gracious One (*al-Raḥmān*); by whichever name you call upon Him, His are the most beautiful names.[35] Do not utter [the words of] your ritual prayer aloud, nor too low, but seek a Way between." (17:110)

Nineteen Verses from the Sūrah of the Cave (*al-Kahf*)

"Make yourself patient with those who call on their Lord morning and evening, seeking His countenance, and do not turn away your eyes from them, desiring the pomp of the life of this world; do not obey him whose mind We have caused to be heedless of Our remembrance, who follows his passion, and whose case exceeds all bounds." (18:28)

"Set forth to them [i.e. people] a similitude: Two men. One of them We have provided with two vineyards which We have surrounded with date-palms, and between the two We have placed corn-fields. Each garden yielded its fruits in abundance without failure, and between the two We caused a stream to flow. He possessed [large quantities of] fruit and boasted to his companion: I am more than you in wealth and stronger in respect of men. [On one occasion] he entered his garden doing wrong to himself, and said: I do not think that this will ever perish; I do not think the Hour [of Doom] will [ever] come; even if I am brought back to my Lord, I will certainly find a better resort than this. His companion

35. See *supra*, p. 100, n. 37.

said: Do you deny Him Who created you from dust, then from a sperm-drop, and then fashioned you into a [whole] man? As for me, it is God Who is my Lord, and I do not associate anyone with my Lord, When you entered your garden why did you not say: [Everything comes about] as God wills; there is no power except in God. If you see me less than yourself in the matter of wealth and offspring, it is likely that my Lord will give me a garden better than yours, and may direct against your garden, a thunderbolt, from heaven, converting it into barren slippery ground. Or its water may sink into the earth, so that you will never be able to find it. [So it was]—and all his fruit was destroyed. The garden had fallen down on its trellises, and its owner wrung his hands bewailing all that he had spent on it, and said: Would that I had not associated anyone with my Lord! He had no party to help him, apart from God, and he was helpless. At such time, it is only the protection of God, the True, that can be of avail. He is the best in rewarding and the best in respect of final outcome." (18:32-44)

"Set forth to them [i.e. people] the similitude of the life of this world: It is like the water that We send down from the clouds, and the vegetation of the earth [grows and] mingles with it; then all becomes stubble which is scattered about by the winds. God has full power over everything. Wealth and children are an adornment of the life of this world, but the abiding things, the good deeds, are better in the sight of your Lord both in respect of reward and in respect of expected benefits." (18:45-46)

"Those who believe and do good deeds shall have the Gardens of Paradise as a hospitality. In them they will dwell forever; they will desire no removal from them." (18:107-108)

"Tell [people]: if the ocean became ink for [transcribing] the words of my Lord, surely the ocean would be exhausted before the words of my Lord came to an end, even though We augment it with the like of it." (18:109)

"Tell [people]: I am but a man like you; it is revealed to me that assuredly your God is one God. So let him, who hopes to meet his Lord, do good deeds and let him associate no one in the worship of his Lord."[36] (18:110)

Nine Verses from the Sūrah of Mary (*Maryam*)

"Warn them [i.e. people] of the Day of Remorse [i.e. the Day of Judgement] when the affair shall be [conclusively] determined, while [today] they are heedless and do not believe. Surely it is We Who inherit the earth and all who are therein, and to Us they will [all] be returned." (19:39-40)

"These [i.e. Zachariah, John the Baptist, and Jonah] were the people on whom God has bestowed His favours from among the prophets, of the posterity of Adam and of those whom We carried [in the Ark] with Noah, and of the posterity of Abraham and Isrā'īl; they were of those Whom We guided and chose. When the words of the Gracious One were recited to them [their hearts were moved so much that] they fell down into prostration, weeping. Then they were followed by a people who laid aside the ritual prayer and followed their lower desires; they will soon be seized with ruin, except those of them who repented, believed and did good deeds; these will enter Paradise, and no wrong whatsoever will be done to them." (19:58-60)

"God increases in guidance those who follow guidance; and the lasting things, good deeds, are better in the sight of your Lord in respect of reward and in respect of the end." (19:76)

"The Gracious One will surely create love for those who believe and do good deeds. So assuredly We have made it [i.e. the Qur'an] easy in your [i.e. Muḥammad's] tongue that you may convey thereby glad tidings to the righteous, and warn thereby a stubborn people. How many generations have We

36. This means that one must not worship God partly for God and partly for ostentation (*riyā'*); worship of God must be purely for God. The Prophet (ṣ) called ostentation the lesser polytheism (*al-shirk al-aṣghar*). See Aḥmad ibn Ḥanbal, *Musnad*, V, 428, 429. For an account of ostentation see Quasem, *Ethics*, pp. 133-136.

destroyed before them [because they disbelieved in such messages as the Qur'an]; Can you perceive a single one of them, or hear [even] a whisper of them?" (19:96-98)

Nineteen Verses from the Sūrah of ṬāHā

"[God said to Moses:] I have chosen you; so carefully listen to what is revealed: Verily I am God; there is no god but I; so worship Me alone, and perform the ritual prayer for remembrance of Me. Surely the Hour [of Doom] is coming—I would almost conceal it [i.e. its knowledge I would not make widespread]—that everyone may be recompensed according to his endeavour. So never let him who does not believe in it and follows his passion, turn you away from [believing in] it, lest you perish. [God asked:] What is that in your right hand, Moses?" (20:13-17)

"They [i.e. the magicians] said [to Pharaoh]: We can never prefer you to the clear signs that have come to us, and to Him Who created us. So decree what you will decree; you can but decree concerning this present life. We have believed in our Lord, that He may forgive us our offences and the sorcery you have forced us to practise. God is the Best and Most Abiding." (20:72-73)

"Anyone who comes to his Lord a sinner will most certainly be in Hell; he will neither die there nor live. But anyone who comes to Him a believer having done good deeds, for such shall be the highest ranks [in Paradise]." (20:74-75)

"Anyone who turns away from remembrance of Me, his will certainly be a life of narrowness [in the grave], and on the Day of Resurrection We shall raise him up blind. He shall ask: O my Lord, why have You raised me up blind, while I had good sight before? God shall say: Thus it is. Our signs came to you, and you did disregard [lit. forget] them; in like manner you will be disregarded on this day. Thus We recompense him who goes beyond the limit and does not believe in the signs of his Lord. The chastisement of the life to come is certainly more severe and more lasting." (20:124-127)

"Does it not serve as a guidance to them [i.e. the disbelievers] how many a generation We destroyed before them, in whose dwellings they now walk? In that indeed are signs [of Our power] for those who possess reason. Were it not for a word already gone forth from your Lord, and a term already fixed, their punishment would have been inevitable [in this world]." (20:128-129)

"So be patient under what they [i.e. disbelievers'] say and glorify your Lord with His praise before the rising of the sun and before its setting; and glorify Him in the watches of the night and at parts of the day, so that you will be well pleasing. Never look covetously upon the embellishment of this worldly life which We have given to some class of them for a brief enjoyment, so that We try them thereby. The provision bestowed upon you by your Lord is better and more lasting. Bid your family to perform the ritual prayer, and be constant in it. We do not ask for provision; it is We Who provide for you. The [good] end is for righteousness." (20:130-132)

Ten Verses from the Sūrah of the Prophets (*al-Anbiyā'*)

"In the name of God, Most Gracious, Ever Merciful. The time of reckoning is drawing near to people, yet they are heedless and turn away. Wherever any fresh admonition comes to them from their Lord they listen to it and make sport of it. Their minds are indifferent towards it." (21:1-2)

"We have indeed written in the Book [revealed to David], after the exhortation that My righteous servants will inherit the earth. Most surely in this is a message for those who are devoted to God." (21:105-106)

"We have sent you [i.e. Muḥammad] only as a mercy for the worlds. Proclaim: Assuredly it is revealed to me that your God is only one God. Will you, then, surrender [to Him]? If they turn away tell them: I have proclaimed to you all alike, and I do not know whether that which you are promised is near or distant. Surely God knows that which you say openly and [also] knows that which you conceal. I do not know; probably it [i.e. delay of punishment] is a trial for you and an enjoyment for a while. He [i.e. Muḥammad] said: My Lord, judge with truth; our Lord is the Most Gracious One Whose help is to be sought against that which you describe [of Him]." (21:107-112)

Fifteen Verses from the Sūrah of the Pilgrimage (*al-Ḥajj*)

"Among men there is such a one as worships God upon the very edge—if good befalls him, he is content with that; but if a trial befalls him, he turns over on his face [i.e. idolatry or infidelity]. He loses in this world as well as in the world to come. That is indeed a clear loss. He calls, apart from God, upon that which can neither harm him nor profit him. That is indeed straying far away. He calls upon him whose harm is nearer than his benefit. How bad indeed is such a patron and how bad indeed is such an associate"! (22:11-13)

"Surely God will admit those who believe and do good deeds into Paradise beneath which rivers flow. Surely God does that which He wills." (22:14)

"That [is the admonition]. Anyone who venerates the sacred signs of God [can be sure that] his veneration originates from the righteous condition of his soul. You may draw benefits from them [i.e. the animals designated for sacrifices in pilgrimage] for an appointed term; then they must be conveyed for sacrifice to the Ancient House. For every people We have appointed a holy rite, so that they may pronounce God's name over the quadrupeds of the class of cattle that He has provided for them. Your God is one God; so to Him submit yourselves wholly and give glad tidings to the humble whose hearts tremble [for fear and awe of God] when God is mentioned, and to those who endure patiently whatever befalls them, and to those who perform the ritual prayer and spend [for the pleasure of Us] out of that which We have provided for them." (22:32-35)

"The flesh of them [i.e. the sacrificed animals] can never reach God, nor their blood[37]; on the contrary, it is your righteousness that reaches Him. Thus has He subjected them to you, that you may magnify God for guiding you, and give glad tidings to those who do good deeds. Certainly God will defend those who believe; surely He does not love the perfidious or the disbeliever." (22:37-38)

"If We establish them [i.e. the persecuted people] in the earth, they will perform the ritual prayer, pay the divine tax, and enjoin good and forbid evil. With God rests the final issue of all affairs." (22:41)

"Those to whom knowledge has been given should realize that the Qur'an is the truth from your Lord, so that they may believe in it and their minds may fully submit to it. Most surely God guides those who believe to the straight path." (22:54)

"O you who believe bow down and prostrate yourselves [in ritual prayer], worship your Lord, and do good, that you may be successful. Strive in the path of God a perfect striving; He has chosen you and has laid no hardship upon you in [the matter of] religion. [Follow] the religion of your father Abraham. God has named you Muslims in this [Qur'an] and [also] before it. [i.e. in previous scriptures], so that the Messenger may be a witness to you and that you may be witnesses to mankind. Then observe the ritual prayer, pay the divine tax and hold fast to God. He is your Master. How excellent a Master and how excellent a helper He is!" (22:77-78)

Twenty-two Verses from the Sūrah of the Believers (*al-Mu'minūn*)

"In the name of God, Most Gracious, Ever Merciful. The

---

37. This is a denial of the primitive Semitic idea (found in the Old Testament) that God is made favourable to men by the physical qualities of the sacrificed animal, e.g. its smell. What really pleases God is the sincere intention of the man offering a sacrifice, his observance of the stipulations of piety in sacrificing.

believers shall be prosperous. They are those who are humble in their ritual prayer, who avoid what is vain, who pay the divine tax, who safeguard their sex—except with their wives and with those whom they own [i.e. slave women, for they are not to be blamed for satisfying their sex with them]; but anyone who seeks anything beyond that is a transgressor—who are watchful of their trusts and covenants, and who strictly observe their ritual prayer. These are the [true] heirs who will inherit Paradise; they will dwell there forever."[38] (23:1-11)

"O [Our] messengers, eat of the things which are pure and perform good actions. I have the fullest knowledge of that which you do. This community of yours is one community, and I am your Lord; so keep your duty to Me. But their people have cut up the guidance into bits among themselves, each party rejoicing in what they have. So leave them in their confusion for a time." (23:51-54)

"Do they imagine that Our helping them with wealth and children is to make them advance rapidly in good? On the contrary, they are not aware [of its real reason]. Surely those who tremble with fear of their Lord, those who believe in His signs, those who do not ascribe partners to Him, and those who give [to others] what they give, with hearts trembling with fear because [finally] they will have to return to their Lord—these are the people who [really] advance rapidly in doing good, and they are foremost in this respect." (23:55-61)

Twelve Verses from the Sūrah of the Light (*al-Nūr*)

"Those who love that turpitude should spread among those who believe, will surely have a painful chastisement in this world and the world to come. God knows, and you do not know. But for the bounty of God and His mercy upon you, and

38. In these verses several important duties of believers are mentioned. Fulfilment of these duties will result in admission into Paradise in the Hereafter.

that God is Compassionate and Ever Merciful, [you would be undone"]. (24:19-20)

"O you who believe, do not follow in the footsteps of Satan; whoever follows in the footsteps of Satan [should know that] he only enjoins indecency and wrong. But for the bounty of God and His mercy upon you, none of you would ever be purified; but God purifies whom He pleases. God is All-hearing, All-knowing." (24:21)

"Let not those who are possessed of bounty and plenty among you resolve by oath to withhold their bounty from their kindred, the poor, and those Who have migrated from their houses in the cause of God, [because of some default on the part of the recipient]. Let them pardon and forgive. Do you not love that God should forgive you? God is Most Forgiving, Ever Merciful." (24:22)

"[The light of God illumines] houses which God has ordained that they be exalted and in which His name is commemorated. In them is He glorified mornings and evenings by men whom neither trade nor traffic diverts from the remembrance of God, performance of the ritual prayer, the payment of divine tax; they fear a day [i.e. the Day of Resurrection] on which hearts and eyes will be agitated; [they do all this] so that God may bestow upon them the best reward of their deeds and give them more out of His bounty. God provides for whomever He wills without measure." (24:36-38)

"As for those who disbelieve, their works are as a mirage in a wide plain. A thirsty one imagines it to be water until, when he comes up to it, he finds it to be nothing and near him he finds God Who then pays him his account in full. God is swift at reckoning. Or, [their works are] like darkness upon a vast and deep sea, the surface of which is covered by waves rolling upon waves, above which are clouds; layers of darkness exist one upon another [so thick that] when a person holds out his hand he can hardly see it. For him whom God grants no light, there is no light at all." (24:39-40)

"The believers, when they are called to God and His Messenger that he may judge between them, are only to say:

We hear and we obey. It is they who will prosper. Those who obey God and His Messenger, and fear God and have awe of Him, are the ones who will be successful." (24:51-52)

Fifteen Verses from the Sūrah of the Criterion (*al-Furqān*)

"The true servants of the Most Gracious One are those [a] who walk upon the earth with humility and when they are addressed by the ignorant ones they say: Peace; [b] who pass the night in prostration and standing before their Lord; [c] who entreat: Our Lord, avert from us the chastisement of Hell, which is surely a terrible torment; it is indeed an evil resort and dwelling place; [d] who, when they spend, are neither extravagant nor niggardly but keep a balance between the two,[39] [e] who do not call upon any god beside God, nor destroy a life whose destruction God has forbidden except by right, nor fornicate, for anyone who does that will meet with the punishment of sin—his punishment will be intensified on the Day of Resurrection and he will abide in it disgraced, except for those who repent, believe and do good deeds, whose evil deeds God will convert into good ones, God being Most Forgiving, Ever Merciful (and he who repents and does good deeds indeed turns to God with true repentance); [f] those who do not bear false witness and when they pass by anything vain, they pass by with dignity; [g] who, when they are reminded of the signs of their Lord, do not fall down at that deaf and blind [but keep standing and attend to them]; [i] who implore: Our Lord, grant us of our spouses and our offspring the delight of our eyes, make us a leader of those who keep their duty to God. These are the ones who will be rewarded with rooms in Paradise, because they were patient, and they will receive there greetings and salutations of peace, dwelling therein forever. Excellent it is as a resort and dwelling place"![40] (25:63-76)

---

39. See *supra*, p. 85, n. 19.

40. The distinguishing qualities of true servants of God are mentioned in

"Say [to the disbelievers]: What would my Lord care for you, were it not for your prayer? You have regarded [Him] as false, and the punishment will soon cleave to you." (25:77)

Fourteen Verses from the Sūrah of the Poets (*al-Shu'arā'*)

"Do not call upon another god with God lest you become one of those who are chastised. Warn your nearest kinsmen, and extend kindness and affection to those believers who follow you[41]. If they disobey you [in any thing] say [to them], 'I dissociate myself from that which you do', and put your trust in the All-mighty, the Ever Merciful, Who sees you when you stand [for ritual prayer] and your movements in the company of those who prostrate themselves in ritual prayer along with you. Surely it is He Who is the All-hearing, the All-knowing." (26:213-220)

"Shall I inform you on whom the Satans descend? They descend on every lying sinner. They give ears [in hopes of hearing some pieces of genuine revelation] and most of them are liars. It is the erring ones who follow the [evil] poets. Do you not see how the poets wander distracted in every valley and say that which they do not do?—except those [poets] who believe, do good deeds, remember God much, and help themselves [by exacting retribution] after wrong has been done to them. The wrongdoers will soon know to what final place of returning they will return." (26:221-227)

Eleven Verses from the Sūrah of the Ant (*al-Naml*)

"*Ṭā sīn.*[42] These are the verses of the Qur'an and of a clear

---

these verses. The final result of the acquisition of these qualities is also set forth.

41. On the revelation of this verse in Makkah the Prophet (ṣ) started to preach Islam publicly. Prior to this he used to preach secretly.

42. See *supra*, p. 78, n. 10.

Book, a guidance and glad tidings for the believers who perform the ritual prayer, pay the divine tax, and have sure faith in the Hereafter. Those who do not believe in the Hereafter surely We have made their works appear fair to them, so they wander blindly. They are those who will suffer a grievous punishment, and it is they who will be the greatest losers in the Hereafter. Most surely you [i.e. Muḥammad] receive the Qur'an from the presence of One All-wise, All-knowing." (27:1-6)

"Anyone who brings a good deed [to God] will have better than it, and he will be secure against terror that day [i.e. the Day of Judgement]. Anyone who brings [to God] an evil deed shall fall into the Hell-fire face downwards. You will be recompensed only for what you did." (27:89-90)

["Say:] Assuredly I am commanded to worship the Lord of this city [of Makkah] which He has made sacred, and to Him belongs everything. I am [also] commanded to become of the Muslims and to recite the Qur'an. So whoever achieves guidance [thereby] does only so for [the good of] his own self; whoever goes astray say [to him]: I am but a warner. Proclaim [also]: All praise belongs to God. Soon He will show you His signs and you will know them. Your Lord is not heedless of what you do." (27:91-93)

Five Verses from the Sūrah of the Story (*al-Qaṣaṣ*)

"Whatever thing you are given is the enjoyment of the present life and its adornment; that which is with God is better and more lasting. Will you not then understand? Can he to whom We have promised good [in the life to come], and he is going to obtain that promised good there, be like the one to whom We have given the enjoyment of the life of this world, and then on the Day of Resurrection he will be of those who will be brought up [for punishment for their misdeeds]?" (28:60-61)

"Seek the Home of the Hereafter [i.e. Paradise] through that which God has given you, and do not forget [to take] your portion from the present world;[43] do good [to people] as God has done good to you; do not seek to create corruption in the earth; surely God does not love those who create corruption." (28:77)

"That Home of the Hereafter [i.e. Paradise] We bestow on those who do not desire to attain exalted positions in the earth, nor corruption. The [good] end is for those who are righteous. He who does good will obtain better than that; he who does evil, such will not be recompensed except for what he used to do." (28:83-84)

Seven Verses from the Sūrah of the Spider (*al-'Ankabūt*)

"Those who have taken protectors apart from God are comparable to the spider which builds a house, and the frailest of all houses is most certainly the house of the spider, if they but know. Surely God knows whatever they call upon apart from Him. He is the All-mighty, the All-wise. These are similitudes that We set forth for people, but only those who possess knowledge comprehend them. God has created the heavens and the earth in accordance with the requirements of truth and wisdom. In that is indeed a sign [of His existence power and wisdom] for the believers." (29:41-44)

"Recite the Book [i.e. The Qur'an] which has been revealed to you and perform the ritual prayer. Surely the ritual prayer shields [a devotee] against turpitude and evil. The remembrance of God [which is the purpose of ritual prayer] is indeed the greatest thing. God knows well that which you do." (29:45)

"O My servants [i.e. men] who believe, surely My earth is wide;[44] so worship Me alone. Everyone shall suffer death; then to Us you will be returned." (29:56-57)

43. "Your portion From the present world" means acquisition of praiseworthy knowledge and performance of good action, for it is by these two that an individual will be entitled to Paradise.
44. This is an invitation to leave places where worship of God is difficult.

Five Verses from the Sūrah of the Romans (*al-Rūm*)

"Devote yourself single-mindedly to the religion [of Islam], being a man of pure faith; and [thus follow] the original natural disposition given by God on which He has created man. There is no altering the creation of God. That is the right religion. But most people do not know it. [Follow the religion of Islam] completely turning towards Him; keep your duty to Him, perform the ritual prayer, and do not be of those who ascribe partners to Him." (30:30-31)

"When We bestow mercy upon people, they rejoice in it. But if any evil befalls them in consequence of their actions, lo, they are in despair!" (30:36)

"Do they not know that God enlarges the provision for whomever He pleases, and straitens [for whomever He pleases]? In that are indeed signs [of His power and wisdom] for a people who believe. So give the kinsman his due, and to the needy, and to the wayfarer. This is better for those who desire the [glorious] face of God, and it is they who will prosper". (30:37-38)

Nine Verses from the Sūrah of Luqmān

["Luqmān said to his son:] Dear son, God will surely bring forth the slightest action even if it be [of no greater weight than] a mustard seed, and be [hidden] inside a rock or [anywhere] in the heavens or in the earth. Surely God is the knower of the most subtle matters, All-aware. Dear son, perform the ritual prayer, enjoin good and forbid evil, and bear patiently whatever may befall you; that is certainly a matter of firm determination. Do not puff up your cheek with pride before people, nor walk haughtily upon the earth. Surely God does not love any arrogant boaster. Walk with a moderate attitude, and lower your voice; truly the most disliked sound is the bray of the donkey." (31:16-19)

"He who completely submits himself to God and [at the same time] does good is [as if] he has firmly grasped the strongest handle. With God rests the end of all affairs." (31:22)

"O mankind, keep your duty to your Lord, and dread a Day when a father will not be of any avail to his child, and a child will not be of any avail to his father. The promise of God is surely true. So let not the life of this world deceive you at all, nor let the Arch-Deceiver [i.e. Satan] deceive you at all concerning God." (31:33)

"Surely with God alone is the knowledge of the Hour [of Doom]. He sends down the rain, and knows that which is in the womb. No one knows what he will earn tomorrow, and no one knows in which land he will die. Surely God is All-knowing, All-aware." (31:34)

Five Verses from the Sūrah of Prostration (*al-Sajdah*)

"Assuredly those believe in Our signs who, when they are reminded of them, fall down prostrate and glorify their Lord with His praise, and are not proud [against Him]. They withdraw themselves from their beds [in the later parts of the night for prayers], and call on their Lord in fear and hope; they spend out of that which We have given them as sustenance. No one knows what happiness [lit. delight of the eye] is kept hidden for them, as a reward for what they used to do.[45] Is he, then, who is a believer like one who is ungodly? They are not equal. As for those who believe and do good deeds, they will have Gardens of Eternal Abode, in hospitality for that which they used to do." (32:15-19)

---

45. Cf. 1 Corinthians 2:9 (quoting Isaiah 64:4), "eye both not seen, nor ear heard, neither have entered into the heart of man the things which God hath prepared for them that love him." Almost to this same effect there is a well known and oft-quoted Tradition that the prophet Muḥammad said, "God says, 'I have prepared for My virtuous servants what no eye ever saw, no ear ever heard and which never occurred to any man's mind'" (al-Bukhārī, *Ṣaḥīḥ*, Tawḥīd, 35; Muslim, *Ṣaḥīḥ*, Īmān, 312, Jannah, 5-6). This Tradition as well as the Qur'anic verse (32:17) refers to the most intense spiritual pleasure to be derived from gazing upon the glorious face of God for evermore in Paradise. For a brief, discussion of this see Quasem. "Al-Ghazālī's Conception of Happiness," *Arabica*, XXII, 160.

Ten Verses from the Sūrah of the Confederates (*al-Aḥzāb*)

"Among the believers are men who are true to the covenant they made with God. Some of them fulfilled their vow by giving their lives [in holy wars], and others are still waiting. They have not changed in their resolve in the least; that God may reward the truthful for their truth, and punish the hypocrites if He so pleases, or turn to them in mercy. Surely God is Most Forgiving, Ever Merciful." (33:23-24)

"Men who wholly submit themselves to God through Islam and women who wholly submit themselves to God through Islam, men who believe and women Who believe, men who are obedient and women who are obedient, men who are truthful and women who are truthful, men who are patient and women who are patient, men who are humble and women who are humble, men who give alms and women who give alms, men who fast and women who fast, men who guard their private parts and women who guard [their private parts], men who remember God much and women who remember God much—for them [all] God has prepared forgiveness and a great reward." (33:35)

"It is not open to a believing man or a believing woman, when God and His Messenger have decided a matter, to have their own choice in it. Anyone who disobeys God and His Messenger falls into manifest error." (33:36)

"O you who believe, remember God very much, and glorify Him in the morning and in the evening. He it is Who blesses you, and His angels [do the same], that He may bring you forth from darkness into light. He is Ever Merciful to the believers. On the Day when they meet Him, their greeting will be: Peace. He has prepared for them a noble recompense." (33:41-44)

"O you who believe, keep your duty to God and say the straightforward thing. He will enable you to do good deeds and will forgive your sins. Anyone who obeys God and His Messenger achieves a great success." (33:70-71)

"Surely We offered the Trust [i.e. the responsibility of faith and action] to the heavens, the earth and the mountains, but they refused to undertake it and were afraid of it. But man undertook it. Surely he is very unjust, very ignorant." (33:72)

One Verse from the Sūrah of Sheba (*Saba'*)

"It is not your wealth nor your children which will bring you near to Us. Only those who believe and do good deeds [will draw near]; for them is manifold reward for their deeds and they will be secure in lofty chambers [of Paradise]." (34:37)

Seven Verses from the Sūrah of the Originator (*Fāṭir*)

"O mankind, God's promise is certainly true; so never let the life of this world deceive you at all, and never let the Arch-Deceiver [i.e. Satan] deceive you at all concerning God. Satan is surely your enemy; so treat him as an enemy. Assuredly he calls his adherents that they may become inmates of the Blazing Fire." (35:5-6)

"O mankind, you are dependent upon God, while He is the One Who is All-sufficient, the All-laudable. If He pleases, He can destroy you and put [in your place] a new creation; that is not difficult for God." (35:15-17)

"No one burdened can bear the burden of another. If a heavily burdened one should call [another] to carry his load, nothing of it will be carried [by the others] even though he be a kinsman.[46] You can warn only those who fear their Lord in the unseen and perform the ritual prayer. Anyone who purifies himself does so only for his own good. To God is the final return." (35:18)

"Surely those who recite the Book of God, perform the ritual

---

46. This verse emphasizes the individualistic character of the Last Judgement; a man cannot be helped or supported even by "a kinsman." For this sort of teaching, Islam, Christianity, and all other revealed religions are regarded as individualistic in nature.

prayer and spend, secretly and openly, out of that which We have provided for them, are pursuing a commerce that never suffers any loss, so that God will give them their full rewards and He will give them [even] more [than what they deserve by their deeds] out of His bounty. Surely He is most Forgiving, Most Appreciating." (35:29-30)

Eight Verses from the Sūrah of the Rangers (*al-Ṣāffāt*)

"He [i.e. Abraham] said: I am going to my Lord; He will surely guide me. My Lord, grant me righteous progeny, So We gave him the glad tidings of a forbearing son [i.e. Ishmael]. When the boy reached [the age of] running about with him, Abraham said [to him]: Dear son, surely I have seen in my dream that I am to slaughter you in sacrifice to God, so consider what you think of it. The boy replied: Father, do what you are commanded; you will find me, if God pleases, one of those who patiently endure. When both had submitted themselves [to the will of God], and Abraham had thrown his son down on his forehead, We called to him: Abraham, you have indeed fulfilled the dream. Thus We do recompense the gooddoers. That was most surely a manifest trial." (37:99-106)

Six Verses from the Sūrah of Ṣād

"O David, We have made you a deputy in the earth; so judge between people with justice and do not follow passion, lest it should lead you astray from the path of God. Surely those who go astray from the path of God will have a severe punishment because they have forgotten the Day of Reckoning." (38:26)

"We have not created the heavens and earth and that which is between them in vain. That is the view of those who disbelieve. Woe, then, to the disbelievers because of [the punishment of] Hell, Shall We treat those who believe and do good deeds, like those who do corruption in the earth? Shall We treat those who keep their duty like the transgressors? This [Qur'an] is a book which We have revealed to you and which is blessed, that people may reflect over its verses and that those gifted with understanding may take heed." (38:27-29)

["O Prophet] say [to people]: I do not ask of you any recompense for it [i.e. conveying God's message to you], nor am I one given to affectation. This [Qur'an] is nothing but a reminder for all people, and you will most certainly know its tidings after a while." (38:86-88)

Seven Verses from the Sūrah of the Companies (*al-Zumar*)

"Is he who is devout [in prayer], prostrating and standing, during the hours of the night, being afraid of the Hereafter and hoping for the mercy of his Lord, [to be accounted equal with him who is not such]? Ask [them]: Can those who know be equal to those who do not know? It is only those possessed of understanding who take heed." (39:9)

"Say: O servants of God [i.e. men] who believe, keep the duty to your Lord. For those who do good in this life there is good [reward]. God's earth is wide. Assuredly, those who patiently endure will be given their reward without measure. Say [also]: I am commanded to worship God, making my religion sincerely for Him,[47] and am commanded to be the foremost of the Muslims." (39:10-12)

"God has sent down the best message as a Book [i.e. the Qur'an], resembling itself [i.e. self-consistent] in its oft-repeated [verses]; by it the skins of those who fear their Lord are set tingling, then their skins and their minds soften into the remembrance of God. That [Book] is God's guidance; with it He guides whom He pleases. He whom God leads astray has none to guide him." (39:23)

"Say [to people]: O my servants who have committed excesses against your own selves, do not despair of the mercy of God; surely He forgives all sins; surely He it is Who is Most

47. See *supra*, p. 175, n. 36.

Forgiving, the Ever Merciful.[48] Turn to your Lord and submit yourselves to Him before the punishment overtakes you and no one is able to help you. Follow the best of that which has been sent down to you from your Lord, before the punishment overtakes you suddenly while you are unaware." (39:53-55)

Two Verses from the Sūrah of the Believer (*al-Mu'min*)

["A believer from the people of Pharaoh said:] O my people, the life of this world is but a temporary provision; the Hereafter is surely the Permanent abode. Anyone who does evil will be requited only with the like of it; anyone who does good—be he male or female—and is a believer, will enter Paradise, and will be provided there without measure." (40:39-40)

Four Verses from the Sūrah of Ḥā Mīm al-Sajdah[49]

"Who speaks better than one who calls [people] to God, does good deeds, and says: Surely I am of the Muslims.[50] Good and evil are not equal. Repel [evil] with that which is the best; then he between whom and you was enmity becomes as though he were a warm friend. But none attains to this except those who are steadfast; none attains to this save those who possess a great share [of good]." (41:33-35)

"If a provocation from Satan should provoke you, do seek refuge with God. Surely He is the All-hearing, the All-knowing." (41:36)

48. The Prophet (ṣ) said that this verse was more beloved to him than the possession of the entire world together with all that is in it. See al-Zamakhsharī, *Op. Cit.*, III, 403.
49. Another name for this sūrah is *Fuṣṣilat* (the Distinguished) which is given in the official Egyptian edition of the Qur'an.
50. See *supra*, p. 111, n. 11.

Nine Verses from the Sūrah of Ḥā Mīm 'Ayn Sīn Qāf[51]

"Anyone who desires the harvest of the Hereafter, We give him increase in his harvest; anyone who desires the harvest of this world, We give him of that, but in the Hereafter he has no share." (42:20)

"He it is Who accepts repentance from His servants [i.e. men], forgives sins, and knows all that you do. He responds to those who believe and do good deeds, and bestows upon them an increase [in their belief and good deeds] out of His bounty. For the disbelievers there is severe punishment." (42:25-26)

"Were God to enlarge greatly the provision for His servants [i.e. men] surely they would behave arrogantly in the earth; but He sends down according to the measure He pleases. Surely He is fully aware of His servants and sees them fully well." (42:27)

"Whatever you have been given is only a temporary provision of this life, but that which is with God is better and more lasting for [a] those who believe and put their trust in their Lord, [b] those who avoid the grave sins and sexual offenses and when they are angry they forgive, [c] those who respond to their Lord, perform the ritual prayer, whose affairs are administered by mutual consultation, and who spend out of that which we have provided for them and [d] those who, when a great wrong is done to them, defend themselves. The recompense of an evil is an evil similar to it [in proportion]; but he who forgives and effects a reform [thereby], has his reward with God. Surely He does not love the wrongdoers."(42:36-40)

Five Verses from the Sūrah of Ornaments (*al-Zukhruf*)

"Is it they [i.e. the disbelievers] who distribute the mercy of your Lord? It is We Who distribute among them their livelihood in the life of this world, and We exalt some of them above others in rank so that some of them may take labour from others;

51. This sūrah is also called *al-Shūrā* (Counsel).

the mercy of your Lord is better than that which they amass." (43:32)

"Were it not that mankind would [in consequence] be one nation [of disbelievers], We would have provided those who disbelieve in the Most Gracious One, with roofs of silver for their houses, and stairways [of silver] by which they could climb, [silver] doors of their houses and couches [of silver] on which they could recline, and ornaments of gold.[52] All this, however, is only the temporary provision of the life of this world; and the world to come is, according to your Lord, for those who keep their duty to Him." (43:33-35)

"For him who lives in turning away from the remembrance of the Most Gracious One, We assign a Satan who becomes his boon companion." (43:36)

Six Verses from the Sūrah of Crouching (*al-Jāthiyah*)

"Do those who do evil deeds imagine that We shall make them as those who believe and do good deeds, in life and in death? How evil is that which they judge! God created the heavens and the earth in accordance with the requirements of wisdom, so that every one may be recompensed according to what he has done; no wrong will be done to them." (45:21-22)

"Have you considered [the case of] him who has made his passion his god,[53] whom God has led astray on the basis of his knowledge, and whose ears and mind He has sealed up, and on whose eyes He has put a covering? Who will, then, guide him after God [has thus led him astray]? Will you not then take heed?" (45:23)

---

52. This passage expresses how mean the embellishments of this world are in the estimation of God: These are so insignificant that He would have given them abundantly even to those who do not recognize Him had there been no evil consequence of giving these to them. The evil consequence is that all people, being engrossed in them, will gradually be disbelievers. See al-Zamakhsharī, *Op. Cit.*, III, 487.

53. That is, he follows his passion so much that it is as if he has become its worshipper. The Sufis often quote this verse in support of their doctrine that a novice must oppose his passions and desires, especially during the period of self-training and mortification.

"The evil nature of their [i.e. evildoers'] deeds will become manifest to them [on the Day of Resurrection] and that which they used to mock at will encompass them. It will be said [to them]: Today We forget you as you forgot the meeting of this day of yours; your resort is Hell; you will have no helpers. This is because you made a jest of the signs of God, and the life of this world deluded you. So today they will not be taken out of Hell, nor will they be allowed to make amends." (45:33-35)

Three Verses from the Sūrah of the Sand-dunes (*al-Aḥqāf*)

"Those who [believe and] say, 'Our Lord is God', and then remain firm [on this belief] will have no fear, nor will they grieve [on the Day of Judgement"]. (46:13)

"Endure patiently as did the Messengers possessed of high resolve, and do not desire for their [i.e. disbelievers'] quick punishment. On the Day [of Resurrection] when they see that [punishment] which they are promised, they [will feel] as if they had not tarried [in their life of this world] but for an hour of a single day. [This is] a message [of warning]! None but the ungodly people will be destroyed." (46:35)

Six Verses from the Sūrah of Muḥammad (ṣ)

"Do they not ponder over the Qur'an, or is it that their hearts are locked up from within? Those who have turned back [to their former religion] after guidance became manifest to them, have surely been tempted by Satan who lengthens false hopes for them. That is because they said to those who disliked that which God has revealed: We shall soon obey you in some matters. God knows their secrets." (47:24-26)

"Assuredly the life of this world is sport and pastime, and if you believe and keep your duty to God, He will give you your rewards and will not ask of you your belongings. Were He to ask you of them and to press you [for them] you would be niggardly, and He would bring to light your rancour." (47:36-37)

"Take notice, you are those who are called upon to spend in the cause of God; but some of you are niggardly, and anyone who is niggardly is only so against himself. God is Self-sufficient, and you are needy. If you turn away [from Him] He will bring in your stead another people who will not be like you." (47:38)

Two Verses from the Sūrah of Victory (*al-Fatḥ*)

"He it is Who has sent His messenger [Muḥammad] with guidance and the religion of truth, that He may cause it to prevail over all other religions. God is sufficient as a witness." (48:28)

"Muḥammad is the messenger of God. Those who are with him are hard towards the disbelievers, [but] compassionate towards one another. You see them bowing and prostrating [in ritual prayer] seeking His bounty and pleasure. Their mark is visible on their faces in the impression of prostration. This is their likeness in the Torah.[54] Their similitude in the Gospel is: Like a seed[55] that sends forth its sprout and then strengthens it; it then becomes thick and stands firm on its stem, delighting the sowers; that through them God may enrage the disbelievers. God has promised forgiveness and a great reward to those of them who believe and do good deeds." (48:29)

Six Verses from the Sūrah of Apartments (*al-Ḥujurāt*)

"O you who believe, avoid too much suspicion, surely some suspicion is a sin. Do not backbite one another; would any of you like to eat the flesh of his dead brother?; you would dislike it. Observe your duty to God. Surely God is Oft-

54. Cf. Deuteronomy 11:18: "... as frontlets between your eyes"; 6:8 "... as frontlets between thine eyes."
55. Cf. Mark 4:26-29: "... cast seed into the ground...."; 30-32: "... like a grain of mustard seed, ..."

returning [with compassion], Ever Merciful." (49:12)

"O mankind, surely We have created you from male and female; We have divided you into races and tribes, that you may know one another. Surely the most honoured among you in the sight of God is he who is the most righteous among you.[56] Surely God is All-knowing, All-aware." (49:13)

"The believers are only those who believe in God and His Messenger and then do not doubt, but strive hard with their wealth and their persons in the cause of God. It is they who are truthful." (49:15)

"Say [O Messenger to the bedouins who have just accepted Islam]: Will you acquaint God with your religion, while God knows whatever is in the heavens and whatever is in the earth, and God has the fullest knowledge of everything? They behave as if they have done you a favour by embracing Islam. Tell them: Do not deem your accepting Islam a favour done to me. On the contrary, God has done you a favour in that He has guided you to the faith, if you are truthful. God knows the unseen of the heavens and the earth. God sees well all that you do." (49:16-18)

Two Verses from the Sūrah of Qāf

"Patiently endure that which they [i.e. the Christians] say; and glorify your Lord with His praise, before the rising of the sun and before its setting, and glorify Him during the night and after prostrations [of ritual prayer]." (50:39-40)

Three Verses from the Sūrah of the Scatterers (*al-Dhāriyāt*)

"I have not created jinn[57] and mankind except that they

56. This verse serves as the Islamic criterion of goodness, nobility, excellence, and so on. Muslims, especially the Sufis, often cite this verse in their books, sermons and religious discourses, There are several prophetic traditions containing the theme of this verse. See al-Zamakhsharī, *Op. Cit.*, III, 569.

57. See *supra*, p. 84, n. 18.

should worship Me.[58] I do not desire any sustenance from them, nor do I desire that they should feed Me. Surely it is God Who is the All-sustaining, the Possessor of power, the Strong." (51:56-58)

Two Verses from the Sūrah of the Mount Sinai (*al-Ṭūr*)

"Adhere steadfastly to the command of your Lord, for you are in front of Our eyes, and glorify your Lord with His praise when you are standing in ritual prayer. [Also] glorify Him during the night and at the setting of the stars." (52:48-49)

Eight Verses from the Sūrah of Iron (*al-Ḥadīd*)

"What ails you that you do not spend wealth in the path of God, while to God belongs the heritage of the heavens and the earth? Those of you who spent wealth [in the path of God] and fought before the victory [over the Makkan infidels] are not equal to those who spent and fought after the victory; the former are higher in rank. To each [of the two groups] God promised the best reward; God is fully aware of that which you do." (57:10)

"For the men who give alms and the women who give alms, and those who lend to God a goodly loan [by spending in His cause], that which they spend will surely be increased manifold, and theirs will be a generous reward. Those who believe in God and His messengers are the most truthful and the witnesses in the sight of their Lord. They will have their reward and their light. Those who have disbelieved and denied Our signs will be the inhabitants of Hell." (57:18-19)

"Know that the life of this world is but sport, pastime, adornment, a subject of boasting among you, and rivalry in

58. This verse is often cited by Muslims as proof of the view that the aim of man and jinn in this life is worship of God and knowledge of Him. Although knowledge of God is not explicit in this verse, it is included in it because worship of God is not possible without knowledge of Him. See al-Ḥujwīrī, *Kashf al-Maḥjūb*, trans. by R.A. Nicholson, Leyden, 1911, p. 267.

multiplying riches and children. It is like a rain—vegetation produced by it rejoices the disbelievers; then it withers, and you see it turning yellow; then it becomes broken particles of stubble. In the Hereafter there is a severe chastisement, and forgiveness from God and His pleasure. The life of this world is but illusory enjoyment. Vie with one another in seeking forgiveness from your Lord and for Paradise, the breadth of which is like the breadth of heaven and earth, and which is prepared for those who believe in God and His messengers. That is the bounty of God; He gives it to whomever He pleases. God is the Possessor of a great bounty." (57:20-21)

"No affliction befalls in the earth or in yourselves, but it is recorded in a Book [i.e. the Preserved Tablet][59] before We created it. Surely that is easy for God. [Thus it is,] so that you may not grieve over that [good] which you miss nor rejoice in that [good] which has come to you. God does not love any vainglorious, boastful person, who is niggardly himself and bids others to be niggardly. Anyone who turns away [should know that] God is the Self-sufficient, the All-laudable." (57:22-24)

Two Verses from the Sūrah of the Gathering (*al-Ḥashr*)

"O you who believe, keep your duty to God, and let everyone consider that which he has laid up for the morrow [i.e. the Day 1 of Judgement]. Keep your duty to God, surely He is fully aware of that which you do; do not be like those who forgot God, and so He caused them to forget [the good of] themselves. It is they who are ungodly." (59:18-19)

Two Verses from the Sūrah of the Rank (*al-Ṣaff*)

"O you who believe, shall I direct you to a commerce that will save you from a painful chastisement? [It is that] you believe in God and His messenger [Muḥammad], and fight in the path of

59. See *supra*, p. 82, n. 15.

God with your wealth and your persons. That is better for you, if you know." (61:10-11)

Four Verses from the Sūrah of Congregation (*al-Jumu'ah*)

"Tell [the Jews]: The death from which you flee will overtake you. Then you will be brought back to the knower of the unseen and the seen, and He will inform you of that which you had been doing." (62:8)

"O you who believe, when call is made for [the midday] prayer on Friday hasten to the remembrance of God and leave off all [forms of] business. That is better for you, did you but know. When the prayer is finished, disperse in the land, seek of God's bounty, and remember God much that you may prosper. When they [i.e. your companions] saw a matter of commerce or amusement, they drifted away from you, [O Muḥammad], towards it and left you standing.[60] Tell [them]: That which is with God is better than any matter of amusement or commerce. God is the Best Provider." (62:9-11)

Four Verses from the Sūrah of the Hypocrites (*al-Munāfiqūn*)

"O you who believe, let not your wealth nor your children divert you from the remembrance of God. Those who do that are those who are the losers. Spend [in the cause of God] out of that which We have provided you before death comes upon one of you and he should say: My Lord, why did You not grant me respite for a while, that I could give alms and be among those who do good deeds? God will never grant respite to one when his appointed term has come. God is fully aware of that which you do." (63:9-11)

---

60. On a Friday a caravan of goods arrived at the time of the Friday Assembly Prayer which the Prophet (ṣ) was leading in his mosque, and all except a dozen of the Muslims left the mosque to look at the caravan. Then this verse was revealed. See Muslim, *Ṣaḥīḥ*, Jumu'ah, 11.

Eight Verses from the Sūrah of Mutual Fraud (*al-Taghābun*)

"Whichever affliction befalls is only by the permission of God. God guides the mind of whoever [truly] believes in Him. God has the fullest knowledge of everything." (64:11)

"Obey God and the Messenger. If you turn away, the duty of Our Messenger is only to convey [the message] clearly. God is He besides Whom there is no god; so in God should the believers put their trust." (64:12-13)

"O you who believe, of your wives and your children some are your enemies; so beware of them. But if you pardon, overlook and forgive, then surely God is most Forgiving, Ever Merciful. Your belongings and your children are only a trial [for you]; but with God is a great reward. So keep your duty to God as far as you can, listen and obey, and spend [in His cause] for the good of yourselves. Those who are guarded against the avarice of their souls are they who will be prosperers. If you lend to God a goodly loan, He will multiply it for you, and will forgive you. God is Most Appreciating, Most Forgiving, Knower of the unseen and the seen, the Mighty, the All-wise." (64:14-18)

Four Verses from the Sūrah of Divorce (*al-Ṭalāq*)

"God will prepare a way out [of his difficulties] for him who keeps his duty to God, and will provide for him from where he does not expect. God is sufficient for him who puts his trust in Him. God is sure to attain His purpose. God has appointed a measure for everything." (65:2-3)

"God will provide facilities in the matter of him who keeps his duty to God. That is the command of God which He has revealed to you. God will efface the evil deeds of him who keeps his duty to God, and will enlarge his reward." (65:4-5)

One Verse from the Sūrah of the Forbidding (*al-Taḥrīm*)

"O you who believe, turn to God in sincere repentance. It may be that your Lord will acquit you of your evil deeds and admit you to Paradise beneath which rivers flow, on the Day when God will not humiliate the Prophet (ṣ) and those who believed with him. Their light will run before them and on their right hands. They will pray: Our Lord, perfect our light for us and forgive us; surely You have the fullest power over everything." (66:8)

Seventeen Verses from the Sūrah of the Stairways (*al-Maʿārij*)

"Surely man is created [such that he is] fretful. When evil afflicts him, he is impatient; but when good befalls him, he is grudging; except [a] those who perform the ritual prayer and are constant in their ritual prayers; [b] those in whose wealth is a known right for the beggar and the outcast; [c] those who affirm faith in the Day of Judgement; [d] those who are fearful of the chastisement of their Lord—surely the chastisement of their Lord is something from which one cannot feel secure; [e] those who guard their private parts save from their wives and those whom they posses [i.e. slave-concubines]—such are not to blame, but those who seek to go beyond that are they who are the transgressors; [f] those who keep what is entrusted to them and [fulfil] covenants; [g] those who are steadfast in testimonies; and [h] those who strictly observe their ritual prayers. [All] these [categories of people] will be honoured in Paradise." (70:19-35)

Eight Verses from the Sūrah of the Jinn (*al-Jinn*)

"If they [i.e. jinn] had adhered to the straight path, We would have provided them with abundant water to drink, that We might try them thereby. Anyone who turns away from the remembrance of his Lord, is thrust by Him to rigorous chastisement. All places of worship belong to God; so do not call [there] anyone along with God. When the servant of God [i.e. Muḥammad] stood up praying to Him, they [i.e. jinn] were almost upon him in swarms." (72:16-19)

"Tell [people]: I pray only to my Lord, and I do not associate anyone with Him. Say [to them also]: Surely I have no power to do you any harm or to grant you rectitude. Tell [them further]: Surely none can ever protect me against God, nor can I ever find any place of refuge apart from Him. [My duty is] only to convey [that which I receive] from Him and His messages. For those who disobey God and His Messenger there is surely the fire of Hell, in which they will dwell forever." (72:20-23)

Nine Verses from the Sūrah of the Enwrapped One (*al-Muzzammil*)

"O you wrapped up in your mantle, pass the night in worship except a small part of it, half of it, or a little less, or a little more, and recite the Qur'an slowly and distinctly. Surely we are about to charge you with a weighty word[61]. Surely getting up at night for worship is the most potent of means of subduing the self and of achieving effectiveness in discourse. Surely you have much occupation during the day. Remember the name of your Lord, and devote yourself wholly to Him. [He is] the Lord of the East and the West; there is no god but He; so take Him as your guardian. Endure patiently whatever they [i.e. non-believers] say, and forsake them in a good manner."[62] (73:1-10)

Seven Verses from the Sūrah of the Enmantled One (*al-Muddaththir*)

---

61. The word of God is said to be weighty because the commands are difficult to carry out.
62. In this verse God asked us to break off or to have no friendly dealings with non-believers.

"O you enmantled, arise and warn; magnify your Lord; purify your clothes; flee from idolatry, do not do favour in the expectation of receiving more in return; and endure patiently for the sake of your Lord." (74:1-7)

Seven Verses from the Sūrah of Man (*al-Insān*)

"Surely it is We Who have revealed the Qur'an to you. So adhere patiently to the command of your Lord, and do not obey any sinful, ungrateful one from among the people. Remember the name of your Lord morning and evening; prostrate yourself before Him at night and glorify Him for a long part of the night." (76:23-26)

"Those [ungodly] people certainly love this transitory world, and disregard the hard Day [of Judgement] ahead. We have created them and made their joints strong; We can completely replace them with others like them, when We will." (76:27-28)

Surely this [Qur'an] is a reminder; so whoever wishes may take to the way leading to his Lord. But you can wish only if God pleases. Surely God is the All-knowing, the All-wise. He admits to His mercy whom He pleases, and for the evildoers He has prepared a painful chastisement." (76:29-31)

Seven Verses from the Sūrah of the Pluckers (*al-Nāzi'āt*)

"When the great catastrophe comes, on the Day when man recalls all that he strove for, and Hell is made manifest to him who can see, then for him who rebelled [against God and His messengers] and preferred the life of this world, it is Hell which will certainly be his resort. But for him who feared the [condition of] standing before his Lord [for judgement] and forbade his carnal soul to follow its passions, it is Paradise which will certainly be his resort."[63] (79:35-41)

63. This verse is of tremendous importance to the Sufis, for it alone contains the whole of their general method of character-refinement. This

Three Verses from the Sūrah of the Rending (*al-Inshiqāq*)

"O man, you, surely having striven hard towards your Lord, will meet Him. Then He in whose right hand is given his book [in which all his actions were recorded], will soon have an easy reckoning, and will return to his people rejoicing." (84:6-9)

Six Verses from the Sūrah of the Most High (*al-A'lā*)

"He who purifies himself, and remembers the name of his Lord and so offers ritual prayers, will surely prosper.[64] But you prefer the life of this world, whereas the Hereafter is better and most lasting. Surely this is set forth in the earlier scriptures, the scriptures of Abraham[65] and Moses." (87:14-19)

Six Verses from the Sūrah of the Dawn (*al-Fajr*)

"As for man, [his nature is such that] whenever his Lord tries him, honours him and favours him, he says [in boastful attitude]: Even my Lord honours me! But when He tries him and limits his provision, he says [lamenting]: My Lord has despised me. Not so, but you do not honour the orphan, you do not urge one another to feed the poor, you squander inherited wealth extravagantly, and you love wealth inordinately." (89:15-20)

---

method consists in opposing passions and desires. For a discussion of this method see Quasem, *Ethics*, pp. 92-95.

64. This verse too is of special importance to the Sufis. It constitutes the Qur'anic proof for their theory that it is on the purification of the soul that happiness in the Hereafter is dependent and that all bodily acts really aim at inward purification. There are other verses on this same theme.

65. Abraham was a prophet or messenger of God and so he received a revelation from God, which was written down. This is referred to in the Qur'an as the Leaves of Abraham. The Leaves are lost and there is no mention of them in the Bible.

Seven Verses from the Sūrah of the City (*al-Balad*)

"Man has not attempted the scaling of the height. What will teach you what the scaling of the height is? [It is] the freeing of a slave, or feeding, on a day of hunger, an orphan near of kin or a poor person in misery; and to be of those who believe, exhort one another to patience and exhort one another to mercy. These are the people of the right. Those who disbelieve in Our signs are the people of the left.[66] They will be punished with furnace fire." (90:11-20)

Four Verses from the Sūrah of the Sun (*al-Shams*)

"By the soul and that which has proportioned it and then inspired it to lewdness and righteousness, he who purifies it, shall prosper and he who corrupts it shall be ruined."[67] (91:7-10)

Ten Verses from the Sūrah of the Night (*al-Layl*)

"Surely your strivings are divergent. He who spends [in the cause of God] and keeps duty, and takes as true [the teaching about] that which is best [i.e. Paradise], will soon have his way to the happiness [of Paradise] made easy by Us. But he who is a miser, considers himself independent [of God because of his wealth] and rejects as false [the teaching about] that which is

---

66. In the Qur'an human beings are classified into three broad categories, namely, the people on the left (*aṣḥāb al-shimāl*), the people on the right (*aṣḥāb al-yamīn*), and those drawn near to God (*al-muqarrabīn*). The first consists of those who deny God and His messengers (*al-mukadhdhibīn*). They are also called those who have gone astray (*al-ḍāllīn*). The second category is made of believers. At the last category are placed those who are most pious believers. They are also called those who are foremost (*al-sābiqīn*). See Qur'an 56:7-94; 7:36-53.

67. To the Sufis this verse is of the same importance as the verse 87:14 cited on *supra*, p. 155. The reason for the importance of both verses is also the same and is mentioned on *supra*, p. 205, n. 64.

best [i.e. Paradise], will soon have his way to misery [of Hell] made easy by Us. His wealth will not avail him when he perishes. Most surely it is for Us to provide guidance, and it is to Us that the Hereafter and this world belong. So I have warned you of a flaming Hell." (92:4-14)

Three Verses from the Sūrah of the Forenoon (*al-Ḍuḥā*)

"As for the orphan, do not oppress him. As for the beggar, do not drive him away. As for the favour of your Lord tell [people] about it." (93:9-11)

Seven Verses from the Sūrah of the Blood-clot (*al-'Alaq*)

"Read in the name of your Lord Who created [everything]; created man from a blood-clot. Read,[68] since your Lord is Most Beneficent, Who taught by the Pen, taught man that which he did not know." (96:1-5)

"By no means. Surely man does indeed transgress, for he considers himself self-sufficient. Surely to your Lord is the [final] return." (96:6-8)

Two Verses from the Sūrah of the Earthquake (*al-Zalzalah*)

"Anyone who will have done the smallest particle of good will see it [on the Day of Judgement], and anyone who will have done the smallest particle of evil will [also] see it [on that Day]." (99:7-8)

Six Verses from the Sūrah of the Chargers (*al-'Ādiyāt*)

"Most surely man is ungrateful to his Lord, and most surely he bears witness to this. Most surely he has strong love of

68. See *supra*, p. 141, n. 88.

wealth. Does he not know that when those in the graves are raised and their very secret thoughts are exposed, on that Day [also] their Lord will most surely be fully Aware of them?" (100:6-11)

The whole Sūrah of Rivalry (*al-Takāthur*)—Eight Verses

"Rivalry in increasing worldly possessions diverts you [from God and the Hereafter] till you reach the graves [for being buried]. This should not happen at all; you will soon come to know [how mistaken you are]. Again—this should not happen at all; you will soon come to know [how mistaken you are]. This should not happen at all. If you knew with the certainty of knowledge, you would most surely see Hell [in this life]. Then you will most surely see it with the certainty of sight [on the Day of Judgement]. On that Day you will most surely be called to account concerning the delight [you enjoyed in this life]." (102:1-8)

The whole Sūrah of Time (*al-'Aṣr*)—Three Verses

"I swear by time, surely man suffers continuous loss, except those who believe, do good deeds, exhort one another to hold fast to the truth, and exhort one another to patience." (103:1-3)

Three Verses from the Sūrah of the Backbiter (*al-Humazah*)

"Woe to every backbiter, slanderer, who amasses wealth and keeps counting! He thinks that his wealth will make him immortal." (104:1-3)

The whole Sūrah of Charity (*al-Mā'ūn*)—Seven Verses

"Do you not see him who disbelieves this religion? That is the one who drives away the orphan and does not urge the feeding of the poor. Woe to those who perform the ritual prayer but are unmindful of their ritual prayer and pray to make show [to other people] and they [also] refuse divine tax"! (107:1-7)

All Three Verses from the Sūrah of Help (*al-Naṣr*)

"Now[69] that the help of God and [the consequent] victory [i.e. the conquest of Makkah] have come and you have seen people join the religion of God [i.e. Islam] in large numbers, then glorify your Lord with His praise, and seek forgiveness of Him. Surely He is Oft-returning [to man with compassion]." (110:1-3)

The whole Sūrah of the Daybreak (*al-Falaq*)

"Say: I seek, the protection of the Lord of the daybreak, from the mischief of what He has created, from the mischief of darkness when it gathers, from the mischief of the women who blow on knots [i.e. malignant witchcraft], and from the mischief of an envious person when he envies."[70] (113:1-5)

The whole Sūrah of Man (*al-Nās*)—Six Verses

"Say: I seek the protection of the Lord of mankind, the King of mankind, the God of mankind, from the mischief of the slinking whisperer, who whispers into the minds of people, whether he be from jinn [i.e. Satan] or from man." (114:1-6)

---

69. This sūrah was revealed during the Farewell Pilgrimage about three months before the Prophet's death. In this sūrah God indicated that his death was approaching and asked him to prepare for it by additional devotional acts.

70. This and the following sūrah are together known as the *Mu'awwidhatān* (the sūrahs of taking refuge with God) and are incantations or protective formulae to ward off evil, especially demonic suggestions. The practice of taking refuge with God is commanded at various points in the Qur'an.

Conclusion on the two classes of verses

Why the discussion of Qur'anic verses has been confined to the classes of jewels and pearls

Know that for two reasons we have confined ourselves to the discussion of Qur'anic verses classified as jewels and classified as pearls. The first reason is that the remaining types of verses are more than can be enumerated: The second is that these two classes of verses are the most important ones of which no one can ever be free, because the basis of religion is knowledge of God (may He be exalted!), and after this is traversing the path to Him. As for the matter of the Hereafter, general belief in it is sufficient, because one who knows God and obeys Him will surely have a place of return which will make him happy, and one who denies God and disobeys Him will surely have a place of return which will make him miserable. Knowledge of the details of this, however, is not a stipulation for traversing the path of Him. Yet this knowledge adds to the perfection of yearning [for happiness] and warning [against misery].

Sometimes you will see the jewels and the pearls strung all together in some verses; we have left them unmentioned, except those in which the mention of the two intended classes predominates. You must continue your reflection on these two classes, for it is by this that you will obtain the highest degree of happiness.

May God make you and us among those whom He has made happy through His bounty, generosity, power, and extensive mercy! Surely He is the Most Generous, Most Compassionate, and Ever Merciful.

Bibliography

Abū Dāwūd, Sulaymān ibn al-Ash'ash al-Sijistānī. *Sunan*. 2 vols. Cairo, 1935.

Al-Abyārī, Ibrāhīm. *Ta'rīkh al-Qur'ān*, Cairo, 1965.

Al-'Asqalānī, Ibn Ḥajar. *Tahdhīb al-Tahdhīb*. Hyderabad, India, 1325 AH.

Azad, Mawlana Abul Kalam. *Basic Concepts of the Qur'an*. Prepared by Syed Abdul Latif. Hyderabad, India, 1958.

Bakker, Dirk. *Man in the Qur'ān*. Amsterdam, 1965.

Barth, J. "Studien sur Kritik and Exegese des Qorāns." *Der Islam*, VI (1915-1916), 113-148.

Al-Bayḍāwī, 'Abdallāh. *Anwār al-Tanzīl wa Asrār at Ta'wīl*. Egypt, 1923.

Bell, Richard. "The Origin of 'Īd al-Aḍḥā." *Moslem World*, XXIII (1933), 117-120.

—. "Who were the Ḥanīfs?" *Ibid.*, XX (1930), 120-124.

The Bible. Authorized version. Oxford, n.d.

Birkeland, Harris. *The Lord guideth: studies on primitive Islam*. Oslo, 1956.

Al-Bukhārī, Muḥammad Ibn Ismā'īl. *Ṣaḥīḥ*. 9 vols. Egypt, 1377 AH.

Causse, Maurice. "Théologie de rupture et de la communauté: étude sur la vocation prophétique de Moïse d'après le Coran." *Revue de l'histoire et de la philosophie religieuses*, I (1964), 60-82.

Coulson, Noel J. *Conflict and Tensions in Islamic Jurisprudence*, Chicago, 1969.

Cragg, Kenneth. *The Event of the Qur'ān*. London, 1971.

—. *The Mind of the Qur'ān*. London, 1973.

Darrāj, Muḥammad 'Abdallāh. *Al-Nabā' al-'Aẓīm*. Egypt. 1379/1960.

Al-Dhahabī, Muḥammad Ḥusayn. *Al-Tafsīr wa al-Mufassirūn*. 3 vols. Cairo, 1381/1961.

Fahd, T. "Ibn Sīrīn." *Encyclopaedia of Islam* (new ed.), III, 947-948.

Faris, Nabih Amin. "The Iḥyā' 'Ulūm al-Dīn of al-Ghazzāli." *Proceedings of the American Philosophical Society*, LXXI (1939), 15-19.

Al-Fayrūzābādī. Abū Ṭāhir Muḥammad ibn Ya'qūb. *Al-Qāmūs al-Muḥīṭ*. 4 vols. 3rd ed. Cairo, 1344/1925.

—. *Tanwīr al-Miqyās min Tafsīr Ibn 'Abbās*. 2nd ed. Egypt. 1370/1901.

Gardet, L. "Al-Asmā' al-Ḥusnā." *Encyclopaedia of Islam* (new ed.), I, 714-717.

Al-Ghazālī, Abū Ḥāmid. *Al-Arba'īn fī Uṣūl al-Dīn*. Egypt, 1344 AH.

—. *Iḥyā' 'Ulūm al-Dīn*. 5 vols. Beirut, n.d.

—. *Al-Imlā' 'alā Ishkālāt al-Iḥyā'* in *Mulḥaq Iḥyā' 'Ulūm al-Dīn*. Beirut, n.d.

—. *Al-Iqtiṣād fī al-I'tiqād*. Cairo, 1320 AH.

—. *Al-Maḍnūn bih 'alā Ghayr Ahlih*. On the margins of *al-Insān al-Kāmil* by 'Abd al-Karīm al-Jīlī. Egypt, 1949.

—. *Al-Maqṣad al-Asnā fī Asmā' Allāh al-Ḥusnā*. Translated by Robert Stade under the title *Ninety-nine Names of God*. Ibadan, Nigeria, 1970.

—. *Mi'yār al-'Ilm fī Fann al-Manṭiq*. Egypt, 1329 AH.

—. *Al-Qisṭās al-Mustaqīm*. Edited by al-Yasū'ī. Beirut, 1959.

—. *Tahāfut al-Falāsifah*. Edited by Sulaymān Dunyā. Cairo, n.d.

—. *Al- Wajīz*. Cairo, 1317 AH.

Al-Ḥujwīrī, 'Alī Ibn 'Uthmān. *Kashf al-Maḥjūb*. Translated by R.A. Nicholson. Leyden, 1911.

Ibn 'Abd al-Barr. *Al-Istī'āb*. 4 vols. Egypt, 1960.

Ibn Abū Dāwūd, Abū Bakr 'Abdallāh. *Kitāb al-Maṣāḥīf*. Edited by Arthur Jeffery. Egypt, 1355/1936.

Ibn al-Ḥajjāj, Muslim. *Ṣaḥīḥ*. 16 vols. Cairo, 1929.

Ibn Ḥanbal, Aḥmad. *Musnad*. 6 vols. Cairo, n.d.

Ibn al-Jawzī, 'Abd al-Raḥmān. *Zād al-Masīr fī 'Ilm al-Tafsīr*. 6 vols. Beirut, 1384/1964.

Ibn Kathīr, 'Imād al-Dīn Abū al-Fidā' Ismā'īl. *Tafsīr al-Qur'ān al-'Aẓīm*. 4 vols. Egypt, n.d.

Ibn Khallikān, Abū al-'Abbās. *Wafayāt al-A'yān wa Anbā' Abnā' al-Zamān*. Cairo, 1299 AH.

Ibn Mājah, Muḥammad Ibn Yazīd al-Qazwīnī. *Sunan*. 2 vols. Edited by Muḥammad Fu'ād 'Abd al-Bāqī. Cairo, 1952-1953.

Ibn al-Manẓūr Jamāl al-Dīn Muḥammad Ibn Mukarram al-Anṣārī. *Lisān al-'Arab*. 20 vols. Cairo, 1308/1901.

Ibn al-Nadīm, Muḥammad. *Kitāb al-Fihrist*. Edited and translated by Bayard Dodge. 2 vols. New York & London, 1970.

Ibn Taymiyyah, Taqī al-Dīn. *Muqaddimah fī Usūl al-Tafsīr*. Edited by 'Adnān Zarzūr. 2nd ed. Beirut, 1392/1972.

—. *Al-Tawassul wa al-Wasīlah*. Beirut, 1390/1970.

Al-Iṣfahānī, Abū al-Qāsim al-Rāghib. *Al-Mufradāt fī Gharīb al-Qur'ān*. Edited by Muḥammad Sa'īd. Tehran, n.d.

Izutsu, Toshihiko. *Ethico-Religious Concepts in the Qur'ān*. Montreal, 1966.

Jomier, Jacques. "Le nom divin 'al-Raḥmān' dans le Coran." *Mélanges Louis Massignon*, Damascus, 1957, II, 361-381.

Al-Jurjānī, Abū al-Ḥasan al-Ḥusayn. *Al-Ta'rīfāt*. Edited by G. Flügel. Leipzig, 1845.

Macdonald, D.B. *Development of Religious Attitude and Life in Islam*. Beyrit, 1965.

—. and Masse, H. *et al.* "Djinn." *Encyclopaedia of Islam* (new ed.), III, 546-550.

Al-Marāghī, Aḥmad Muṣṭafā. *Tafsīr al-Marāghī*. 10 vols. 2nd ed. Egypt, 1373/1953-1380/1961.

Al-Muzanī, Abū Ibrāhīm Ismā'īl ibn Yaḥyā. *Al-Mukhtaṣar al-Ṣaghīr*. Bulaq, 1321-1326 AH.

Al-Nasā'ī Abu 'Abd al-Raḥmān ibn Shu'ayb. *Sunan*. 8 vols. Egypt, 1383/1964.

Penrice, John. *A Dictionary and Glossary of the Kor-ān*. London, 1873.

Quasem, M.A. *The Ethics of al-Ghazālī: a Composite Ethics in Islam*. Foreword by W. Montgomery Watt. Revised Ph.D. thesis. Malaysia, 1975.

—. "Al-Ghazālī's Conception of Happiness." *Arabica*, XXII, 153-161.

Al-Qur'ān al-Karīm (bi al-Rasm al-'Uthmānī). Edited in Egypt, n.d.

Al-Qur'ān al-Karīm. Translated into English by Abdullah Yusuf Ali. Lahore, Pakistan, 1938.

—. Partly translated into English by A.J. Arberry, London, 1953.

—. Translated into English by A.J. Arberry. London, 1955.

—. Translated into English by E.H. Palmer. Delhi, India, 1880.

—. Translated into English by George Sale. London, 1887.

—. Translated into English by J.M. Rodwell, London, 1909.

—. Translated into English by Mohammed Marmaduke Pickthall. London, 1930.

—. Translated into English by Muhammad Karim Jauhar, Calcutta, India, 1974.

—. Translated into English by Muhammad Zafrulla Khan. London, 1971.

—. Translated into English by N.J. Dawood. 4rth ed. London, 1974.

—. Translated into English by Pir Salahud-din. Eminabad, Pakistan, n.d.

—. Translated into English by Richard Bell. Edinburgh, Scotland, 1937, 1939.

—. Translated into English by Syed Abdul Latif. Hyderabad, India, 1969.
Al-Qushayrī, Abū al-Qāsim. *Laṭā'if al-Ishārāt*. Edited by Ibrāhīm. 5 vols. Cairo, n.d.
Rahbar, Daud. *God of Justice: a study in the ethical doctrine of the Qur'ān*. Leiden, 1960.
—. "Reflections on the Tradition of Qur'anic Exegesis." *Muslim World*, LII (1962), 269-307.
Ringgren, Helmer, "The Conception of Faith in the Qur'ān." *Oriens*, IV (1951), 1-20.
Roberts, Robert. *The Social Laws of the Qor'ān*. 2nd ed. London, 1971.
Al-Ṣāliḥ, Ṣubḥī. *Mabāḥith fī 'Ulūm al-Qur'ān*. 5th ed. Beirut, 1968.
Shahid, Irfan. "A Contribution to Koranic Exegesis." *Arabic and Islamic Studies in honour of Hamilton A.R. Gibb*. Leiden, 1965, pp. 563-580.
Al-Shamma, S.H. *The Ethical System underlying the Qur'ān*. Tübingen, 1959.
Al-Suyūṭī, Jalāl al-Dīn. *Al-Itqān fi 'Ulūm al-Qur'ān*. 3rd ed. Cairo, 1370/1951.
—. *Lubāb al-Nuqūl fī Asbāb al-Nuzūl*. 2nd ed. Egypt, n.d.
—. and al-Maḥallī, Jalāl al-Dīn. *Tafsīr al-Jalālayn*. On the margins of al-Qur'ān al-Karīm (bi al-Rasm al-'Uthmānī). Beirut, n.d.
Al-Ṭabarī, Muḥammad Ibn Jarīr. *Jāmi' al-Bayān 'an Ta'wīl Āy al-Qur'ān*. 12 vols. 2nd ed. Egypt, 1373/1954.
Al-Tahānawī, Muḥammad 'Ali. *Kashshāf Iṣṭilāḥāt al-Funūn*. Bairut, 1966.
Al-Tirmidhī, Abū 'Isā Muḥammad. *Sunan*. 13 vols. Egypt, 1931-1934.
Walī Allāh, Shāh. *Al-Fawz al-Kabīr fī Uṣul al-Tafsīr*. Karachi, Pakistan, n.d.
Watt, W. Montgomery. *Companion to the Qur'ān*. London, 1967.
Al-Zajjāj. *I'rāb al-Qur'ān*. 3 vols. Edited by Ibrāhīm al-Abyārī. Cairo, 1384/1965.
Al-Zamakhsharī, Abū al-Qāsim Jārallāh. *Al-Kashshāf 'an Ḥaqā'iq al-Tanzīl*. 4 vols. Egypt, 1385/1966.
Al-Zanjānī, Abū 'Abdallāh. *Ta'rīkh al-Qur'ān*. 3rd ed. Beirut, 1388/1969.

General index

Index of Qur'anic sūrahs and verses[1]

1. Numbers within parentheses refer to Qur'anic verses.